The Real Options Solution

Founded in 1807, John Wiley & Sons is the oldest independent publishing company in the United States. With offices in North America, Europe, Australia, and Asia, Wiley is globally committed to developing and marketing print and electronic products and services for our customers' professional and personal knowledge and understanding.

The Wiley Finance Series contains books written specifically for finance and investment professionals as well as sophisticated individual investors and their financial advisors. Book topics range from portfolio management to e-commerce, risk management, financial engineering, valuation and financial instruments analysis, as well as much more.

For a list of available titles, please visit our Web site at www.WileyFinance.com.

The Real Options Solution

Finding Total Value in a High-Risk World

F. Peter Boer

John Wiley & Sons, Inc.

Published by John Wiley & Sons, Inc., New York.

Published simultaneously in Canada.

This publication is designed to provide accurate and authoritative information in regard to the subject matter covered. It is sold with the understanding that the publisher is not engaged in rendering professional services. If professional advice or other expert assistance is required, the services of a competent professional person should be sought.

Library of Congress Cataloging-in-Publication Data

Boer, F. Peter, 1940–
    The real options solution : finding total value in a high-risk world / F. Peter Boer.
      p. cm.—(Wiley Finance series)
    Includes bibliographical references and index.
    ISBN 0-471-20998-8 (cloth : alk. paper)
      1. Options (Finance). 2. Financial futures. 3. Risk management. I. Title. II. Series.

HG6024.A3 B63 2002
332.64'5—dc21

                        2001045645

Printed in the United States of America.

10 9 8 7 6 5 4 3 2 1

To those who gave all in the tragic events
of September 11, 2001

Preface

The Real Options Solution offers a new approach to the valuation of businesses and technologies based on options theory. It provides a *quantifiable* approach to the problem of the strategic premium—the gap between apparent economic value and actual value as determined by the marketplace. *Total value* is the sum of economic value and the strategic premium created by real[1] options.

The wild rise of Internet stocks, which peaked shortly after the millennium opened and the severe correction that followed have made clear to everyone what some have known all along—there is a crisis in how companies, especially technology companies, are valued. Accounting systems based on historical costs can't do it. Discounted cash flow models can't do it when positive cash flow is nowhere in sight. Dubious comparables, such as "price-to-sales ratios" or "eyeballs," lose track of value and beg the question of whether the stocks to which one is comparing are correctly priced.

The gap between market value and economic value has been trending upward for some time as the economy becomes increasingly service- and information-based. The gap reached record proportions at the height of the Internet bubble; it is still very substantial after the correction and is likely to grow again. Dismissing the phenomenon as simply the madness of crowds wastes the opportunity to analyze the dynamics of how great value is being created and destroyed by innovation in the modern economy.

■ THE VALUATION SOLUTION—PLANS ARE OPTIONS

This book is based on a straightforward central idea: *plans are options*. A plan is unlike the physical or financial asset it is intended to produce because the owner of the plan has freedom to modify the plan as circumstances change. This freedom has value, which can be analyzed quantitatively. The implications of the idea are considerable because options are valued differently than securities. The idea is powerful because it provides a universal valuation method—one that applies equally to the dullest old-economy company and to a wild new Internet start-up. It also creates a framework for the special valuation issues that occur when brilliant innovations are being made within a traditional operating business.

No radical assumptions are required to use this approach. The discounted cash flow (DCF) model is fundamentally sound for operating businesses and is the core first step. And DCF analysis is also the first step in valuing innovative business plans—whether of a new business-to-business (B2B) model, a promising drug in the research pipeline, or a new type of fuel cell. But because these plans are subject to both unique and market risks and because management has considerable flexibility in their execution, such plans are correctly evaluated as real options. The value of such options under the dual conditions of rapid growth and high volatility can be huge—and unquestionably higher than one might intuitively guess.

Plans are certainly not correctly valued by the prevalent, and seriously flawed, notion that they are future cash flow machines to which an arbitrary risk-weighted hurdle rate can be applied.

Why does this insight make a difference? Simply because

DCF analysis alone can lead an investor to pass up a financially attractive opportunity. In the past, executives used the word *strategic* to label intuitively attractive investments that failed to earn the cost of capital. Options theory allows one to *calculate* the strategic premium to obtain total value.

■ WHO SHOULD READ THIS BOOK?

Those who are investing for above-average returns and those who are trying to create these above-average returns should read on. Among the former will be venture investors and those legions of individual investors who are willing to take investment risks to enjoy superior returns. The latter includes executives of New Economy start-ups or of old-economy firms seeking to reinvigorate their companies. The book should be of special interest to those in research and development (R&D).

Potential readers may be frustrated by the mumbo jumbo terminology that aims to justify large premiums based on a "first-mover" principle, impressive intellectual capital, or a supposedly unassailable market position. But just how does one determine what these premiums are worth? If you are willing to think about a new approach, read on.

■ RISK IS MORE PREVALENT THAN WE GENERALLY REALIZE

I am a high-risk investor and have been in the employ of high-risk investors. But I have not thought about myself this way all along, nor has my new perspective developed by conscious choice. After all, I was for most of my career in the employ of solid Fortune 100 industrial companies. I viewed my personal investments as growth oriented, but reasonably safe. These assumptions proved to be illusions.

The lights came on in the 1980s when a misguided news report temporarily destroyed about 25 percent of my paper net worth. The picture became even clearer when modest investments in new technology grew quickly into major investments, while my "value" investments underperformed for a decade. And it became crystal clear when a young relative with an idea created significant personal wealth in the space of one very wild year.

Investors have become inured to massive changes in market valuation triggered by a single business news item, whether it is an announcement about a deal, an earnings warning, or government intervention. It is similarly common to see daily changes in our personal stock portfolios equivalent to months of salaries earned from solid labor. Nonetheless, many of us, old and young alike, have come to prefer being rewarded with equity, especially stock options, rather than with cash.

And despite our anxiety about this irrational and high-risk world, on the whole we are more prosperous than ever. It seems we must live with risk; and if we must, it's best to enjoy the ride.

■ ORIGINS OF THE BOOK

This book is an outgrowth of two major influences. The first was my earlier book,[2] *The Valuation of Technology*, which was conceived in 1997 and published in 1999. Broadly speaking, that work aimed to bridge the communications gap between scientists and engineers and the business and financial community through the concept of valuation. More narrowly, the book linked the familiar algorithms used by the R&D community, where I spent much of my professional career, with the algorithms used by those more directly concerned with shareholder value: investors, senior executives, and board members.

The Valuation of Technology is a quantitative book, replete with graphs, tables, equations, and detailed examples. It is aimed at practitioners of and investors in technology. I came away from the task of writing it with the conviction that some of its key concepts had broad usefulness and could eventually be the core of a book aimed at a wider audience. In particular, I recognized that the techniques used to manage the extraordinarily high-risk world of R&D were applicable to other important problems in the business world.

The second influence for this book has been my exploration of the concept of real options. I have been exposed to the general concept of R&D as a form of real option[3] for over a decade. My initial reaction as a practitioner was that the idea had conceptual merit but was too abstract to use as an effective communications tool in a real company (and I was a senior executive of a real company at the time). Nevertheless, I included the basics of options analysis in my original book, included a number of quantitative cases to show why the idea could be important, and referenced some of the current thinking in the field.

The epiphany about the consequences of options thinking came in a classroom situation, when, in the role of a professor, I was trying to explain the value of embedded options in a business proposal, using a case taken from a corporate finance textbook. The example described a proposal to make a new computer product, which implied the further option to introduce a second-generation computer three years later. Coincidentally, the talk of the business community at the time was about the extraordinary and seemingly irrational valuations being placed on Internet stocks. The fact that my young relative was deeply involved in a dot-com compounded my interest. I decided to plug typical Internet growth rates and volatilities into the textbook case. These new conditions produced some extraordinarily high valuations,[4] yet the results all were derived using standard financial theory.

While these results demonstrated a very plausible linkage of market valuation to embedded options, the most important message was that the options *were visible to some and invisible to others.* In the original textbook case, the chief executive officer (CEO) had rejected a proposal to make the new computer because it failed to meet his hurdle rate. But an analyst pointed out that making a first-generation machine carried with it an option to build a second-generation machine a few years later. In other words, she had identified and valued a strategic premium that reversed a flawed decision derived from economic value alone. How to identify, structure, and exploit such hidden options is one of the ambitions of this book.

■ FIVE KEYS TO A LOCK

The immediately following paragraphs offer a crisp summary of the book's five premises and how they can unlock the mystery of value. The book will explore a wide range of cases that illustrate the consequences of these ideas.

The first key to the lock is the concept of value, that new capital is created in direct proportion to the degree to which returns on capital exceed the cost of capital. This idea is widely accepted today, but hardly universally understood. It needs development.

The second key is that value creation cannot occur in the absence of risk and, indeed, is dependent on the assumption of risk and its intelligent management. These general ideas are not really original, but the actual algorithms linking risk and value for the innovation process may be novel and are central elements in *The Valuation of Technology.*

The third key is that human capital and intellectual capital are important, and sometimes dominant, parts of the valuation of modern companies. The idea of intangible capital assets has a reasonably long history, and its extension as "intellectual capital" to explain the gap between accounting and marketplace values has gained adherents during the past decade. Nevertheless, there is considerable confusion about just how intellectual capital is converted into shareholder value. This book outlines a solution.

The fourth key is that strategic capital resides in an organization's plans and options for future actions. The implications of this fact are largely unexplored. Previous approaches tended to look at intellectual capital as an extension of quantifiable intellectual property, such as patents, trademarks, and copyrights. To these were added more subjective forms of intellectual capital, such as learning and knowledge, business processes, and technical know-how. However, the weakness of this approach is that it is not intellectual capital itself but the ability to translate it into business plans that creates value in the marketplace. There is no other way to determine which patent, which ad campaign, or which employee will add the most value.

The fifth key—perhaps the missing key—is that plans begin as real options and are transformed into tangible capital when the options are exercised. This idea is new, particularly in the context of the fourth premise, and is a promising approach to the valuation of strategic capital.

An important consequence is that to value the opportunity (and therefore the strategic premium), the analyst must carefully separate unique risk from systematic risk. This technique for evaluating options is not new to options theorists, but it is only just beginning to be understood and applied in the world of real business and investment.

■ PLAN OF THE BOOK

Part One of the book provides a new perspective on value by developing the concepts on which an integrated value model is built. The introductory chapter retells a high-seas adventure story from the viewpoint of a high-risk investor and recapitulates the enormous prosperity (the Total Value) triggered by that investment.

A foundation for a new approach is built in Chapter 2, where the crisis in valuation noted earlier is reviewed, and the differences between book capital, economic capital, and strategic capital are reviewed. This structure is more useful than the notion that the difference between market value and book value is accounted for by "intellectual capital." Why? Because those intangibles that support the current economic processes of the firm must be distinguished from those other intangibles that create a strategic premium. Without that distinction, valuation of a strategic premium is hopeless. Some recent business cases are used to illustrate the point.

Chapter 3 has two purposes. The first is to review the methods and the limitations of conventional (DCF) economic valuation, which is the foundation on which the Total Value approach is built. The second purpose is to imprint a fundamental understanding of the powerful link between sustainable growth and value creation. Yet, it is easy to go badly astray with DCF analysis, leading to serious undervaluation or, almost as easily, to overvaluation.

The Real Options Solution comes together in Chapter 4. Here, an ambitious, integrated valuation model combines *economic* valuation based on forecast cash flows with *strategic* valuation based on option theory. The chapter also discusses how strategic capital can be converted into economic capital, and vice versa. The model has the advantage of universality: It does not require separate yardsticks for established operating companies and innovative new businesses; it can smoothly accommodate a mix of the two—a common situation. And it holds true for both microeconomic and macroeconomic conditions. Chapter 4 reduces the concepts just introduced to a practical, six-step method for determining total value. It begins with a brief summary of the method. It then defines and discusses the underlying concepts in each step, beginning with the core concept of economic value and its relationship to growth rates. To complement theory with a concrete example, the economic value of a very straightforward business is calculated. This business model then becomes a platform to which a single strategic option is added. The value of the option is calculated, the sum of economic capital and strategic capital is added, and a total value for the business is obtained.

Options are an extremely useful way to manage risk, the subject of Chapter 5. This chapter reviews the basics of financial options and shows why they are closely analogous to business situations that contain what are called *real options*. (The term *real* is coming into increasing use, in the titles of books, articles, and management conferences, to distinguish those options that arise in ordinary business from financial options relating to securities or commodities.) It demonstrates why, in situations characterized by a combination of high growth and high volatility, options can take on extraordinary values. Investors need to understand the dynamics by which this remarkable phenomenon occurs. But financial options are risky—they can expire with the full loss of the premiums paid for them—and the wild ride of Nasdaq stocks in 1998 and 2001 amply demonstrates a corresponding risk for real options.

Chapter 6 explores the proposition that strategic capital resides in an organization's plans and options for future actions. This assertion is the foundation for a quantitative approach to the valuation of strategic capital. However, to make the equation *Plans = Options* useable, it is important to recognize *that plans are neither forecasts nor dreams*. In a nutshell, one must realize that *Position* is a necessary although not sufficient condition for plans to be actionable.

Part Two of the book describes how *diminishing returns, risk,* and *innovation* affect the integrated value model introduced in Part One and in particular outlines why the management of risk and innovation is the foundation of modern prosperity.

Chapter 7 deals with the law of diminishing returns and shows how its consequences have driven organizations to stagnation and devolution through value destruction. Investors and executives can be slow to accept the inevitable deterioration of once-successful business models, which leads to serious misallocation of scarce resources.

The acceleration of economic growth and widely spreading prosperity have been the most extraordinary of modern phenomena. Chapter 8 explores the causes. What is different today from the stagnation typical of past eras? I argue that one difference is a far superior understanding of risk, which has led to a new balance between innovation and diminishing returns.

Risk is the subject of Chapters 9 and 10. Traditional risk management (think of a bank or an insurance company) does not translate easily to the high-risk environment of breakthrough innovation. So what is it that we have learned about risk management? We are beginning to understand that the management of systematic (market) risk requires different techniques (and provides different profit opportunities) than the management of unique (private) risk. And we have developed new value-creating management techniques pioneered for a high-risk environment, such as the aggressive use of the option to abandon troubled projects. We are also learning to apply what financial experts have called the "last free lunch," diversification, to technology and other high-risk portfolios.

Chapter 11 returns to the subject of human and intellectual capital—the key to value creation in a modern economy. It explores the mechanics by which human and intellectual capital are translated into economic capital on the one hand and into strategic capital on the other. After reviewing traditional intellectual property, including patents and copyrights, the chapter turns to the more complex issues of valuing R&D and new business opportunities. The situational nature of intellectual capital valuation is emphasized throughout.

Innovation is our weapon for overcoming the law of diminishing returns and is tied to the ability to frame real options. Innovation is the subject of Chapter 12. The technological S-curve and the appearance of disruptive technologies are two critical features of how innovators create value for themselves and destroy value for others. Innovation itself appears to be in a stage of exponential growth based on the accelerating number of combinatorial possibilities generated by the increasingly frequent emergence of new technologies. One of the most promising investment strategies is to place chips where such combinatorial possibilities are greatest.

Governments have an important role in creating or in destroying prosperity. We examine their role in Chapter 13. Strong governments have historically provided important contributions by enhancing security and reducing risk. Governments also provide services, sometimes efficiently and sometimes less so. They invest in education, infrastructure, health, and technology. But while governments may adopt policies that favor value-creating investments, they are perfectly capable of misguided policies that systematically destroy value. Some examples will be presented.

The Epilogue deals with three of the central issues of our time. The first is the Keynesian nightmare—that we will run out of attractive investment opportunities. The second is the notion that the planet itself imposes serious limits on our future prosperity. The third is that the complexity of modern-day decision making will overwhelm human intellectual limits. However, there is ample reason to believe that our age of prosperity is far from over.

■ STYLE OF THE BOOK

This book is appearing at what will one day be viewed as the denouement of the Internet gold rush, a very unique time in U.S. economic history. There is an obvious peril in dispensing business wisdom that is the product of a unique era—it may fit the times, but times soon change. So I will mix contemporary examples with historic examples to test whether the central premises are useful in a broader context.

For the contemporary examples, I did not have the full advantage of hindsight. But I did have the advantage of abundant stores of financial and economic data, plus my own direct experience. The historic examples are just the opposite—we know how the story turned out; but there may never be enough data, especially regarding profit margins, to confirm, or possibly disprove, the arguments. Given my seemingly safe position in the latter cases, I can still hope that the readers will gain new insight into the economic forces that have shaped our past and amusement from how classic examples translate into modern business jargon!

To increase the readability of this book, I have also chosen to minimize tables, formulas, and charts.

■ ACKNOWLEDGMENTS

The development of this book owes much to conversations I have held with members of my classes at the Yale School of Management and with many professional colleagues with whom I have discussed the implications of options theory.

Three people deserve special thanks. Ranch Kimball, formerly a partner at Boston Consulting Group (BCG) and a managing director of Tiger Scientific, Inc., made many contributions to the book in terms of its organization and provided several specific case studies based on his extensive consulting experience. Ranch in particular helped me articulate the notion that position is a prerequisite for plans and was a major contributor to Chapter 6.

Andrew Boer, through our many discussions of real-world situations, deserves the credit for my introduction to the special dynamics of high technology during the Internet bubble. Andrew, after founding in 1997 the Internet nonprofit TRUSTe, which dealt with issues of Internet privacy, moved on to found the distinctly for-profit corporation Emptor in 1998. Emptor was funded by two prominent Silicon Valley venture capital firms, changed its name to Accept.com in 1999, and was sold to Amazon.com for $180 million.

Louis Hegedus of Atofina, a veteran R&D practitioner and my former associate, was kind enough to read the draft in full and provided highly useful critical tests of its assertions and assumptions.

I also wish to thank Richard Luecke for skillful professional assistance in reviewing the book and arranging for its publication. The unstinting support of Jeanne Glasser and the splendid Wiley team, Judy Cardanha, and Jamie Temple is gratefully appreciated. May Adams, my assistant for two decades, has been an invaluable helper, not only in the preparation of some of the materials used in this book, but also in organizing my many activities to ensure that the book stayed on track.

Finally, my wife, Ellen, has undoubtedly wondered why, after one book was completed, I still felt that there was enough left unsaid to justify the time spent on yet another. Surely, I neglected to tell her that, having done one, I might go for another. Her continued support and enthusiasm, and her conversion to the cause, are deeply appreciated. Even more important, since Ellen is an inveterate high-risk investor, I hope she concludes that reading the final version will be another winning investment.

F. PETER BOER

Village of Golf, Florida
January 2002

Contents

Chapter

Introduction

One of the great business stories, a tale of vision, risk, value creation, prosperity, and eventual decapitalization, is too often told only as a history lesson. This reading should not surprise us because the participants were not consciously thinking in business terms.

In this story, Queen Isabella became the most successful venture capitalist of her time. She encountered an entrepreneur and bankrolled his story. The entrepreneur in this case was an Italian visionary named Christopher Columbus, who happened to possess not only a visionary idea but also formidable skills as a navigator, a sailor, and a manager.

The expedition involved substantial risks, from seemingly random events such as storms and disease and from Columbus's own errors. Of course, these were mostly errors in hindsight, but it was predictable that he would make at least a few given the scarcity of good information.

■ FROM KNOWLEDGE TO VALUE

Columbus targeted a large market, and his discoveries created great total value, although not in the way he planned. His investors, the Spanish crown, were able to use these riches to advance Spain from an impoverished feudal power, emerging from a desperate struggle to reconquer Andalusia, to Europe's dominant Renaissance power under Charles V and Philip II.

The process of value creation began with the easy plunder of gold and silver; but when the plundering business encountered diminishing returns, the Spanish turned to mining the richest beds of ore, at sites such as San Luis Potosi in Mexico. In time, the friars and conquistadors built a mixed agricultural and resource-driven economy in the New World. They had a bias for operations, but their enterprises stagnated fairly quickly.

Spain soon encountered competition. Portuguese caravels found entirely different routes to the riches of Southern Asia, the East Indies, China, and Japan by rounding the Cape of Good Hope. Brazil was colonized for good measure. King John of Portugal found his own entrepreneurs in great sailors such as Bartholomew Diaz and Ferdinand Magellan. The Portuguese were less interested in operations, but they had their own formula for creating value, as merchants and traders. Great wealth appeared in sixteenth-century Lisbon. Then, when Spain under Philip II acquired Portugal in the seventeenth century, Portuguese competition diminished and the splendors of the past never returned there.

The later competitors, the English, the Dutch, and the French, were another matter. They competed for these same territories and staked out new developments in North America, Australia, and Africa. They had excellent operating, trading, and administrative skills and soon surpassed the Spanish in value creation—witness the successful colonies of North America, the plantations of the Dutch East Indies, and the highly profitable colonization of the Indian subcontinent by the great East India Company.

Englishmen, such as Drake, could be highly successful in the plundering business when they put their minds to it; but their booty was not, and could never be, the foundation of long-lasting prosperity.

Something else happened—something that initially had little connection with the colony business, but surely affected it. A burst of innovation—the Industrial Revolution—took hold in England, France, and North America. It spread to other places in Europe and even to Japan, but was very slow to reach Spain, Portugal, and their colonies. Diminishing returns from natural resources and the failure to innovate in agriculture and industry inexorably sucked value from Spain and Portugal; and by the advent of the twentieth century they were relatively poor cousins within the family of European nations.

The economic cycle from the point of view of the Iberian countries is illustrative. The greatest wealth was created shortly after the period of greatest risk. Diminishing returns and competition took their toll. With time, the return from operations dropped to the cost of capital and below, new investment slowed, and the Iberian economies withered. More modern enterprises—the railroad, steel, and auto industries—have endured an analogous cycle. Similar problems, in all probability, will one day be encountered by the enterprises that are creating the most value today.

Whereas innovation can create great wealth for the innovator, it can at the same time destroy the wealth of others. There is an interesting argument that the beginning of the end for Italian Renaissance prosperity coincided with Italy's loss of the profitable European spice trade, which was dominated by Venice and Genoa. That trade involved many expensive transfers of cargo from the Philippines to India to Egypt and finally to Europe.

The first step was by boat across the Indonesian archipelago and the Bay of Bengal to the Malabar Coast of India—a trip that required tribute to local rulers and was subject to aggressive piracy. From India, the goods entered the Arabian Sea, dominated by the Sultan of Egypt. From the coast of the Red Sea, the spices were transferred by land caravan to the Nile, again subject to banditry. There they were loaded on transport ships to the Mediterranean, where they could expect the protection of Venetian fleets. Spice cargoes went on to Venice for transshipment to continental merchants such as the Fuggers in Augsburg. The cost of tribute and physical losses and the inevitable markup of goods as they changed hands added enormous overhead to this trade.

When Portuguese caravels passed the Cape of Good Hope and made their way to both India and the Spice Islands, the need for middlemen was virtually eliminated. The entrenched competitors tried to resist, but the Portuguese were formidable fighters for their day. Their cannon mounted on stout oaken caravels easily overcame the reed ships of the Sultan of Egypt and his European allies at the naval battle of Diu in 1535.

The Italians of Genoa and Venice were indisputably great sailors and great businessmen, easily capable of managing serious marine expeditions. But the Italian powers were not yet interested in risky new ideas; and Columbus—one of their own captains, had to go to Spain to find venture capital for his bold idea.

■ COLUMBUS'S BUSINESS PLAN

Columbus presented Queen Isabella with a straightforward business plan: Make an investment in ships and men for the first voyage (she invested[1] the modern equivalent of $14,000 in May 1492) and reap an uncertain amount of cash when the ships return home. As it turned out, two of the three ships returned in

March 1493 with a small amount of gold. From an accountant's perspective and considering the risks, this was a paltry return. The fact that gold had been discovered in the New World, however, attracted a great deal of interest.

To a venture capitalist, the significance of the voyage was not in its immediate return on capital but in the fact that it carried with it the *option* to invest in further voyages. Isabella surely understood this potential at the outset. In other words, the embedded option was worth far more than the operating business—the initial voyage of discovery. Clearly, it was not possible to plan the second voyage until the first had been made. And with the discovery of gold, investment capital was readily available. Columbus made three more voyages with indifferent success; but others who followed, particularly Hernando Cortez and Francisco Pizzaro, found fabulous wealth.

Put another way, the strategic premium of being the first to know that there was a New World, and how to get there, was very valuable indeed. Ironically, this piece of intellectual property was instantly shared with the Portuguese because Columbus, with the *Nina* in bad shape, made his initial landfall in the Portuguese Azores and then in Lisbon's outer harbor!

For all practical purposes, Columbus's business plan was an option, one that would have closed "out of the money" if Isabella's ships had been lost or if he had discovered only inhospitable islands with nothing but nuts and berries. Nuts, berries, and tough aboriginal warriors were all that Leif Erickson and his Vikings found in Newfoundland and North America in the late tenth century. The fame of their discovery did not spread over Europe and, indeed, was doubted until the recent discovery of compelling archeological evidence at L'Anse-aux-Meadows. The enterprises of these intrepid Vikings attracted little subsequent investment. For the time being at least, the plunder and farming businesses closer to home in Europe seemed to offer Norsemen better returns.

So on a net, net basis, Columbus returned with part of his initial investment (two ships), a small amount of treasure (tangible capital), and an enormous store of intellectual capital.

■ RISKS IN THE PLAN

It is also worth reflecting on the risks. Economic analysis depends on distinguishing between unique risks (which are specific to the venture and tend to dominate in innovative ventures) and systematic risks (which are defined as risks out of the venture's control).

In Columbus's plan the unique risks were identifiable. Storms were certain—the intrepid skipper overcame a very dangerous one on his return trip near the Azores. Going aground was another unique risk—the *Santa Maria* ran aground on a coral reef during good weather. The hostility of natives was a third risk—indeed they seemed to have wiped out the men Columbus left behind at Navidad, the New World's first colony. The potential hostility of the Portuguese was a huge risk, which Columbus fortunately managed with skill. Disease was another, although it did not seriously affect this voyage. The unique risks were well known to mariners, but of course their magnitude could not be readily judged in an unknown region.

There were also systematic risks that could have affected the value of the voyage. Probably the most important was the power of Spain. If Spain had suffered serious financial or military reverses, the option to invest in further voyages may have been severely diminished. But we shall see that there is an upside to systematic risk—things can turn out better than expected. So it seemed to be in Spain. Isabella and her husband Ferdinand were on a roll—the Moors had been expelled and the kingdoms of Castile and Aragon consolidated, making unified Spain unusually well positioned to exercise its option.

The point about risk should not be dismissed simply because it didn't happen. Just such a policy reversal was encountered by the "Chinese Columbus." In 1414, fewer than a hundred years before Columbus, the Ming Dynasty commissioned an armada of 62 huge sailing junks, many times the size of either a Spanish caravel or a nao. The largest Chinese galleons had three decks on the poop, nine masts, and twelve sails and are believed to have measured 440 feet long by 180 feet wide. Their 1500-ton displacement dwarfed the *Nina*'s 60. Under the eunuch Admiral Zheng He, the fleet sailed west as far as the east coast of Africa, where ample archaeological evidence of contact between Chinese travelers and native Africans has been found.[2] The capability to reach Europe and America might have been within reach within the century. But a naval effort on this scale was hugely expensive, and a decision was made in the imperial court to disband the navy and to focus on the internal affairs of the kingdom. So the option was lost through no fault of Zheng He, and the rich game of global exploration was ceded to Europe.

Part One

A New Perspective on Value

Chapter 2

The Crisis in Valuation

It is a beautiful spring day in backcountry Connecticut as I compose these sentences. The lilacs and tulips have just started to fade, but the azaleas are in full glory; and there is more glory to anticipate as the rhododendron blooms emerge. I am looking forward to a fine dinner with old friends, perhaps of venison and red wine. I am enjoying a very physical world, just as my ancestors centuries ago might have done.

At the same time, I am adding bits of information to a magnetic disk and contemplating how much of my existence is virtual and how much of the world with which I am concerned has become the same. Not all, certainly, but almost infinitely more than those ancestors could have contemplated.

At heart, this book is about capital, tangible and intangible, real and virtual. In an age of information, it is the intangible, invisible part of capital that is the most rapidly growing, the most interesting, and the most perplexing. While we perceive our physical surroundings, we are surrounded by and acted on by very real forces that we cannot see and cannot measure. A virtual economy encircles us. There are ghosts in the garden.

■ THE NATURE OF THE CRISIS IN BRIEF

The term *valuation* as used in this book means assigning a quantitative value, in dollars, for example, to an asset, whether that asset is a share of stock, an oil painting, or an invention. Valuation is important not only in driving transactions (parties will agree on a price based on their respective valuations) but also in decision making. A central thesis of my book *The Valuation of Technology* is that technical managers trained in the language of science must translate their ideas into the language of finance to be clearly understood by nontechnical decision makers. This point is of no small import in the information age, because technological forces are now driving over half of the growth of Western economies.[1] Poorly informed decisions squander resources, whereas good decisions about value creation create wealth.

■ THE FIRST CRISIS IN VALUATION

The root of the valuation problem dates back to the rise of modern commerce in Renaissance times,[2] which was accompanied by the acceptance of accounting systems based on historical cost.[3] This innovation was no bad thing. Indeed, it was vital to the progress of that era. As long as most transactions involved physical goods and tangible assets, the accounting approach to valuation worked well.

Financial statements, as prepared by accountants, attempt to measure transactions in the physical and the financial worlds. They are not necessarily accurate measures of income or wealth, even in a narrow sense, because of various accounting conventions relating to depreciation, to treatment of poorly defined liabilities, and to unrealized changes in the value of property and securities. The accountant is confined to dealing with actual transactions in actual currencies, ignoring many other aspects of transactions. But financial statements are at least precise and reasonably stable measures of one part of the economic beast. Even if some of the rules no longer make sense, the objective, consistent nature of accounting remains a cardinal virtue.

Accounting results have an important effect on valuation. We have all seen how a shortfall of about 10 cents per share in quarterly earnings can cause a change in market valuation of 10 dollars or more for a stock. Investors are usually shocked when it happens. After all, the book value of the firm has only changed by 10 cents versus the expectation. But the concern that drives the market will be that the latest data point may indicate a change in the long-term growth projection for the firm and hence in its economic value. (*Economic value* or *economic capital* is defined in this book as the present value of future cash flows; *strategic value* or *strategic capital* is defined as the value of unrealized opportunities.)

The effects of changes in long-term growth rates on economic value are discussed in depth in Chapter 3; for now it is important to note that changing trends in earnings can be detected only by careful, consistent, and honest accounting.

So conventional accounting still plays an extremely important role in valuation. Managers and investors still seek accounting advice, and the profession will continue to thrive. But only tax collectors intent on determining income, sales, and value-added taxes (VATs) wholly rely on accounting, whereas investors and managers ignore the virtual, or intangible,[4] economy at great peril.

But as the information sector of the economy grows to a size beyond even manufacturing in importance, it becomes obvious that the earnings power of many firms bears little relationship to the historical costs of their assets. It is no longer unusual to see the market value of a stock exceed its "book" value by a factor of

10 or even 20. This state of affairs implied that 90 percent to 95 percent of the value of a company might be derived from what is not on the books—thus, poring over financial statements and footnotes will be totally inadequate for purposes of valuation.

So, the first, and continuing, crisis in accounting arose from the growing differences between the marketplace and the accountant's perspective of valuation based on historical cost.

■ THE INTELLECTUAL CAPITAL "SOLUTION"

In attempts to close the valuation gap, in the 1990s, a host of articles extended the venerable concept of intellectual property to the concept of intellectual, or knowledge, capital, which added an important new dimension to intangible assets. Consider, as a starting point, this statement in a 1988 accounting textbook: "Assets can provide future benefits without having physical form. Such assets are called *intangibles*. Examples are research costs, advertising costs, patents, trade secrets, know-how, trademarks, and copyrights."[5]

From this base, the extended concept included the knowledge of the organization and its employees and the firm's ability to learn, and thus it went far beyond the more limited concepts of know-how and trade secrets. Most important, there was recognition that intellectual and human capital could far outweigh tangible capital for valuation purposes. This insight was important, yet not very definitive.

> But the idea of intellectual capital is a new one, P.H. Sullivan wrote. It brings to the foreground the brainpower assets of the organization, recognizing them as having a degree of importance comparable to the traditional land, labor, and tangible assets. If a survey were conducted, there would be agreement that many modern companies are filled with intellectual capital: law firms, consulting firms,

software companies, computer companies to name but a few. But if the survey went on to ask people to define what intellectual capital is, there would be a wide range of answers. These answers would not converge onto one straightforward definition of intellectual capital, but rather on many. The range of views and the number of terms used to describe and define intellectual capital are broad, without a clear focus, and often confusing. Once a firm understands that it has intellectual capital, how does it convert it into something of value? The answer is that it depends![6]

Or, as two Ernst and Young commentators put it: "So-called intangible assets such as brand equity, intellectual capital, corporate culture, employee skills, patents, and trademarks—to name a few—were regarded as important, but lacking the pragmatic substance necessary to build them objectively into the valuation equation."[7]

In an effort to overcome these inherent difficulties, Professor Baruch Lev and his associates have pioneered in measuring intellectual and human capital. Lev defines *intangible* (knowledge) *capital* as the present value of the future stream of knowledge earnings. He does this by creating a model whereby the economic performance of a company is based on separate contributions from its physical, financial, and knowledge assets. Among the knowledge assets are past investments in research and development (R&D). He then applies a mathematical technique called linear regression to a corporate database to get a best fit to the overall operating profit and thus to measure the rate of return on each class of assets, including the intellectual ones. In a study of the chemical industry, for example, his work indicates a 16.5 percent after-tax return on R&D and a 9.8 percent after-tax return on physical assets. His work also shows some interesting correlations between the time at which an R&D investment was made and its effect on the bottom line (3 to 5 years for maximum effect) and the size of the company making the R&D investment (higher returns for larger companies).[8]

These results conform to my intuition about the chemical industry, in which I spent a large part of my career. It suggests that the chemical industry does not return its cost of capital (today, typically 10 percent to 12 percent) with investments in physical assets alone; instead, it is that the combination of R&D and physical capital that earns an economic return. In other words, shiny new plants are commodities, and only those with proprietary technology (or an otherwise "unfair" advantage) can earn a competitive edge. Those who make physical investments only will lose money!

The numbers also tell us that the larger chemical companies, such as Dow, DuPont, 3M, and Bayer, which typically spend more on R&D, get a higher return from their spending. This harsh reality can only force industry consolidation, which has in fact been the long-term trend in the industry.

Lev's work is reassuring to those of us concerned with making an economic profit. But his results are still tied to historical spending patterns, and they are aggregated across the industry. They make no distinction between research that paid off big and research that failed utterly—although such things make all the difference in which companies prosper and which diminish in time. In other words, Lev's results are inadequate to explain either the situational differences *between* companies or the ways in which relationships between the investments (say, R&D programs and new production facilities) play off on one another. Investors are interested in the future, and they will look beyond past economic performance in selecting their investment strategies. They will seek to move beyond economic value and to anticipate *market value*. Although some of the difference between book value and economic value can be accounted for by Lev's intangible/knowledge capital, market value often moves far beyond economic value and will always be affected by the reaction of investors to business prospects.

Some writers even choose to *define* intellectual capital as the difference between market value and the value of the tangible assets. This approach is exemplified by this quotation from promotional material for a conference on intellectual capital: "The greatest challenge facing any organization today is in understanding the huge differential between its balance sheet and market valuation. This gap represents the core value of the company—its Intellectual Capital."[9] This comment will lead us astray for two reasons. The first is comparatively trivial—the undervaluation of economic assets on the balance sheet. Consider first *undervalued physical assets*. A forest products company might have purchased timberlands for $2 an acre in the nineteenth century. Though these acres will be worth hundreds or even thousands of dollars today, their balance sheet value will remain at $2 an acre; and the true value does not show up on the books of the company. The value is enhanced in part because of inflation, but also because a century or more of development may have turned wilderness into prime real estate. If the timberlands are sold, however, the company will receive a sum reflecting market value. Or if another company acquires the forest products company, it will pay a premium above historical cost for these woodlands (but the premium will show up on the books as "goodwill" and not as a new value for the acreage). Similarly, undervalued physical assets can prop up a mediocre retail operation, such as a supermarket chain that cannot earn the cost of capital from its operations. Its stock market valuation may be derived more from its ownership of prime commercial locations than from the cash flow from its failing business model.

The second reason why intellectual capital does not account for the difference between book value and market value is profound, and it will be developed in the next two chapters. For there are two very different ways of deploying intellectual capital: (1) as *economic capital* that directly increases cash flow and (2) as *strategic capital* to exploit new opportunities. In other words, intellectual capital is involved *both* in the cash-generating processes that underpin the economic value of a company and in the plans and options that create its strategic premium. Lev's work, as described earlier, encompasses only the former but gives intellectual capital due weight for its contribution to economic value.

However, we must turn to strategic capital when the marketplace insists on an enormous price/earnings ratio or creates a positive market capitalization even when cash flow is negative. Furthermore, these two forms of capital—economic and strategic—have different characteristics; and their values are best analyzed separately, the former by discounted cash flow techniques and the latter by options theory applied to a coherent business plan. The results should be additive and should account for the total value of the enterprise.

In brief, the intellectual capital solution weighs intellectual capital by difference with reference to market value. The result is useless to an investor or a decision maker. The real options solution implemented through the concept of total value weighs intellectual capital directly. This solution affords a way for investors to determine whether total value exceeds market value or falls short of it. The first circumstance broadly translates to "invest," the second to "divest."

■ EXPLOITING STRATEGIC CAPITAL: THE JAPANESE ATTACK ON THE U.S. AUTO MARKET

One of the great industrial battles of our time can be characterized in terms of total value versus economic value. The outcome of that battle had to do with much more than economic advantage or intellectual capital. In the 1970s, Japanese automobile manufacturers began their onslaught on the U.S. Big Three—Ford, General Motors, and Chrysler—that led to an increase in market share from near 0 percent to just short of 30 percent. The attack began at the low end of the market, where the Toyota

Corolla, the Honda Civic, and the Datsun offered good quality at low cost. These cars had been perfected for Japanese urban driving conditions and translated reasonably well to the needs of urban commuters in parts of the United States. The energy crises of the 1970s greatly boosted their appeal, while their advantages in quality translated into good resale value and repeat purchases. U.S. manufacturers attempted to fight back with their own small cars, the Pinto and the Vega, for example, but the U.S. companies proved too inexperienced in this sector to reply with a convincing value proposition for the consumer. More important, Detroit's heart was not in the game: Its experience was, and still remains, that small cars offered only low profit margins and that large cars loaded with options were the foundation for their prosperity.[10]

This analysis was of course based on an economic value model. It ignored the strategic premiums associated with both technical knowledge (here, the knowledge of how to build value into a small car) and an important consumer franchise. Detroit gave the Japanese the opportunity to grow up-market with their customers and to introduce more expensive and hugely successful models, such as the Honda Accord and the Toyota Camry. In time they targeted the last bastion, the luxury market; and by 1998, Lexus, a Toyota subsidiary, was outselling Cadillac by a large margin.[11]

In the context of this book, the Japanese could justify an assault on the small-car market, even if initially unprofitable, because it created the option to enter the middle and the luxury markets! Whether such a plan was explicit or unspoken is only of historic interest; the option was there, and it was profitably exercised. The total value formulation prevailed over the economic value model.

This case also brings home the point that a sound approach to valuation not only is of importance to investors, but also is essential for managers if they are to make correct business decisions.

■ THE SECOND CRISIS IN VALUATION

The explicit recognition of the value of intellectual capital is an important advance in bridging the world of finance with the world of technology. It has a host of nuances, and an understanding of its dynamics will be of paramount importance to wealth creation in the twenty-first century. Chapter 11 is committed to a discussion of some of the more important issues involved in intellectual capital.

Unfortunately, previous attempts at fathoming the value of intellectual capital have not always improved the understanding of market value. This situation became crystal clear with the second crisis in valuation—the explosion of the Internet. The concept of intellectual capital needed to be stretched very far to explain the huge valuations created by Internet start-ups or, for that matter, the corrections that followed. Analysts were in disarray—many resorted to new metrics, while others dismissed the phenomenon as an example of the madness of crowds. For example, the stock of Doubleclick, a company that serves ads and tracks the patterns of Internet users, rose from about $10 in June 1998 to over $120 at the height of Internet fever in early 2000. That peak represented a market capitalization of about $15 billion. By December 2000, it was trading as low as $8. A promising business-to-business (B2B) company, FreeMarkets, Inc., was trading as high as $370 on January 3, 2000, soon after going public, and attained a valuation of about $15 billion. A year later, shares of Freemarkets stock could be purchased for $20.

Dot-com fever threw a wrench into the established machinery of valuation practice. Companies with nothing but operating losses achieved valuations of $10 billion to $50 billion. In the absence of earnings, the traditional yardsticks of value—price/earnings (P/E) ratios, price-to-operating income, and price-to-operating cash flow—could not be applied. The discounted cash flow method remained applicable; but to reconcile the results with market values, wildly optimistic cash flow projections had to be made. Internet analysts began to use "price-to-revenues" ratios; and strange and mystical metrics such as "price-to-vision" ratios, "eyeballs," and "click-throughs" came into vogue. There was also talk of a "New Economy" characterized by "increasing returns," in contrast to what the dismal science of economics had taught us about the inevitability of diminishing returns. The "comparables" were no longer companies with operating track records; they were other recent start-ups. Old hands began to speak of tulips and bubbles.

Meantime, a river of money poured into venture capital: New venture financing, which had attracted less than $5 billion per year a decade earlier, topped $60 billion. And it's no wonder—for a brief period some venture capitalists were earning over 100 percent per year annual returns. This was a far cry from the "good" old days when a 20 percent average annual return was considered good performance in venture capital.

The AOL Time Warner deal was probably the peak: a calculation by sophisticated businesspeople, subsequently well-accepted by professional investors, that merging an old-economy content-and-services provider with its Internet counterpart was good business. It seemed to validate the valuation.

Briefly, we wondered whether the dot-coms could take over the world. Business-to-business exchanges such as FreeMarkets had valuations (as measured by market capitalization) of billions of dollars, higher than many of the traditional companies they purported to serve. Could AOL Time Warner presage the New Economy taking over the old?

In April 2000, the bubble burst. The Nasdaq dropped from 5000 to well below 2000. This contraction was painful—more painful for some companies than others.

The issue is much deeper than whether Internet stocks were overvalued or whether one should own them or shun them. The phenomenon that occurred was a real one, and its details are well documented. Every investor and every business executive (again valuation is important not only for transaction purposes but also for decision making) now needs to consider the remarkable dynamics by which incredible value creation and, subsequently, value destruction proceeded. In my opinion, this sequence of events was no aberration, and similar value dynamics are likely to challenge us more frequently in the future.

■ THE THREE LEVELS OF VALUATION: BOOK, ECONOMIC, AND TOTAL

The issues posed in the preceding section can be resolved without introducing any radical financial concepts or metrics, but they do require a clear understanding of the differences among three types of valuation. The first is very familiar: book value as represented by a balance sheet prepared according to accepted accounting principles. The second is standard fare in business schools and corporate finance courses: economic value as calculated from a discounted sum of forecasted cash flows. The third is far less familiar and at the heart of this book: the use of options theory to value positions subject to uncertainty. The application of options theory to general business decision making is growing rapidly, and the literature is quickly identified under the term *real options*. Fortunately, the principles required to evaluate business positions and plans are not very different from those used to value financial options and other derivatives, traded daily in enormous quantities around the world.

■ THE MISSING PIECE: STRATEGIC CAPITAL

To find total value, it will be very helpful to use a new term, which I call *strategic capital*. It was defined earlier as the value of unrealized opportunities. It encompasses the human and intellectual capital that creates options for adding value to a business. It also requires the fundamental business positions that enable these options.

Although strategic capital may include a great deal of intellectual capital, it is emphatically not the same thing as intellectual capital. So in this framework, where is intellectual capital to be found? The short answer is that some of it is included in economic capital, some of it is found in the realm of strategic capital, and what is idle and not contributing to value can be safely ignored.

Strategic capital is an integrating concept because it allows a common approach to valuation whether one is dealing with the old economy or the new. An unimaginative manufacturing company may have little strategic capital. Many Internet start-ups were valued entirely for their strategic capital. A traditional industrial company that has an innovative and productive R&D effort will derive value from both economic capital and strategic capital.

Because strategic capital is based on options, it is inherently more volatile than economic capital. After all, it is perfectly possible for the value of an option to increase by 100 percent when the price of the underlying stock changes by 10 percent. And so it should be no surprise that volatility increases as the mix of capital swings from primarily economic to primarily strategic.

Financial textbooks[12] have long referred to intangible assets, including patents, copyrights, trademarks, know-how, and trade secrets. These comprise the domain known as *intellectual property*. The term *intellectual capital* began to recognize the tremendous values that could be created by shrewd investments in such intangibles as R&D, training, and advertising, which do not show up on a balance sheet because they are fully accounted for as expenses when incurred. But, as Lev has shown, some intellectual capital is built into the *economic* valuation of an operating business, even if it is not shown on the accounting balance sheet. It is included in the value-creating processes of the company, those processes that permit a return above the cost of capital and that sustain long-term growth. But the strategic capital that pertains to new opportunities is generally not in the economic equation.

Perhaps strategic capital has been ignored because, in principle, the predictable creation of many small incremental opportunities can be included in an economic model; incremental growth has been explicitly the corporate strategy of traditional "growth" companies, such as 3M and IBM. But the economic approach to growth will not work as well when the value of the opportunity is comparable to, or greater than, the value of the current operations.

The case for strategic capital can be formulated in a manner entirely congruent with what is taught in finance textbooks. There it is taught that the valuation of a company should be based on its *cash flow in a no-growth situation plus the net present value of its opportunities*.[13] Opportunities in this context are *all* opportunities to invest additional capital to grow the business— the classical situation. We shall see that it is straightforward to include in the base valuation *forecast* growth rather than *no-growth* to obtain the economic value of the company. "Opportunities" are then redefined as those business options that create value above forecast. The mechanics are discussed and illustrated in Chapter 4.

In this approach, some intellectual capital supports forecast growth, which is built into the economic value of an enterprise. Valuing the additional opportunities that go beyond the expected is less straightforward. But it is precisely in the realm of the unexpected that advantage can be gained and new value created. The history of Searle illustrates this point. G. D. Searle was a moderately successful pharmaceutical company that could be reasonably expected to grow at a normal rate and earn returns typical of the drug industry. From an analyst's viewpoint, these parameters, adjusted for his or her opinions of Searle's strength relative to the rest of the industry, would have been sufficient to define the company's economic value. When its R&D labs discovered the sweetener named aspartame, a blockbuster new product for the beverage industry, it acquired a valuable option to pursue a unique strategic opportunity not yet factored into its economic value.

For high-risk investors, the really important contributors to strategic capital are *the plans and the capabilities of the firm to exploit new opportunities*. Such unrealized opportunities may be valued on the stock market, but they are not found in financial statements.

■ COMPARING THE THREE APPROACHES TO VALUATION

Table 2.1 summarizes the distinctions being made here between book value, economic value, and total value. In a completely efficient marketplace, total value should equate to market value. Let's look at the top tier first—*Economic Capital*, assets that relate to the current operations of the company.

The first column shows the typical accounting characteristics of a "virgin" company—one that has not made any acquisitions. The accountants will value its fixed assets at cost less depreciation. They will then value its working capital—its inventory,[14] based on last in–first out (LIFO) or first in–first out (FIFO) methods, plus its receivables. Finally, they will add up cash in the bank, plus any securities or other investments made by the company. That's all. The sum of these numbers is book value.

The second column shows the economic value of the firm. The method used is typically discounted cash flow (DCF) valuation. A forecast is made of the cash payouts of the firm, with future payments discounted at the cost of capital. Economic value is what drives a financial investor (who could be an acquiring company) to pay a premium above book value in the

Table 2.1   A Comparison of Historic, Economic, and Strategic Approaches to Valuation

	Type of Applicable Valuation Method			
	Historical or Book Value (Accounting)	Economic Value (Cash Flow)	Strategic Premium (Options)	Transaction Accounting (Mark-to-Market)
Type of Capital				
Economic Capital				
Fixed capital	Yes	Yes	No	Yes
Working capital	Yes	Yes	No	Yes
Cash, securities, and investments	Yes	Yes	No	Yes
Goodwill	No	No	No	Yes
Income-producing intellectual property	No	Yes	No	Yes
Value processes	No	Yes	No	No
Strategic Capital				
Business plans		No	Yes	
Strategic assets				
Conventional intellectual property		Cost	Yes	Yes
In-process R&D		Cost	Yes	Yes
Goodwill		Cost	No	Yes
Strategic alliances		Cost	Yes	
Unused financial capacity		Cost	Yes	
Transformation processes		Cost	Yes	

first place. That investor expects a future cash flow stream with a value above the book value of the assets as determined by the accountants.

Why might the company be worth more than book value? Again, it may have assets such as real estate that were purchased at prices well below current market value. Also, the company is likely to own intellectual capital not shown on the books, above the more tangible assets of fixed capital, working capital, and financial capital that appear on the balance sheet. Intellectual capital will include the value-creating processes used by the company, the skills of its employees, unique commercial franchises, intellectual property, and so forth. Because these assets all contribute to cash flow, they create economic value.

The items in the third column, labeled "strategic premium," are generally not relevant to current operations and are not included among balance sheet assets. These assets do not contribute to current cash flow; on the contrary, they often incur a cash flow penalty. They are shown in the table's second tier—*Strategic Capital*. These are the assets that are of interest to a *strategic investor*—one who is interested in creating opportunities above and beyond the values derived from forecasted cash flow. Strategic capital is embodied in the plans that have been put in place to create that value. It is also embodied in those intangible assets that are retained to enable those plans. Typically these strategic assets include R&D, patents, strategic alliances, some unused financial capacity, and managers and professionals capable of blending these components into a successful commercial operation. Usually all of these are required: They are part of the plan and the plan cannot be executed without them. Chapter 4 illustrates how these elements can be combined to calculate a quantifiable total value to guide investment, acquisition, and strategy.

The strategic premium can be quite large—and can sometimes be the whole ballgame. As I pause in writing, I surf over to the profile of a company with six thousand employees and a prior-year *loss* measured in nine figures on *revenues well under a billion dollars*. As a cash flow machine, it is still a loser. Its economic value is negative. But at the time I first wrote this paragraph, it had a market capitalization fluctuating between $50 billion and $100 billion! More than 90 percent of that value was created in the previous year. At this time, the marketplace had placed a huge value on its strategic capital—on its business plan and on the abilities of its key employees to execute.

■ WHEN MARKET VALUE DOES NOT FOLLOW ECONOMIC VALUE

The difference between economic value and market value separates strategic investors from value investors. This same difference helps explain why the market often reacts to news in surprising ways—when market value decreases as economic value increases, or vice versa. For example, let's assume a firm has just announced the layoff of one hundred R&D employees. The intent of management is to improve cash flow by perhaps $10 million per year and, in principle, to create economic value added (EVA) of $100 million or more. If the stock market felt those employees were not doing anything particularly useful, the stock would move to a higher level. Market value added (MVA) should follow EVA.

But MVA sometimes moves in a direction opposite to EVA! If it were felt that the R&D layoff reflected management's pessimism about future prospects, the strategic investors might downgrade their estimate of the strategic capital of the firm sufficiently that the stock would drop. Naturally, this circumstance would be more likely to occur in a technology stock carrying a large strategic premium than in a more traditional company with fewer strategic options.

Table 2.1 dissects this relationship for us. It shows book value in the first column, as a point of reference. In the second column is the economic value of the firm. As we have discussed, the difference between book value and economic value (first and second columns) can be attributed to the intellectual capital of the firm embodied in its value processes plus any undervalued tangible assets. The third column indicates the firm's strategic capital. *Total value* is the sum of the second and third columns. In a rational marketplace, total value should equal market value. When the market pays a strategic premium above the economic value of the firm, it perceives opportunities not reflected in the cash flow forecast of its current operations, and it is recognizing strategic capital.

To use the layoff example again, those R&D employees represent a cost in the second column, but they also represent an option to execute business plans that require their skills. Abandoning that option will reduce strategic capital in the third column. The marketplace will judge whether the net effect is expected to be a loss or a gain. Of course, unwise innovation can extract a penalty. Boeing had committed resources to the option to build a new jumbo jet, dubbed the 747-X, capable of carrying over 500 passengers. It had communicated this option to investors and potential customers. Then, in early 1997 it announced that it was canceling the program, which was costing $3 million per day.[15] The stock rose several points. Clearly, the stock market viewed the 747-X project as a likely destroyer of value (the Asian market looked dubious at the time) and welcomed Boeing's exercise of its abandonment option and the boost to its free cash flow.

On the other hand, a firm has ways to try to increase MVA other than to increase EVA. It may announce a hot new product or an attractive new deal. New strategic capital becomes evident in such plans, and total value should increase even if there is no immediate increase in economic value. But, as always, if the plans imply a decrease in cash flow, investors will weigh the negative economic impact against their perception of the value of the new opportunity. The stock market frequently surprises management in this situation as well, as when the announcement of an acquisition decreases the share price of the would-be acquirer.

■ TRANSACTION ACCOUNTING: MARKING ECONOMIC AND STRATEGIC CAPITAL TO MARKET

There is one important case in which virtual and strategic assets may suddenly, and sometimes uncomfortably, find themselves on the balance sheet.

Assume our company loses its virginity: It acquires a similar firm and pays a premium above book value for it. This situation is summarized in the fourth column, as "transaction accounting." Accountants view a transaction as history and mark the difference between the book value of the acquired assets and the market price paid to the latter value. The difference is typically accounted for as "goodwill."

Because goodwill can only be written off over a 40-year period, it is very unproductive capital, providing only a tiny tax shield. Businesspeople and investors hate it, and accountants have obliged them by finding ways to reduce goodwill: One way is to use pooling accounting. Another way is to appraise the value of patents and other intellectual property and to depreciate these over their useful life. A third way is to attribute some of the premium above book to "in-process R&D." This sum may then be written off and used immediately as a tax shield.[16] The practice is understandably unpopular with the Securities and Exchange Commission (SEC) and with the tax authorities. Changes in this area are to be expected in the future.

In the ordinary course of business, events involving strategic capital are financially invisible. But as ghosts are rumored to materialize from time to time, virtual (or strategic) capital can materialize as well. When a company is bought at a premium above its economic value, it implies that a buyer has put a value on its strategic options that is above and beyond the value inherent in its cash flow. This situation will occur, for example, if GE pays cash for an Internet company that has zero or negative cash flow. Its characteristics are shown in the second tier of the fourth column of Table 2.1. The strategic premium can be recorded as goodwill, as in-process R&D, or as intellectual property. And the gain above historic cost realized by the previous owners will be taxed at the capital gains rate. There is nothing virtual about a tax! On an ongoing basis, no one yet attempts to tax intellectual "income," say as contributed by a successful R&D program. But the strategic capital created will be taxed when financial gains are realized.

■ THE LBO OPTION

The special case of a leveraged buyout (LBO) is introduced at this time because it so clearly illustrates the differences between the valuation approaches that are at the core of this book. A leveraged buyout is a transaction in which debt is used to fund all or most of the price paid to buy a business. LBOs are used both by managers who want to take a business private and by acquisition-minded investors who want to acquire publicly owned companies.[17] The LBO strategy is a nearly sure way to create wealth when the company can be purchased so cheaply that its own cash flow can be used to pay down the interest and principal of the loan, leaving the acquirers with ownership of the company with a minimum personal investment. In many actual cases, management must take drastic steps to boost the cash flow sufficiently to make the LBO plan feasible.

The strategy will often be triggered when the marketplace ceases to believe that a company's continuing investments in strategic capital will pay off, and the resulting low share price opens a shorter and surer route to wealth creation. An opportunity then becomes apparent to buy the company with borrowed money and to pay off interest and principal from the company's cash flow. The role of diminishing returns in setting the stage for an LBO is discussed in Chapter 7.

To a company employee, an LBO is a very cold bath. It means the termination of many initiatives, many commitments, and many fellow employees. But to an investor, it is a logical leap from one investment strategy to an entirely different one. Consider how a steely-eyed "value" investor, especially an LBO investor, may view strategic capital as illustrated in the bottom tier of the second column of Table 2.1. She will assign zero value to the opportunities implicit in plans since her immediate priorities are to maximize cash flow. Previous management may have invested substantially in growth-creating opportunities that are still consuming cash, such as introducing new products. These investments are now expendable. Eliminating them increases cash flow and shortens the time until the debt is paid down.

R&D programs that once fit into future business plans but require cash investments also do not fit the new strategy. Patents may be dropped, or licensed, to save maintenance costs. A line of credit to facilitate acquisitions may be reduced to save money. The costs of maintaining a network of strategic alliances and memberships in industry groups may be seen as needless overhead. The most costly assets comprising strategic capital are people—the skilled staff required to transform opportunities and plans into operating capital. They may be R&D employees, market researchers, central engineering staff, commercial development experts, strategic planners, and so forth, who were hired to facilitate the process of transforming strategic capital into operating cash flow. In an LBO they are among the first to go.

In a sense, the classic LBO strategy is the last option: Its value is realized by abandoning all the other options, thus increasing cash flow.

■ STRATEGIC BUYERS VERSUS FINANCIAL BUYERS

The bifurcation of value between economic capital and strategic capital becomes apparent in another financial arena as well—

that of mergers and acquisitions. In this field the distinction is commonly made between "financial buyers" and "strategic buyers." Almost by definition, a strategic buyer is one who will pay more for an asset than a financial buyer will. The strategic buyer will pay more because he or she sees opportunities or options that the financial buyer does not.

This behavior is mirrored in the world of auction galleries. The buying population at an auction consists of dealers and nondealers. In essence the bidders are financial buyers and strategic buyers. Art, furniture, and rug dealers typically buy goods at auction and mark them up to a higher price in their shops. Because they must hold inventory and bear costs associated with running their shops, they have learned through experience that they can only make a profit if their average markup reaches a certain level.

Assume that a dealer's strategy is to sell a rug at twice what he pays for it. Therefore, if he sees an oriental rug at auction that he thinks he can sell for $5,000, he may drop out of the bidding at $2,500. However, he may be fairly flexible about which $5,000 rugs he may bid $2,500 for. A private party may be looking at the same rug and recognize that dealers are asking about $5,000 for similar ones. The nondealer, however, is looking for a rug about 8 feet by 10 feet that matches the blue upholstery in her den. She will not bid on a rug of the wrong size or color but is prepared to bid up to $4,000 (less than the retail cost) for the right item. She is a strategic buyer—she perceives enhanced value in the synergy between her decorating plans and a particular rug.

In business, the financial buyer is akin to the LBO specialist discussed earlier. She will be prepared to borrow the selling price for an asset if she is confident that the cash flow from that asset can pay back the interest and the principal of the loan. Cash flow is everything—she is unlikely to jeopardize her financial strategy by diverting much of that cash flow to growth opportunities. As soon as the loan has been paid down sufficiently, she may seek a strategic buyer and realize her profit.

However, a strategic buyer may see opportunities that the financial buyer does not. For example, a competitor may see the opportunity to realize savings by combining sales forces and eliminating redundant office facilities and people. The enhanced cash flows from these savings are termed "synergies" and can in principle be capitalized. The strategic buyer can afford to top the bid of a financial buyer by the value of these synergies. Of course, he will try to get the lowest price available—hopefully just above the financial buyer's bid.

In effect, the strategic buyer has an option, or opportunity, that neither the seller nor the financial buyer has. That option is embedded in the existing sales organization. If his synergy is substantial and if he does not have to bid against another strategic buyer in this auction, he can create substantial value for his firm. That value premium is comprised entirely of strategic capital.

■ INVESTMENT STYLES: GROWTH VERSUS VALUE

The distinction between economic investing and strategic investing is mirrored at a higher level in investment styles. However, the terminology used is different and, I believe, misleading. The two styles are designated as *growth* and *value*—and mutual funds are typically labeled as following one style, the other style, or a "balance" of the two. It has long been observed that in some years "value funds" outperform "growth funds," and in other years the reverse is true. The number of years in which one style or the other is superior appears to be about equally divided.

At the time this book was conceived, growth investors had been on an unprecedented winning streak, and some commentators are perplexed by the phenomenon. Renowned value investors such as Julian Robertson and Laurence Tisch had been hurt by the market and professed to be bewildered by the market valuations of New Economy stocks. "People don't realize this is a unique period in American financial history. . . . We've gotten to such an extreme in the market that a correction would be of such major proportions, it could do economic harm to the country."[18]

The chairman of the Federal Reserve Bank characterized these valuations as "irrational exuberance." The phenomenon is frequently compared to tulip mania in seventeenth-century Holland and to the South Sea bubble in eighteenth-century England. The implication was that a future crash is as unavoidable as the certain fact of the crashes of 1637 and 1720. This is the *rejectionist* school of thought. Its underpinnings are well summarized by an investment veteran, indeed, a veteran of the crash of 1929: "The most important single factor in shaping securities markets is public psychology."[19] The high volatility of New Economy securities naturally reinforces the concept that they are dangerous investments. The arguments of the skeptics are worth considering seriously, especially because of the 60 percent correction to the Nasdaq that followed its fast run-up in value; but there are equally serious reasons for thinking the skeptics may have missed the point.

The other school of thought derives from the *efficient market hypothesis*: This assumes "that information is widely and cheaply available to all investors and all relevant and ascertainable information is already reflected in security prices."[20] It is time to consider the possibility that the marketplace judgments may be reasonable *for the time at which they are made* and that the financial tools being used to render judgment are the problem. There are typically two pieces missing in the rejectionist analysis: One is strategic capital, the second is the nature of risk.

The word *growth* no longer defines the issue, but confuses it. To be sure, there is a clear linkage between economic growth and economic value,[21] which can be readily demonstrated using discounted cash flow techniques and which we describe in Chapter 3. But this formula is intellectually consistent with value investing, as long as the sustainability of that growth is credible. However, an increasing portion of the valuation of the market is related to strategic capital. That amount has been reckoned as up to 75 percent.[22] Most of that strategic capital happens to be attributed to the growth sector. And as long as strategic capital grows faster than economic capital, the growth sector must outperform the value sector. This phenomenon can only result in higher price/earnings ratios because the P/E metric is tied to current economic performance. That is what we have been observing in the current marketplace.

Is a bias toward value investing synonymous with a bias toward investing in companies with few opportunities (which should have lower P/E ratios)? In a world where change seems to be accelerating (a subject discussed in the last chapter), this approach may be more dangerous than investing in situations where management has significant opportunities to adjust to change. Maturing industries, such as railroads, steel, and paper, seem to be caught in this trap. I have a close association with the plastics industry: In the 1960s and 1970s our industry had large opportunities to replace metal, glass, and paper. It was fun to be part of it. In the 1980s and 1990s many or most of those options were exercised and the value realized. Identifying new opportunities of the same quality is increasingly challenging. If value investing means investing in mature industries that can no longer earn the cost of capital, it will be delusional.

Although market setbacks are inevitable, there is no way to predict when the winning record of growth stocks might come to an end. But it is time to recognize that stocks with high P/E multiples might be better characterized as stocks that have proportionally high levels of strategic capital supporting their valuations. If exceptional growth is indeed driven by strong strategic capital positions, then there is no mystery. The core issue becomes whether the strategic capital, which should be valued using real options theory, has become overvalued.

It also stands to reason that the ability of strategic capital to drive growth is considerably more situational (real options reflect managerial flexibility) than the ability of economic capital to generate cash flow. Therefore the value of strategic capital is likely to be more volatile as conditions change. Hence, it is to be expected that stocks carrying a large strategic premium will have some terrible years.

Closing the valuation gap is far from hopeless. Valuation of intellectual property is sophisticated in some areas (licensing), while primitive in others. And the development of real options theory gives us important tools for understanding the relationship between risk and value. However, the game may be getting away from us—because the role of human and intellectual capital is rapidly increasing in modern society and because risk levels also rise when competition involves a battle of ideas and standards rather than the efficient use of conventional assets.

Incidentally, this phenomenon is hardly restricted to the high-technology and biotechnology sectors of the economy. Entertainment giants like Disney, brand name franchises such as McDonald's and Coca-Cola, law firms, consultants, and a host of other important businesses, each for different reasons, must count intellectual property among their most highly valued assets. Their market capitalizations reflect these values, though their financial statements do not. The most successful of these companies leverage the power of their brand names and brainpower to create strategic capital. So Disney leveraged movies into theme parks and theme parks into residential real estate. Andersen leveraged accounting into a leading position in enterprise software consulting.

■ WHY TOTAL VALUE IS NOT MARKET VALUE

In the preceding discussion, I have proposed that in an efficient market place total value should equate to market value. In this and the following section, I will discuss two reasons why the market is not efficient and why discrepancies occur. These discrepancies, of course, represent profit opportunities.

The first reason is discontinuities in supply and demand. So far, I have treated the stock market with great abstraction. But it is not an abstraction at all; it is a microcosm of existing and potential investors. The public market for a particular company's stock—its buyers and sellers—is made up of many kinds of players. Participants include employees who know a great deal about their company's plans and capabilities; professional analysts who influence institutional holdings and who write broker recommendations; and individual investors who are, for whatever reason, knowledgeable about the company's line of business (people whose judgment I, in general, respect). Each of these groups attempts to forecast the economic performance of the firm, which is difficult, and also attempts to assess a strategic premium, which is even more difficult. Because these players trade with each other, the market price will, in part, reflect a balance of views regarding a reasonable strategic premium. A new fact can dramatically shift that balance and move the price.

The market also consists of day-traders, momentum investors, and the followers of "technical" analysts (whose judgment I respect less, but whose behavior is important). There is smart money and less-smart money among these players.

Institutional players may distort an efficient market through policies, such as holding only large caps, avoiding commodities, or pursuing a social agenda. The profile of the buyers and the sellers is not constant: It shifts with fashions in the marketplace, it responds to changing investment objectives, and it is even affected by the time of year.

Beyond the activities of the public market, there are hidden private options for value creation. A firm may divest operations, it may become an acquisition target, or it may negotiate with lenders to go private as a leveraged buyout. The existence of these options provides bounds for valuation. A stock should not drop much below a point at which an LBO is a financial sure thing. And the valuation of General Motors must consider the firm's options to divest a Hughes Electronics.

For all of these reasons and for others to be discussed later, total value cannot be congruent with market price. Rather, market price reflects an imperfect process seeking to integrate all available information to estimate total value. From this viewpoint, an investment whose total value is greater than market price is attractive, and one whose market price exceeds total value may turn out badly.

■ THE TWIN CAUSES OF INVISIBILITY: DARKNESS AND FOG

The second barrier to an efficient market is that strategic, or virtual, capital—the ghost in the garden—can be very hard to measure. So investment in high-risk businesses can never be easy. Call the reasons darkness and fog. Darkness occurs because the key information is available only to insiders. Fog occurs when it is obscured by a host of confusing factors.

First, *darkness*. For competitive reasons, a firm will keep its most valuable intellectual property (excepting issued patents) secret—not only its intellectual assets but also its *plans* for deploying them. Firms in the public sector vary considerably in what they will tell investors and the public. Some large firms seem to be instinctively secretive; they produce annual reports replete with glossy photographs of happy suburban housewives shopping for consumer goods and with highly aggregated financial statements. Others provide detailed descriptions of the performance of each of their divisions, their ongoing capital projects, the specifications of their products, and even their environmental records.

There are good, and straightforward, reasons for both approaches. Secretiveness enhances competitive advantage. Openness keeps investor interest at a peak and can reduce the cost of capital. Every chief executive officer (CEO) must decide on the right balance.

Many small firms have to tell more than they prudently should, simply because "selling" a good business plan is part of the process of attracting seed and venture capital. Other firms, large and small, that are not seeking capital may be very opaque for reasons of privacy as much as for competitive strategy.

Outsiders have opportunities to glimpse into the darkness— they can read public documents such as patents and permits, look at help-wanted advertising, study industry statistics, and consult experts. Competitors may delve this deeply, but few investors or even investment analysts have time to do it.

Second, *fog*. The information that matters is hidden in an enormous mass of other information, some of which is only partly communicated or documented. Much of it is so specialized that only an expert can interpret it. Some of it is erroneous, wrong-headed, or deliberately crafted to mislead. There are simply too many people, too many relationships, and too much technical material in even a medium-sized company for any individual, even an insider, to analyze all the options comprehensively.

And more information emerges every day. In the world of research every experiment enhances or diminishes a key project's chance for success. A division president may be planning to propose a brilliant acquisition or product introduction, but until he or she feels confident about the last critical piece of information, even the CEO may not be told of it.

As a senior executive and as a board member—a classic insider by definition—I have sat through endless business reviews analyzing financial statements, market trends, and new developments. That information was very useful from the viewpoint of supporting individual business decisions. But it was less useful in short-term valuation of the total enterprise. While insiders were addressing exciting new opportunities or cutting losses on what now seemed to be unproductive investments, outsiders were reacting to different information and often had very different issues on their minds than those that concerned management. So, excepting the special case of inside information about an announcement that would surprise the public (information on which it is illegal to trade), I never felt fully confident in predicting the next move in the stock price. Even when the lights were turned on and most vital economic information was accessible, there was still plenty of fog to contend with.

So given the darkness and fog, why is it worthwhile for a high-risk investor to try to value strategic capital? The first answer is that an analysis of real options is one of the few ways in which an investor can use his or her intelligence and insight to beat the market. Second, some of the larger options may be obvious and amenable to quantitative analysis. Third, because options can only have positive values, the neglect of real options by other investors may result in undervaluation (but never overvaluation).

■ GENENTECH: A DRESS REHEARSAL FOR THE NEW ECONOMY

The valuation problem created by the New Economy caught everyone's attention, but it was hardly unprecedented. In fact, it had played out years earlier with the emergence of the biotech industry. With the benefit of considerable hindsight, it is instructive to review that earlier episode.

Genentech was founded in 1976 by venture capitalist Robert Swanson and university biochemist Herbert Boyer, a co-inventor of seminal gene-splicing technology. By 1979 Genentech had cloned three important human proteins: (1) somatostatin, (2) human growth hormone, and (3) insulin. However, the firm faced many years of expensive development (read "negative cash flow") to turn a cloned sequence into a commercial product. It went public in 1980 with a $35 million offering, and the stock surged from $35 to $88 per share in the first hour. Before long Genentech's market capitalization was just under a billion dollars. I took careful note of this development because my employer at the time, the American Can Company, could boast leading market positions in packaging and consumer goods, a hundred-year long history, many profitable operations, and revenues that placed it in the Fortune 50. But American Can's market capitalization *was less than Genentech's.* Was this "irrational exuberance"?

With no short-term cash flow in sight, Genentech's valuation was based purely on its intellectual property. And that property was formidable—several potential new drugs in the pipeline, a technology lead over its competition, and, above all, the ability to attract the best biochemists and molecular biologists that the university community could produce. Scientists flocked to Genentech and its competitors because of the opportunity to get in on the ground floor of a hot new field and to build their resumes by working on some highly visible and exciting projects. And, as in the case of the dot-com boomlet, the allure of stock options was a huge factor. American Can did not offer stock options to junior employees.

It appeared that Genentech had a huge number of opportunities, not only to invent and produce human pharmaceuticals, but also to apply biotechnology to animal health, specialty chemicals, diagnostics, and so on. On the downside, it had no experience in commercial operations, and many wondered whether any of its products could be brought to market unaided. In addition, rival biotechnology companies were proliferating at the time, and many wiser heads predicted that it would only be a matter of time until Big Pharma muscled in or bought out the pioneers. One analyst observed that the market capitalization of biotechnology stocks hoping to cure cancer exceeded the total global anticancer drug market many times over!

What does hindsight tell us? Most important, it tells us that Genentech was fairly valued: Its market capitalization today of more than $30 billion has rewarded patient investors handsomely. It earned a double-digit return for long-term investors. It needed to capitalize on only a few of its options to survive and prosper. And it did so. These included the successful licensing of human insulin to Eli Lilly (marketed in 1982) and the introduction of its first commercial recombinant product, human growth hormone, in 1985. Other opportunities emerged with time, and today Genentech retains a leadership position in the industry.

Some options were not exercised, such as the idea of using genetically engineered organisms to produce specialty chemicals. Other options were captured by competitors. Despite Genentech's general lead, the most successful new biotech drug, erythropoietin, was commercialized by Amgen, which thereby retained its independence and became a successful manufacturing and marketing company.

The risks were indeed high and the road was bumpy. Two of the early leaders in biotechnology, Genex and Cetus, failed; and Genentech itself was compelled to sell a majority interest to Hoffman-LaRoche.

But what about American Can? Most of its operations were, indeed, sound; and in the end it proved somewhat undervalued. It did not survive as a corporation, however; and all of its operations were purchased, either by LBO specialists (the ultimate cash flow managers) or by more agile competitors. Nothing like $30 billion in market value was ever created. American Can had *few options*. The majority of its businesses were mature, and pricing was too competitive to allow returns on new investments that were much above the cost of capital. Its access and receptiveness to new ideas were limited, and its access to capital was squandered when management gambled wildly on the acquisition of retail music businesses. These businesses hemorrhaged cash, and the company was forced to divest its core packaging operations.

What do these cases tell us about options? We know that options are especially valuable in situations of high growth and high volatility. High volatility equates to high risk. We also know that options are all about flexibility: Management has the ability to make investments but no obligation to do so. It can wait and see whether the market conditions and the technology factors look favorable or otherwise. One of the ingredients is intellectual capital; another is access to financial capital. These are the conditions that created wealth at Genentech. American Can was in low-risk, virtually recession-proof, low-growth businesses. These conditions failed to create much wealth.

■ THE AGRACETUS CASE

Let us use option terminology to look at another example in which I was a participant. The Agracetus name was an ingenious composite that included the name of the founding company, a leading biotechnology firm then named Cetus Corporation; the connotation of agriculture (the target market); and the letters "grace" representing my firm, W. R. Grace and Company. In many ways Agracetus had a typical business history, with some very uncertain moments, but a generally good outcome.

A major biotech industry, with publicly traded stocks, was created in the early 1980s to exploit the now-apparent potential of genetic engineering to create new products for health care, agriculture, and specialty chemicals. The leading companies at that time were Genentech (described earlier), Cetus (now part of Chiron, but the largest of the four), Biogen, and Genex. Genex was not a survivor, but Genentech and Biogen continue in the industry as leading players, to be joined by Amgen and many others.

These companies started with no meaningful operating revenues, huge R&D budgets, and some great ideas. To survive, they needed continuing infusions of cash from investors or support from strategic partners with deep pockets. All planned to transform themselves into independent operating companies before their cash ran out. None of the first group fully succeeded, though Amgen did, and Genentech came close. The situation was in many ways an early parallel to the Internet stock situation today.

Cetus created a subsidiary in 1981, originally called Cetus Madison, in Madison, Wisconsin, to exploit the potential of its genetic technology for agriculture. A distinguished scientist recruited from the University of Wisconsin, Dr. Winston Brill, headed Cetus Madison; and a small but very talented scientific staff was assembled.

In need of financing, Cetus approached W. R. Grace in 1983 with a proposal to create a joint venture (JV) in the field of agriculture. The heart of the deal was this: In return for Grace financing the R&D costs of the operation for five years, Cetus would donate to the JV the results of Cetus Madison research, full access to all Cetus technology, and excusive rights to that technology in the field of agriculture. In option terms, Grace was asked to purchase a five-year call, at a cost of five years of research support, to enjoy half the income generated by the venture.

Grace had strategic reasons for being interested: It was enjoying peak cyclic earnings in agricultural chemicals at the time, based primarily on its commodity fertilizer business. Grace Agricultural Chemicals had only minimal R&D programs in agriculture but an extensive distribution network and a feeling for the market. Opportunities to invest its cash in more fertilizer assets were unattractive at the time, so other alternatives were sought to improve the future of the business. Also, developing a corporate window on biotechnology was seen as a good long-term investment for the company as a whole.

As I recall the initial meeting of these firms, two things stand out. The first was a presentation by a young and very articulate Cetus executive of a business plan by which Agracetus would create five or six high-margin businesses, mostly in genetically engineered crops. The revenues of these hypothetical businesses were projected to exceed $100 million in a few years, and growth thereafter would be powerful. The young executive had no operating experience; and the Grace executives there, including myself, were profoundly skeptical that the plan could be executed, if from a timing standpoint alone. And about that we were right.

The second memorable event was a presentation by Cetus scientist Kary Mullis that showed a new way to amplify small gene segments called PCR (for polymerase chain reaction). Mullis was awarded the 1993 Nobel Prize for this work, which became arguably the most valuable intellectual property owned by Cetus. Under the terms of the deal, Agracetus was to own exclusive rights to PCR in agriculture.

Before long, the deal was done.

During the next five years, Agracetus worked diligently to commercialize new products based on the nitrogen-fixing bacteria called *rhizobia*, which were in the field of Brill's expertise. These products ultimately failed. But two other important things happened: First, the scientific staff made substantial progress in learning how to genetically engineer plants, and they began to accumulate a portfolio of potentially valuable patents. The best of these concerned cotton. Second, Agracetus acquired rights to radical new technology, originally called Biolistics™ (as in "ballistics") and later trademarked by Agracetus as Accell™. It had been invented at Cornell University. The idea was to coat small strands of DNA onto tiny gold particles and then to shoot these particles into living cells using a "gene gun"—a mechanical device. The tiny holes made by the gold particles were usually repaired quickly by the target cells, and the DNA that was delivered could be taken up by the cells to produce proteins not normally made by the target organism. Although the method was neither efficient nor predictable, it had the advantage of not involving any viruses. These advantages could be useful not only in plants but also in human applications, such as gene therapy and genetic vaccines.

Agracetus had some new options, although they would be expensive to exercise.

According to the deal, when the five years were up, Grace and Cetus would split subsequent expenses. But as that date approached, it was clear that Cetus was having serious financial difficulty and could not afford the cash drain from Madison. It was also now clear that PCR was going to be of high value and that Cetus would need to monetize that asset. But Grace's partial ownership of PCR for agriculture might encumber that value from Cetus's viewpoint. Thus, a new deal was engineered: Grace would acquire Cetus's share of Agracetus in exchange for Grace's rights to PCR and a small amount of cash.

In view of changing circumstances, the strategic alliance no longer made sense. Grace now had Accell, the plant program, and the plant patents; and Cetus had PCR and the ability to move on. Cetus was soon acquired by Chiron, which sold the PCR patent to Hoffman-LaRoche for $300 million.

But Grace also had a financial crisis on its hands: A major shareholder decided to sell his 26 percent ownership of the company. To avoid a potential takeover, CEO J. Peter Grace used his line of credit to buy those shares. Cash had to be raised quickly, and Grace decided to monetize the commodity agricultural business. The eventual buyers were financial types who had no interest in Agracetus.

So, to Grace, Agracetus was no longer much of a strategic asset. Some securities analysts began to question top management as to why Grace was continuing to support it. Internally we realized that the negative cash flow of over $5 million per year for the Agracetus program could be a sizeable negative for analysts attempting to value Grace based on its cash flow. On the other hand, I remember one analyst adding an arbitrary 75 cents per share to his valuation of Grace for its Agracetus holding. In general, top management was divided as to whether to continue to invest based on continuing technological promise and a sunk R&D investment of over $30 million or to cut the cord because of the absence of short-term commercial opportunities.

But the marketplace was changing. Grace had once held aspirations of challenging Monsanto and DuPont in the life sciences marketplace, but it was apparent Agracetus was now far behind these giants in overall competitive capabilities. But its patents, particularly in cotton, could still give it a niche position. We used a number of techniques, including a pro forma DCF valuation of a genetically engineered cotton business, to attempt to value the agricultural piece of Agracetus. The values were in the range of $40 million to $70 million. Options methods were not used.

Subsequently, the plant assets were put up for sale. Monsanto was very interested both in the technical capabilities of the research group and in acquiring the critical cotton patents. But another giant, Hoechst-Celanese, was also interested because of the intriguing possibilities of genetically engineering new forms of cotton fiber—and fibers were an important business for them. Both Monsanto and Hoechst held strategic options well beyond what Grace could effect by itself. In the end, the agricultural assets were sold to Monsanto for about $150 million in 1996.

Grace was still left with Accell and the options in medicine (gene therapy and genetic vaccines), veterinary medicine, and improved livestock. Among the genetic vaccine programs were one for HIV, which was under evaluation in chimpanzees, and other potentials for hepatitis B, influenza, malaria, measles, dengue, and rheumatoid arthritis. This research, also no longer strategic to Grace, was continued for a time under the name Auragen Inc. In 1996, it was combined with a stronger partner, privately held Oxford BioSciences Ltd. (UK), to form a new JV, Geniva, Inc.

As a result of these transactions, Grace recovered substantially more than its initial investment from the Monsanto sale alone and was left with a stake in Geniva of indeterminate, but potentially very high, value.

Clearly, all of the value creation here involved strategic capital in the form of risky long-range plans for commercial products based on revolutionary, and usually proprietary, technology. Cash flows were negative throughout the totality of this history. The plans were never particularly realistic, and they were often overtaken by events, some of which had nothing to do with the plans themselves. Nevertheless, the final effect of uncertainty in this case was to *increase* the value of the options.

So we return to the ghost in the garden. All of these events dealt with virtual capital—ideas, patents, and future opportunities. Scientists in the laboratory spent many millions of real dollars, while executives from a half dozen firms maneuvered the assets in attempts to create value. Finally, some of the values emerged from the mists as tangible assets in the form of large cash payments that were recorded on the balance sheets of the technology sellers.

Economic Value: The DCF "Gold Standard" and Its Limitations

The term *value* has both broad and narrow connotations. In this book, I deliberately use one of the narrowest—a purely financial definition. *Valuation* in this framework means putting a quantitative number—a currency will do—on an object. I recognize the existence and the validity of other value systems, but I choose this narrower definition because its implications are powerful. Broader and less materialistic definitions of value, while consistent with the dictionary, for now only muddy the water.

Thus, the value of a dollar is a dollar. The value of a share of Dow Chemical is about what the newspaper says it is. The value of a physical good, such as a painting by Rembrandt, will be appraised at the price it is likely to fetch at auction. The painting's role in the history of art may be part of that value, or it may not.

■ ECONOMIC VALUE

The discounted cash flow (DCF) method is the "gold standard" of valuation.[1] Throughout this book, I use the term *economic value* to mean the present value of projected cash flows. When the financial assumptions are accurate and the business model is complete, there can be no doubt of DCF's validity. Yet in Chapter 2, I identified powerful reasons why economic value is an inadequate explanation of market value. To resolve the apparent paradox, however, I propose not to abandon the economic model, but to build on it. To do that, we need to understand how economic value is created.

■ THE RELATIONSHIP OF ECONOMIC PROFIT TO ECONOMIC VALUE

The concept of economic value added (EVA), or *economic profit,* has a clear definition: It is the amount of capital invested times the rate of return realized after subtracting the cost of capital.

1. Economic Profit = Capital Investment ×
   (Return on Capital – Cost of Capital)

Taxes are a consideration—let's assume they are 40 percent. Jack borrows $1 million at 15 percent and invests it in an auto repair business that earns a profit of $250,000 before taxes and $150,000 after taxes. Because interest is tax-deductible, Jack's cost of capital is 9 percent, or $90,000. His economic profit, or EVA, for this year is $60,000. (After one year, the book value of his business will also be $60,000, which is comprised of the retained earnings and a million dollars of assets offset by a million dollars of debt.)

But what is the economic value of this business? It cannot be determined without making a projection about its future. Let us make the simplest kind of projection—that the business will neither grow nor decline. Then it is an annuity, or perpetuity, throwing off $60,000 per year essentially forever. And a very simple formula governs the value of a perpetuity—it is the annual payment divided by the cost of capital.

2. Economic Value = Annual Income/Cost of Capital

That is $60,000 divided by 0.09, or $666,667. By establishing a successful and apparently enduring business, Jack has made quite a bit of money on paper.

The market may give a different value. Jill observes Jack's success and offers to buy his business for 10 times Jack's after-tax profits of $150,000, or $1.5 million. If Jack accepts her offer and then pays off the loan, he will have made $500,000. That is his market value added (MVA). Because her offer is less than the business's economic value, it is not particularly generous. It's still a lot more than his EVA of $60,000. But he will not realize that MVA unless he chooses to sell, at which time the price may be higher or lower.

How does this metric apply to big companies? EVA can be calculated from financial statements, which are public information. Magazines such as *Fortune* regularly publish EVA rankings. Using this yardstick, we observe some companies create great value each year, while others destroy value. They often destroy value not because they fail to make a profit, but because they fail to return the cost of capital.[2] An 8 percent "profit" earned by a company with a 12 percent cost of capital is a surefire way to destroy economic value.

The MVA yardstick is even more problematical because it compares year-to-year changes in market capitalization. MVA depends on the performance of the share price and changes in the number of shares outstanding. So it is perfectly possible for MVA to far exceed EVA (in a rising market) or for MVA to be down even though EVA rises (as can happen in a falling market). For example, if next year Jill increased her offer by $200,000, Jack would gain an additional $200,000 in MVA, regardless of his economic performance.

A variant of MVA called *total shareholder return* (TSR), in which dividends are added back to MVA, is a widely used indicator of the performance of chief executive officers (CEOs) and their teams. MVA does not depend directly on economic performance and assumes that shareholders care only about the value of and the return from their portfolios.

■ LINKING GROWTH AND VALUE: THE PEGGY SUE SCENARIO, PART I

The link between value and growth is very powerful. For now, it is worth exploring this relationship purely in terms of its financial implications. In Chapter 8, we will discuss the inverse—how the persistent absence of growth over the general course of economic history and the continuing stagnation of large parts of the world today may be linked to an absence of value creation.

Even neophyte investors learn that faster-growing companies carry higher price/earnings (P/E) multiples than slower-growing firms. But we will use the cash flow approach to valuation to derive this result.

Two concepts are required to understand how growth and profitability link to value. The first is *free cash flow* (FCF) and the second is the *cost of capital*.

➤ Free Cash Flow

Free cash flow is the money a business can afford to throw off year after year for purposes other than running the business. It is actual cash flow minus the amount of cash that must be reinvested. From the point of view of the business, it doesn't matter what is done with free cash flow.

Look at the thriving dry cleaning business that Peggy Sue owns in Lubbock, Texas. She bought it with proceeds from her famous divorce several years back and has since found that she has a knack for small business management and effective promotion. The business is not only growing and earning a profit, but is also throwing off cash beyond what Peggy Sue uses to keep the enterprise running or pays herself as an employee. She may spend this free cash flow on luxury cruises to the Mediterranean or on gambling junkets to Las Vegas; she can invest in technology stocks or purchase the minimarket next door.

But how exactly does one determine her FCF? One way is to calculate cash flow and then determine which portion of it is "free." For an operating business, cash flow will equal net after-tax income plus depreciation. Depreciation is cash—it is only an accounting charge against earnings that takes into account a previous capital investment. For example, Peggy Sue invested $400,000 of her life savings in a dry cleaning plant and depreciated it over 10 years, and she has an additional $100,000 tied up in working capital—receivables and inventories—for a total investment of $500,000. Her books show a $40,000 annual depreciation charge for each of those 10 years. If her total cash flow—annual revenues less all cash expenses and taxes—were $130,000, she would report income of $90,000 on the financial statements. But she really has received $130,000 in cash—the reported income plus the depreciation.

There seems to be a higher degree of reality to the cash than to the net income. The cash goes to the bank where it can be counted. The depreciation schedule is arbitrary—her accountants advise that a 10-year useful life for dry-cleaning equipment is a reasonable assumption that will satisfy the tax authorities and anyone else interested in her financial statements. But the machines will probably work for at least 15 years. No matter, she would likely choose the shorter period to defer some taxes.

What about free cash flow—the actual cash flow minus the cash required to sustain the business? If she has *no intention of growing the business* (and she lives in an inflation-free world), she will need to be prepared to replace that aging $400,000 plant some day with a new one. Assume that she will need about $400,000 to do it. In this case, aside from timing issues, her projected capital expenditures match her depreciation. So her FCF turns out to be her net income.

But if her thriving business is going to expand, forecasting FCF will be more complex. She will need to forecast a growth rate, something that is partly under her control. Let's work under the assumption that she plans to grow at 6 percent per annum. That works out to almost 80 percent growth in 10 years. Her dry cleaning equipment will soon be strained for capacity, and she will need to periodically add or upgrade equipment. These expenses will require more capital than her cash flow from depreciation provides. Let's say she learns that it is wise to keep a two-week supply of hangers, plastic bags, boxes, and solvent on hand. She will need to increase her inventory of these consumables by 6 percent per year. If she accepts credit, she will have to finance more of the float between the time the services are performed and the time she receives payment. So both her working capital and her fixed capital needs will increase. The increases mean that FCF will now be less than net income. *In short, free cash flow cannot be forecast independently of a growth plan.*

Let us see how these numbers can work out for the 6 percent growth case. There is a very convenient relationship to guide us:

3. Growth Rate = Return on Invested Capital ×
Reinvestment Rate

For our case, the return on invested capital is $90,000 (net income) divided by $500,000 (total capital employed), or 18 percent. Peggy Sue must invest one-third of her net income, or $30,000, to sustain 6 percent growth. (She must also reinvest her depreciation of $40,000.) In this way, her total capital after one year of operation will increase by 6 percent to $530,000. Her FCF is thus $60,000 ($130,000 cash flow minus $70,000).

> ## Using Cost of Capital to Calculate Economic Value

A second relationship helps us to calculate the economic value of Peggy Sue's growing business. It is the general formula for a *growing* perpetuity:

4. Economic Value = Free Cash Flow/
    (Cost of Capital – Growth Rate)

It is similar to equation 2 for economic value mentioned earlier (Economic Value = Annual Income/Cost of Capital), but instead of dividing the initial cash flow by the cost of capital, we now divide by the *difference* between the cost of capital and the growth rate. As the growth rate increases, the denominator becomes smaller, and the value increases accordingly.

To make this calculation, we need an estimate of Peggy Sue's cost of capital. In the case of Jack's auto repair business, it was easy—his capital was all debt, and the cost of the debt was the after-tax cost of the interest on it. Let's look at an equity case. Assume Peggy Sue, on principle, will not borrow money. But Peggy Sue determines that she can sell her business, or buy a similar business, for about $750,000, based on comparable transactions in West Texas. She reasons that to match her net income of $90,000, she needs to make a 12 percent return on the $750,000. This price defines her *opportunity cost of capital*. If she could find comparable opportunities to invest $750,000 at 13 percent, she could earn more and might choose to sell the business; if she could not, she would continue to operate.

The rest of the calculation is straightforward. Her FCF is $60,000, and the denominator of the equation (cost of capital – growth rate) becomes 12 percent – 6 percent, or 6 percent, which is 0.06. Dividing through, her business is valued at $1,000,000. Note this value is 11.1 times her current net income. This number is equivalent to a P/E ratio of 11.1.

Let us now look at what this business would look like if it grew faster or more slowly. In other words, does increasing the multiplier by growing more quickly offset the increasing penalty for having a lower FCF? The answer is that it does.

But first we need to reflect on this option. Peggy Sue is, by most business standards, doing very well to earn 18 percent on her investment in a reasonably stable business. If she wishes to expand her business faster and to maintain its financial attractiveness, she must find opportunities that also afford an 18 percent return on any additional capital she puts in. It may do her no good to get new business by discounting prices or by opening a new store in a community that already is well served by a competitive establishment. Finding 18 percent return opportunities is not easy, although the most successful businesspeople do it regularly.

First, what if she elected not to grow? Then her reinvestment rate would be zero, and her FCF would be equal to her net income of $90,000. The denominator of the equation would be 12 percent to give a value of $750,000, a multiple of 8.33 times her net income. From a value maximization viewpoint, she is better off investing in growing the business at 6 percent. (Note that equation 2 is just the no-growth version of equation 4!)

What if she could grow faster? Let's assume that with her famous name, sparkling personality, and aggressive promotion, Peggy Sue finds that she can expand her business at 9 percent per year with no loss in profitability. Now her reinvestment rate must be 50 percent of net income. Her FCF drops to $45,000, but the denominator in equation 4 becomes 0.03. The business would theoretically have an economic value of $1,500,000. Because its net income is $90,000, it has an imputed price/earnings multiple of 16.67, exactly double that for the no-growth case.

The trade-offs in play here are very interesting: High growth means lower FCF *but higher enterprise value*. (This proposition has an important "if": The value assumes that the returns on capital can be sustained!) And, the faster she elects to grow, the less will be her FCF. It is not even uncommon for fast-growing profitable businesses to have negative cash flow. Should that be the case, Peggy Sue will surely need external financing. Cruises to the Mediterranean will be out for a while if she plans to open a new shop every two years. Analysts will have a tougher time too because they cannot value her business as a convenient multiple of cash flow as discussed below.[3]

But the take-home point is that to calculate economic value, an investor must make a judgment about the growth of the business. He or she can generally anticipate a choice between an initially smaller FCF stream growing at a faster rate and a larger FCF stream growing at a slower rate.

Although growth is a key factor in value creation, it must go hand in hand with return on capital. Consider a situation in which Peggy Sue's return on investment is materially lower. Let's assume this time that the business still grows at 6 percent, but her return on capital is 13 percent, only one percentage point above her cost of money. The business now turns out to be worth $583,000, only marginally more than the $500,000 Peggy Sue invested.

And as many readers must have guessed, if she earned only 12 percent, exactly her cost of capital, the business would be worth exactly what she put into it, $500,000. This economic fact would be true whether the business grew or did not. There are no gains for investors who earn only the cost of capital. Nor is there any economic profit!

But even earning the cost of capital is not the worst case: If Peggy Sue made 10 percent on her investment, the business would be worth only $333,333 (Net income $50,000, reinvestment $30,000, FCF $20,000 divided by 0.06 in equation 4). It would have an imputed P/E ratio of 6.7. And she would have destroyed $187,000 of value, while ostensibly growing a "profitable" business.

■ THE VALUE MIND-SET

Very seasoned and well-paid executives have fallen into exactly this value trap. They have reasoned that their companies are valued in the marketplace with a relatively fixed P/E ratio. They are able to find "profitable" investment opportunities that do not earn the cost of capital (no great trick). Because these investments increase net income (earnings), they expect their share prices to rise. But they seldom do, because these executives have destroyed value and Wall Street is often sharp enough to spot it.

In modern corporate language, "company value is determined by its discounted future cash flows, and value is created only when companies invest capital at returns that exceed the cost of that capital."[4] This axiom implies that neither top-line nor bottom-line growth is necessarily a value driver. *Top-line* growth refers to growth in revenues (sales), and *bottom-line* growth refers to growth in profits (net income). More commonly they *are* value drivers, but mindless pursuit of either can actually destroy value.

Businesspeople know that in many markets it is possible to grow revenues quickly by cutting price. In other words they can "buy" some customers. However, even that is not so easy, because entrenched competitors may and frequently do elect to match your price cuts. So the revenue gains are more than offset by losses in both net income and FCF. Many industries have learned to discipline themselves against value-destroying price wars for just this reason. Other industries have self-destructed because they failed to learn the lesson.

Always, there is an exception that proves the rule. The barbarians sometimes win. If you can force rational competitors out of the market, which is eminently doable if you are the low-cost supplier and drive prices below your competition's cash cost, you may come to dominate that market. Prices can be raised later; and if they are raised enough, the strategy will be value-creating as defined by the discounted value of FCF. This practice is called *predatory* pricing, and government agencies have been created precisely to prevent it. In terms of our total value model, this kind of business plan has a negative net present value (NPV), but contains an embedded option to raise prices later.

A classic case of an attempt to buy top-line growth or market share was the ferocious attack of Japanese manufacturers on the rapidly growing market for DRAMs—dynamic random access memory chips—in the 1980s. Its lessons are interesting because the effort succeeded but produced unanticipated consequences. Using a theory espoused by the Boston Consulting Group of pricing ahead of the experience curve—pricing with *future* scale-based and experience-based economies built into *current* prices—the Japanese drove virtually all U.S. manufacturers out of the market. Prices were driven below cash costs, even those of the Japanese. Intel was one of the companies that chose to exit DRAM manufacturing; it went on to prosper by focusing on a different kind of chip, the microprocessor, which employed a higher degree of intellectual capital than DRAMs.

The pot of gold that the Japanese anticipated at the end of this rainbow was dominance in a major world market. But that scenario never materialized: Competitive forces, including Taiwanese and Korean manufacturers who learned from the Japanese, have kept DRAM pricing extremely competitive. Circumstances had changed, and the option to raise prices could never be exercised. Unlike the microprocessor, the DRAM became a commodity and would forever remain one. One of the big winners of this development was the personal computer (PC) industry, whose growth benefited enormously from the availability of inexpensive, high-performance memory.

But why is driving the bottom line not necessarily value creating? The answer is that marginal investments will add net income, but they do so by requiring too much capital. If your cost of capital is 12 percent, don't invest in a 9 percent proposal.

While this point seems obvious, it also got lost in the conglomerate craze of the 1960s—a true economic bubble that burst catastrophically. It was driven by focus on bottom-line growth as it appeared on the income statement, without an eye to the balance sheet. In its pure form, companies with higher P/E ratios were able to effect successive mergers with companies with lower P/E ratios. After each merger, the accounting earnings of the conglomerator increased. As a result of the accelerating earnings growth, the P/E ratio of the conglomerator rose, giving it further leverage to make acquisitions.

But while the income statement looked better and better, the balance sheet was encumbered by the premiums the conglomerator had to pay to make successive acquisitions. Those premiums had no economic value, if the acquired companies had been fairly priced in the marketplace before the merger. If the acquiree's stock earned a fair return on capital before the merger, it earned a less-than-fair return after the acquisition premium was paid. Therefore, unless there were large synergies to be achieved between business operations or unless the acquiree's future prospects were grossly undervalued, no new sources of FCF were created in these transactions. (And by definition, a conglomerate is a collection of unrelated businesses affording few synergies.) So the gap between market value, based on an intuitive link between the P/E ratio and the growth rate, and economic value, based on estimates of future FCF, grew and grew until it was clear these corporate emperors wore no clothes.

■ VALUE-CREATING INVESTMENT STRATEGIES

The power of the value mind-set is that it not only prevents plausible but value-destroying strategies from being adopted but also highlights the importance of getting an exceptional return on capital. If one's cost of capital is 12 percent and one has opportunities to make a $200 million investment earning 13 percent or a $100 million investment earning 14 percent, which one should one choose? These investments are theoretically equal from a DCF viewpoint, each creating value of $2 million annually. But I like the second one, because perhaps an opportunity may come along that will also earn 14 percent or more for the remaining $100 million. And if that happy option doesn't materialize, the backup plan would be to invest the remaining $100 million at 12 percent—by buying back stock and retiring debt.

This line of reasoning brings into play the concept of a *hurdle rate*. In this case, a CEO might propose a hurdle rate, perhaps 14 percent or even 16 percent, below which the firm will not make new investments. And with it should come an aggressive search for high-return opportunities—after all, an investment that returns 20 percent creates 4 times the *value* of an equal size investment earning 14 percent!

The discipline of a hurdle rate contrasts with a common business axiom that any investment that earns the cost of capital or that creates value is a good investment. Consider a return of 12.1 percent. It is technically correct that this investment will have a positive NPV when the cost of capital is 12 percent, meeting the academic yardstick for a good financial decision. And such investments are often attractive to executives for non-financial reasons because these investments build the size of the executives' business and hence their prestige. They may even be strategically sound, if they create options for more profitable investments down the road. Thus, when NOVA Corporation invested in TGN, an Argentinian pipeline company that was being denationalized, it earned only a small premium over its cost of capital; but it obtained a foothold in the Southern Cone of the continent that created Gas Andes, a landmark pipeline built to bring Argentinian gas into the heart of Chile.

However, to the degree that capital is thought to be scarce, wasting it on investments that add only a small amount of value may doom a firm to forever lagging its more aggressive competitors.

Risk, though, becomes a consideration. All other things being equal, for the higher-return investments (the 20 percent projects versus the 14 percent projects), one must bear more risk. Thus, the formula for adding value combines two imperatives: (1) a mindset to make the high-return/higher-risk investments and (2) the skills to manage the risks that come with innovation. Those skills are largely encapsulated in real options and diversification—two themes of this book.

Aversion to risk, and aversion to innovation, are the formula for stagnation.

■ THE COST OF CAPITAL AND DISCOUNTED CASH FLOW

In the preceding discussions, we used two simple fictional cases to determine the cost of capital. One was Jack who borrowed money, the other was Peggy Sue who didn't. Peggy Sue might borrow money against her receivables, her inventories, and physical plant if she could find new investment opportunities with an 18 percent return. If she did so, she would be using a mixture of debt and equity. We will find such an opportunity for her shortly.

The financial structure of a real firm is usually much more complex than our examples, but it involves the same considerations. Its treasurer and assistants will spend long hours adjusting the balance sheet to achieve a minimum cost of capital. The cost of capital for a real firm is the subject of a great deal of academic and practical thinking, which is basically outside the aim of this book. We can say briefly, however, that (1) the ratio of debt and equity will be maintained within a range that is typical of the industry and (2) the cost of capital must reflect *current* capital markets, not the historical costs of the actual securities issued by the firm. In practice, when facing a need for additional capital the corporate treasurer will decide whether to go (1) to the debt market or (2) to issue new equity or (3) to construct some complex derivative that has both debt and equity features. In short, although debt may initially be cheaper, it is assumed that new equity will eventually have to be raised. Thus the cost of capital is often considered to be the weighted average cost of capital (WACC), where "weighted" refers to the *market* value of both stock and long-term debt.[5]

We have noted that many companies have market capitalizations that are large multiples of book value; in these cases weighting means that WACC will be dominated by the cost of equity. Consider a company whose balance sheet shows a 1:1 ratio of debt to equity. If the market cap of the stock is 4 times book value, the weighted ratio will be 4:1, which is 80 percent equity.

There is a strong correlation between cost of capital and risk. Financially risky loans bear higher rates of interest. And the appropriate cost of equity for an investment relates to the risk of that investment, not to the average cost of equity for the firm. Thus, it would seem the biotechnology division of a solid old-line company whose cost of capital is 10 percent would have an economic advantage over a publicly traded biotech company whose cost of capital is 20 percent. But not so—perceptive investors would raise the cost of capital for the old-line firm to cover its increased risk. Assume Exxon Corporation has a cost of equity of 10 percent, while an average biotech firm has a cost of equity of 20 percent. If Exxon wants to make an investment in biotech, it must use the 20 percent figure to calculate value, not the 10 percent imputed to its petroleum operations.

The cost of capital, as discussed earlier, is important because it is at the heart of all valuation methods based on discounted cash flow, including the methods used in this book. Many individuals have a poor intuition for it, since they tend to think primarily in terms of debt and interest rates. The cost of capital is the equalizer between a dollar earned today and a dollar earned tomorrow. It is also the equalizer between a dollar spent today and a dollar spent tomorrow. It reflects the financial value of time to a company (or to an individual). This value is different for different situations and different individuals. A low cost of capital also drives value creation through equation 4.

Here's briefly how DCF works. Let us assume that "tomorrow's dollar" is $100 and that "tomorrow" is one year from today. Further assume that we live in a happy world that is free of taxes and risks and where there are plenty of opportunities to earn 10 percent per year on investments. The amount we must invest today to get $100 a year in the future is $90.91; that is, $90.91 plus 10 percent interest of $9.09 returns $100 next year. Viewed in reverse, the present value of $100 a year from now (at 10 percent) is $90.91. Note that this figure is not the same as taking a 10 percent discount on $100, which would yield only $90.00. The correct result is obtained by *dividing* $100 by 1.10.

Now let us consider a case in which we must wait two years to get paid. The present value is now only $82.64. If we invested that $82.64 at 10 percent for one year, we would receive interest of $8.26, giving us $90.91 after one year. This amount will earn

$9.09 during the second year, bringing us up to $100 at the end of the second year. We obtain the present value in this two-year situation by dividing $100 by $(1.10)^2$.

■ THE MAGIC OF GROWTH MULTIPLIERS

The magic by which seemingly small income streams get magnified into huge market valuations is intimately tied up with the arcane mathematics of perpetuities. It sounds dull, but it is well worth understanding because it is the mathematical foundation of Wall Street wealth.

A *perpetuity* is defined as an investment offering a level stream of cash flows forever. What is the value of a perpetuity paying $100 per year forever? Using a cost of capital of 12 percent, it would be the present value of the first payment, plus the second payment, plus the third payment, . . . , plus the fiftieth payment, and so on; that is, $89.29 + $79.72 + $71.18 . . . . The value of the payments gets progressively smaller. The value of the fiftieth payment is only 3 cents!

It turns out that the present value of this stream, no matter how far one goes out in time, cannot exceed $833.33. That number is the free cash flow of $100 divided by the cost of capital, 12 percent, or 0.12—a very simple relationship that we introduced earlier.

Mathematicians say simply that this series converges to a finite limit. This one converges fairly quickly—it reaches 90 percent of the limit in 20 years, and 95 percent in 26 years. So in a practical sense, realizing the value of a perpetuity does not take forever, just a period of time that is consistent with the lifetime of a durable business.

The more interesting businesses are, of course, those that are growing very rapidly, but unfortunately these are impossible to handle using perpetuity formulas. We have seen that a business growing at 6 percent per year in a 12 percent cost of capital environment will be valued at 16.67 times (1/0.12 – 0.06) its FCF. At 9 percent, the growth multiplier will rise to 33.3 times; and at 11 percent, to 100 times. What about rates of 12 percent, 30 percent, and 100 percent?

These projections get pretty heady, and the phenomenon is not unimportant to value creation, but we need to get back to earth for two reasons.

First, there is a mathematical issue about convergence. The value in perpetuity of any business growing at the cost of capital involves dividing by zero. Next year's earnings on a fully discounted basis will be equal to this year's; and so, in an infinity of time, the sum will be infinite. We have created the financial equivalent of a perpetual motion machine. Practically, we also know this scenario cannot happen because sooner or later that business, growing at 12 percent per year, would be larger than the economy as a whole, growing at, say, 3 percent—an impossibility. Other methods must be used that assume that growth rates eventually slow down.[6] The term *fade* applies to adjustments of this type.

Impossibility is preceded by implausibility. As growth rates get close to the cost of money, the number of years it takes for the series to converge to 90 percent or 95 percent of its total value gets longer and longer. Hence, the growth rate in a perpetuity formula, while mathematically sound, stretches our business judgment.

Second, we have so far ignored the fact that high growth rates require high levels of reinvestment in the business and reduce FCF. When FCF goes negative, there is no way to use the perpetuity formula to define a positive economic value.

The preceding walkthrough valuation of a business is so far strictly "old economy." It is actually not very different from how some Wall Street analysts value an operating company. First, they obtain a three- or five-year estimate of FCF from management. This span represents the financial vision of management and defines a "horizon year." Second, they take the FCF in the horizon year, extrapolate from there out as a growing perpetuity, and apply a discount based on the firm's cost of capital. Third, they may elect to tweak the results if they are skeptical about management forecasts.

Because faster-growing businesses with the same net income are substantially more valuable than slower-growing businesses, the choice of the growth rate beyond the horizon year is crucial to the valuation. We have seen the sensitivity of value to the growth multiplier. In many cases, the *horizon value* (that part of the economic value that is created beyond the horizon year) is much more than 50 percent of the company's valuation! Paying attention to how horizon value (also known as "terminal value" or "residual value") is calculated is critical to an accurate economic analysis. That value can be calculated using the FCF multiplier, or an imputed price/earnings ratio: We have seen that the imputed P/E ratio for the dry cleaning business rises from 8.33 for the no-growth case to 16.67 for 9 percent growth.

Higher-return businesses are also much more valuable than lower-return businesses. And the combination of high growth and high return is dynamite.

Our analysis also reveals why seemingly small, and often temporary, changes in a firm's growth rate or profitability cause such large reactions in the stock market. It's not because a dime less of earnings per share is anything but a dime when recorded on the balance sheet. It's because the dime changes all the extrapolations of growth made off the last data point! In effect, the high sensitivity of the growth multiplier amplifies volatility.

■ DEFINING ECONOMIC ASSETS

Because economic value is the foundation on which total value is built, consistency about the kinds of assets that should be included in economic value is of paramount importance. The term *economic assets* is used here to mean those assets that contribute to current cash flow. Other assets are put in place for strategic reasons and are referred to as *strategic assets*. Accounting conventions are not at all helpful: They not only fail to distinguish between economic and strategic assets, but they also omit important classes of assets entirely, such as patents and research-and-development (R&D) investment.

I include in economic capital those assets that drive FCF *at the rate of growth that is reasonably expected*. In other words, I would include the assets that are supposed to generate cash in predictable ways. By this definition, an R&D laboratory that contributes only to sustaining the historic rate of growth of the company is an economic asset. An R&D laboratory that is developing a new product platform that will reinvigorate the company is a strategic asset.

Economic assets include (1) fixed assets (property, plant, and equipment); (2) working capital (inventories and accounts receivable); and (3) the cash, securities, and other financial investments held by the firm that contribute to operating cash flow.[7] These three types of assets are recorded by the accountants on the balance sheet, although on a cost basis rather than current value basis.

A traditional manufacturing business, such as a forest products company, is comprised mostly of such assets. Its properties begin with the woodlands from which raw materials are harvested. A fleet of trucks brings the logs in. Sawmills convert some of the wood to lumber, while the remainder of the wood is processed in a pulp mill. The pulp in turn is fed into paper machines and converted into newsprint, tissue paper, carton board, and other such products. These types of fixed assets are typically labeled "property, plant, and equipment" in financial statements and comprise the first item in Table 2.1 under "Economic Capital." They are likely to be undervalued: The woodlands may have been acquired at lower prices many decades ago, and many pulp mills are almost as ancient. The inventories are very visible: stacks of wood awaiting processing, tanks full of pulp on their way to the paper machine, and warehouses stacked with pallets of toilet tissue or cardboard cartons.

The paper industry is relatively light on intellectual property; it is highly dependent on suppliers of paper machines and converting equipment for its primary processes. Paper engineers are amazingly open about discussing the techniques of their trade. The business does not abound with mainstream opportunities—building a new mill involves making an enormous capital investment in a cyclic market, and the chances of encountering resistance from environmental groups to a new facility are high. There are a few opportunities for innovation, such as new package designs, but these tend to be at the fringes of the business and not in its mainstream.

A retail business also employs fixed assets (land, stores, warehouses, and business equipment), but it will carry relatively higher proportions of its economic capital in the inventory required to serve customer needs. Besides this physical capital, a successful retail business will likely have considerable intellectual capital—its name, reputation, and marketing skills. It will have much lower barriers to opening new facilities.

So far, we have focused on hard economic assets. But intellectual property can generate cash directly, too; and when it does, it is an economic asset. The very name of a retail establishment attracts customers. When the chemical company Union Carbide licensed its patented Unipol polyethylene technology, it was able to generate annual revenues of about $100 million for a 20-year period. Unipol was a huge economic asset. Studios such as Disney and Universal can count on regular revenues from their inventory of old films, such as *Snow White* and *Jaws*; while music companies holding the copyrights to popular standards, such as *White Christmas* or *Whole Lot of Shakin' Going On*, collect royalties each time the song is aired commercially. Such assets are perfectly capable of being appraised and capitalized.

While the term *intangible* has historically been applied to such intellectual property, it is little different in its economic characteristics from physical rental property. Such proven, low-risk moneymakers are economic capital. Hence, the distinction between economic capital and strategic capital is not the same as the distinction between tangible assets and intangible assets.

■ VALUE PROCESSES

Identifiable assets, as we have catalogued them earlier, do not yet make a successful business. Countless fools have bought productive physical and economic assets and operated them into bankruptcy. They ignored the fact that there are *value processes* incorporated in a real operating business. There are many intangibles involved: the talents and experience of all operating employees; the processes by which prices are set, receivables are collected, and materials and services are purchased. Technology can be important; some firms will operate identical physical assets more efficiently than others. The Lev study of the chemical industry discussed in Chapter 2 showed that physical assets alone may not even earn the cost of capital; it is only when they are blended with technology that an economic profit is earned.

Value processes include the human resources function, which addresses how employees shall be recruited, selected, paid, and terminated. In the New Economy, these issues are critical to competitive performance. There is the legal department, which writes enforceable contracts and defends against product liability. Technical service and sales teams keep valued customers in the fold. All of these assets and functions must be managed and coordinated, so even the portion of the executive team assigned to operations are part of the value process.

In short, value processes comprise all of the functions necessary to sustain the operating business at its projected growth rate.

There is financial significance to this distinction because the business will be valued, in part, based on its current FCF and the forecasts one makes about that cash flow in future years. In doing a valuation, we must avoid double counting—if a 5 percent long-term growth is assumed, all the costs and capital required to sustain 5 percent growth must be assigned to the business. And no more.

It should be possible in principle to measure the economic contribution of the value processes of a company: It will be the difference between the total economic value (as determined by DCF) and the value of all physical and intellectual property assets, each individually valued at current market value. The difference will be the contribution of the value processes.

■ THE ISSUE OF TIME HORIZONS

There is no disputing that the discounted cash flow model for valuation of assets is conceptually correct. Why then does it lead so frequently to massive undervaluation?

The first problem has to do with time horizons. The DCF model will not work correctly if the time horizon is too short to include the contributions from assets that have yet to mature as cash contributors. And yet the method is often applied without taking this factor into account. Any growing business whose cash flow is negative (cash flow can be negative owing to growth alone, even though the business is very profitable)[8] initially makes a negative contribution to total cash flow. If growth in perpetuity is applied at this stage, this growing business's contribution to economic value can only be negative. If the analyst is using free cash flow DCF and a three-year or a five-year horizon, he or she must remember that all projects that do not contribute cash in this period are still burning cash. These include successful commercial projects in their high-growth stages, as well as projects still in the R&D pipeline! Hence, the most attractive assets in a company not only may be missed in the calculation, but also may be treated as negatives!

Copeland, an authority on DCF-based valuation, made the point clearly: "Choose a longer rather than a shorter forecast period."[9]

The second problem is that DCF is fine for economic assets whose cash flows can be projected. It fails, however, to recognize the value of strategic assets and the real options they enable. These options justify a premium—the second component of total value.

The Total
Value Model

Conceptually, the Total Value Model is straightforward: Use the discounted cash flow (DCF) method to evaluate the economic capital of the firm. Use options methods to value the strategic capital of the firm. Add the two to get total value. A six-step method is outlined at the end of this chapter to assist the reader in applying the model—whether his or her interest is in evaluating a start-up business, a research-and-development–intensive company, a capital investment, or a hypothetical business problem.

Changes in total value are largely driven by changes in three major factors: (1) risk, (2) diminishing returns, and (3) innovation. They are also mediated by time. Later chapters will discuss how these influences operate on a firm. The important point for now is that each of them is, in principle, measurable and that no new financial methods are required to get a measure of value. Figure 4.1 illustrates the key relationships.

The model is equally applicable to high-risk businesses, which compel a focus on strategic capital, and to more traditional businesses, which typically have real options of their own, though fewer and often less valuable than those of high-risk businesses.

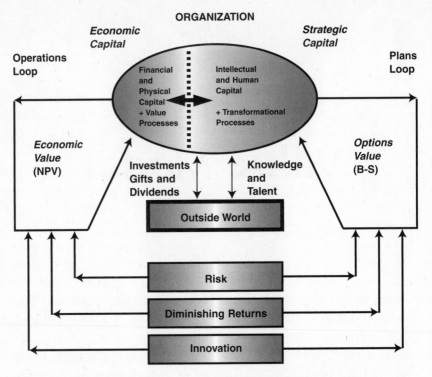

Figure 4.1 Total Value Model. NPV and B-S represent net present value and Black-Scholes valuation methods, respectively.

In this sense, the spectrum from the "growth" and "value" styles of investment is mirrored in the relative values of strategic and economic capital. What is new in this approach is that we include an *explicit* contribution to value, large or small, from the strategic side.

A firm has the ability to transform strategic capital into economic capital by exercising, or selling, real options. It has the inverse ability to transform economic capital into strategic capital by purchasing real options.

Use of the model in real-world situations requires adherence to three rules. The first rule, mentioned at the close of Chapter 3, is to keep the time horizons straight.[1] The second rule, also discussed in Chapter 3, is to separate assets that are built into the DCF valuation of the business from those that are not. If the marketplace is valuing a company based on a 6 percent sustainable growth rate, the research-and-development (R&D) investment required to sustain a 6 percent rate is already counted in the valuation! An additional R&D investment aimed at increasing growth to 8 percent is not. The third rule, applicable to options analysis, is discussed in Chapter 5, and involves the identification and separation of unique risk from market risk.

The model would seem to be general. Although my focus here will be on economic entities, in particular on what we think of as businesses and business units, the principles in this chapter can be applied to almost any organization. The organization can be a political unit, such as a nation, a colony, a state, or a town; or it can be an institution such as a university, a hospital, a church, or even an army. Each has tangible capital, cash flow, and options for future action. Even when we do not think of them as businesses, nearly all institutions have business aspects, and managing these business aspects is vital to their growth and survival. For if the money runs out, they are doomed to oblivion.

■ INSIDE THE MODEL

In Figure 4.1, the central position in the total value model is the oval representing the organization whose value is being determined. The organization is viewed here as a basket of financial, physical, human, and intellectual capital—all of it owned, rented, or otherwise controlled.

Within the oval, the heavy *dashed line* separates the strategic capital of the organization from its economic capital. In this case, that line is drawn deliberately to the left of center because the most interesting examples are those in which the potentialities created by intellectual and human capital outweigh physical and financial capital. The position of the dashed line bears an important message. In a coal mining company it will be far to the right; for a consulting firm it will be far to the left.

That dashed line is more than a passive boundary. It is a transformation engine composed of skilled individuals and management processes that together translate opportunities into business processes. These capabilities come at a cost. When new talent is hired, free cash flow (FCF) is diminished by the costs of that talent. The economic value of the organization will be diminished accordingly on the left side because that value is based on some multiple of FCF. But the intent is that the right side, representing strategic value, will gain even more!

Again, this process is largely reversible: If talent is fired, FCF is increased accordingly, and the left side gains. The critical issue is whether the gain on the left offsets the loss on the right.

Organizational or *corporate culture* plays a huge role in such translations of value. An effective corporation is expert at these trade-offs; a less effective organization may be snared by naïve assumptions. In manufacturing organizations, the trade-off is typically related to investments in technology, especially R&D. Some organizations pride themselves on being innovators (and accept both the costs and the risks), whereas others characterize themselves as "fast followers." The latter reduce their apparent risks and preserve economic capital, but likewise reduce opportunities for innovation. Such predilections explain why culture is so often the critical issue in organizational vitality and survival.

In businesses where star talent is critical to success, the decision to invest, or not, in high-priced talent can be the make-or-break factor in the business. The Miami Marlins under president/entrepreneur Wayne Huizenga amassed a superlative group of ballplayers that took them to a world championship in 1997. The following year, the talent pool was massively decapitalized in a series of trades that resulted in a financially richer but competitively weaker team. Baseball traditionalists were shocked by the organizational culture that fostered this unprecedented series of events.

The dynamics inside this model can be alternatively described as that of value creation and value extraction: Creative processes create value on the right-hand side of the oval, while business processes extract that value and convert it into cash flow on the left. The additional point we are making here is that these business processes begin as plans, whose value can be determined quantitatively by option theory.

➤ Interactions with the Outside World

The box labeled "Outside World" in Figure 4.1 is meant very narrowly to account for sources and sinks of capital that are external to the organization and its operations. It represents the big basket of the rest of the world's capital and human talent. No organization can long remain an island (although some have tried). Among the most important changes are the conditions that make outsiders willing or unwilling to invest, including interest rates. Such changes affect value, yet they are largely independent of the organization's operating and planning loops. Perturbations in this external world are always critical to an organization's development, as the following example will highlight.

Jane Jacobs, in her book *Cities and the Wealth of Nations*,[2] gives a memorable description of Bardou, a French hamlet that thrived as a lead-mining center in Roman times but that has been economically nonviable ever since. Farming on this marginal land goes on, but it is noncompetitive. The hamlet has always exported human capital; young people usually leave for better prospects in Paris. But recently, things have been changing; the hamlet's scenic beauty has attracted a small artist's colony, a cadre of talented and potentially productive people eager to escape the din of automobiles and factories. These sources and sinks for human and intellectual capital are vital to Bardou's future. Whereas the young workers tend to emigrate, the artists immigrate, at least seasonally. The absence of workers may hasten the devolution of the hamlet's economy. But the immigrants bring spirit, energy, knowledge, and, above all, a network to the outside world that has the potential to transform the hamlet.

The hamlet has survived in a marginal way, for example, by remittances by its former residents to aging parents. These payments are, in effect, gifts—a possible source of capital, and an important one for any organization not economically self-sufficient. Subsidies, such as pensions paid by the state, may also provide an important source of capital. The new immigrants are a third source of capital; they are injecting monies earned elsewhere into the hamlet's economy and making modest capital investments in homes and shops.

If times are good and the local economy should start to develop, it is possible that investors will begin to find modest business opportunities in Bardou—perhaps a craft shop or a snack bar. Investors will eventually request a dividend, and any such dividend is a *sink* for the organization's financial capital. So would be gifts made by more prosperous residents to others outside the community.

The external influences described here will in time transform the financial, physical, human, and intellectual assets within the hamlet's oval. That transformation will also be mediated by the culture of the village—perhaps an antipathy to things technological, as in Ms. Jacobs' example.

➤ **The Operations Loop**

The operations loop in the model in Figure 4.1 encompasses the real commercial activities of the organization—buying, selling, distributing, manufacturing, or farming, as the case may be. If a company, or a village, creates or buys raw materials, upgrades them, and sells them, it is operating. If it does so in a way that adds value, the stock of financial and physical capital will grow. If it is inefficient and destroys value in the process, its capital will shrink and the organization will devolve without a source of fresh capital. Bardou, the French hamlet, had no industrial or agricultural exports before the artists came. But it needed to purchase at least a modicum of goods it could not produce—necessities such as medicine and clothing. Its operations were destroying value, and without external sources of income it would inevitably decapitalize.

In a business, all of these activities would be carefully accounted for in financial statements. Sales, minus costs for materials, labor, taxes, and so forth, generate profits or losses. If the profits are sufficient to pay the cost of capital, they can be reinvested to grow the business, paid as dividends to investors, or a combination of the two. In this way, economic value is being added by the operations loop. In a hamlet, or any other nonbusiness organization, these transactions are not aggregated; and the only visible evidence for the process is the improvement or the deterioration of its physical assets. But they take place just the same.

The oval can be drawn to include any definable entity—the nation of Russia, Yale University, the First Methodist Church, or USAirways. The economic activities or services of the entity must in some way earn the cost of capital if the entity is to survive without outside subsidies. The principles are those of microeconomics, but they apply as well to organizations that are more traditionally the subject of macroeconomics.

➤ Influences on the Operations Loop

Obviously, the outside world is much more than a source or a sink for people and capital. It creates an environment that constantly affects the operations loop. For our purposes, the principal ways it does so are through the elements of risk, the law of diminishing returns, and the influence of innovations—the three boxes at the bottom of Figure 4.1.

Risk is such an important concept that Chapters 9 and 10 are devoted to it. We shall see that it is extremely important to recognize whether risk is unique (and diversifiable) or whether it results from marketplace volatility alone. The hamlet is clearly subject to risks—whether the unique risk of a disastrous fire or the market-based risk of a general downturn in the French economy.

The law of diminishing returns underpins most of traditional economics. The hamlet clearly suffered diminishing returns when its lead-mining and smelting operations ceased to be competitive. The law is not an absolute phenomenon because it does not apply under all circumstances or at all times. But because its action always needs to be considered in estimating value, Chapter 7 is dedicated to it.

Finally, the external environment includes a growing pool of knowledge—a constant stream of emerging technologies and new circumstances. Coupled with human ingenuity, these changes create the foundation on which innovation takes place. The positive impact of innovation can more than overcome the law of diminishing returns. Human progress depends on this fact. Both Malthus and the Club of Rome, who focused only on diminishing returns, were proven wrong. The artists of Bardou provided a stimulus for innovative development. In the absence of innovation, for whatever reason, devolution and decapitalization are real possibilities.

Innovation, of course, has a dark side. That is why it is often resisted. Simply stated, innovation can render existing physical capital obsolete. When this occurs the operations loop begins to destroy value. It happened in Bardou. Other materials marginalized and replaced lead. The mines had no chance in the long term. In another time and place, no steam locomotive manufacturers would survive the advent of diesel technology.

➤ The Plans Loop

The plans loop represents the organization's intellectual development. New members, be they employees, immigrants, or recruits, bring knowledge and talent from the outside world; and as they carry on their work, they learn and contribute to the organization's stock of intellectual capital.

We would not expect many such possibilities for a modest hamlet; but even small communities, from Bayreuth in Bavaria to Santa's Workshop in North Pole, New York, have found and developed ingenious ways to develop intellectual property and to turn it into moneymaking businesses. The French artist colony may have the same potential, as its denizens pool their networks of contacts to reach new customers (marketing) and learn from each other's techniques to improve the quality of their offerings (technology). It has happened elsewhere. Former artist colonies, such as Greenwich Village in New York City and St. Tropez, France, are now exemplars of economic prosperity.

Many business firms consciously seek to foster development and exploitation of intellectual capital. They build capabilities that permit the firm to consider courses of action not previously open to it, for example, a traditional manufacturing company may hire an information specialist with experience in e-commerce and simultaneously retain a consultant to implement web site design. The presence of these two people helps effect a plan to begin purchasing over the Internet.

When employees interact with each other, with consultants, with customers, and with suppliers in their day-to-day jobs, they gain relevant experience that adds further value to their plans. So as the e-commerce specialist begins to interact with the company's existing suppliers, he learns relevant information about their plans and what they consider best practices in the industry. He learns what competitors are doing in his new employer's field. He discovers which software works well and which doesn't, and which competitor web sites have the best reputations. The sum of all of this information adds value to the company; and within a year this specialist is far more valuable to his employer than when he first signed on.

At the same time, the specialist makes dozens of new contacts within the firm and learns about the company's operations, cultural patterns, and business vocabulary. As he gains credibility, his recommendations are adopted more readily and his advice is sought in more areas. In an analogy to physical working capital, his intellectual capital is turning over more rapidly, and he is increasingly productive.

The same processes apply to patent lawyers, chemists, and regulatory professionals. Each specialist brings a skill base to the party but then hones those skills on the real problems of the business, building strategic capital in the process. Nevertheless, these skills and insights must be translated into plans for value to be realized. An R&D project is a good example. It is typically aimed at permitting the firm to introduce a new product, for example, a new drug to ameliorate diabetes. The process requires an assessment of markets, an estimate of costs, and the commitment of human resources to translate the idea into a commercial operation. The skills needed to effect this transformation are the dashed line in Figure 4.1. For the diabetes drug, they include a great deal of in-house knowledge about selecting good drug candidates, proving effectiveness and safety in animal and human trials, and bringing a technically effective product into medical channels of distribution. These skills are, needless to say, expensive to acquire and to maintain.

We have just looked at how and why strategic capital grows in an organization's plans loop. There are also at least five ways in which it can diminish.

1. Individuals lose their edge, and their skills become outdated as technology advances and business circumstances change—a virtual form of depreciation.

2. The business plans in which their skills are embedded are implemented and translated into operating businesses. The options are exercised. This result is a desirable one, but it has the effect of eliminating the need for a staff specialist, unless another project plan replaces the need. In effect, an asset has been transferred from the strategic side of the dashed line to the economic side.

3. The decision may be made not to pursue the plan. For example, the firm may cancel its effort to implement web-based business purchasing, making the e-commerce specialist and his knowledge irrelevant. In effect the company abandons its option and writes off its hidden investment in this form of strategic capital.

4. The decision may be made to license or to sell the strategic asset. It is then converted to an economic asset.

5. A key specialist may be recruited by another company, necessitating hiring and training a replacement and hindering the execution of plans—the strategic equivalent of the loss or the theft of a physical asset.

> ## Influences on the Plans Loop

Much of the human and intellectual capital of an organization is embodied in its options for executing future plans. These options are subject to exactly the same forces as operating businesses—risk, the law of diminishing returns, and innovation. But there is one enormous difference. Because the resources involved in plans are not yet committed, *risk* on balance favors the option holder! This may be a way of saying that when life gets less predictable, the most intellectually fit will survive.

The *law of diminishing returns* also applies to the intellectual capital of a firm. As industries and technologies mature, the next element—cost reduction or performance enhancement—becomes increasingly difficult and expensive to achieve. The physical limits of technologies are established and eventually reached. Likewise, intellectual activity, such as R&D in an established field, can become increasingly less productive, to the point where R&D can destroy value after its costs are accounted for.

But *innovation* can break through the impediment of diminishing returns and reinvigorate growth. Often the revolution occurs because new technologies emerge, perhaps initially unrelated to the enterprise at hand. The laser, for example, originated as an important innovation in optics. As its power increased, it became useful as an industrial cutting tool. Surgeons learned to use it for correcting vision. And ultimately, it had a revolutionary effect on the music trade by enabling the CD (compact disc). So an optical development became a dominant technology in acoustics! The CD found its place on computers as the CD-ROM. And as the use of personal computers has been expanding, broadband-data communication over optical fiber (which requires lasers) is rapidly displacing older technologies. Thus, the laser created a circumstance where R&D could create great value in many markets. Such a new opportunity can last for many years, until physical limits are again approached.

Of course, innovation can and regularly does destroy human and intellectual capital. The human capital of knowledge workers (scientists, engineers, computer programmers, accountants, doctors, and lawyers) is steadily eroded by the creation of new information and by technological progress. Specialists need to retool to compete with the more recently educated. In some professions formal requalification is mandatory to permit continued practice.

Intellectual capital can similarly be eroded by innovation. An ingenious competitor may engineer around a patent, or an innovative lawyer may discover how to invalidate the same patent. Hard-won skills in operating first-generation instruments, such as a mass spectrometer, may not be required when those same skills are programmed into the second generation. Customer lists, the crown jewels of every sales organization, become less valuable when customers register on e-commerce web sites.

Navigational skills, once indispensable to national security, were trivialized by the global positioning system (GPS). Twentieth-century navigational technologies, which required enormous physical and intellectual investments in global networks of radio-frequency beacons, atomic clocks, and computers, are being rapidly made obsolete by this satellite-based innovation. The value of the strategic capital of those firms that are based in this older generation of navigational technologies has been as surely reduced as that of the leaders in vacuum tube design or steam locomotives earlier in the twentieth century.

■ ARE IDLE ASSETS OPTIONS?

An interesting issue in valuation is how to treat idle assets. If they are not contributing to cash flow, they belong properly to our realm of strategic capital—the plans loop. The business decision will be whether to sell the option (by liquidating the asset) or to hold it, because its value if held for future operations exceeds its salvage value. (Of course, the economic value of salvage properly includes not only the price received for the asset, but also the capitalized value of what is saved in maintenance costs.) Idle assets can include physical assets (plants, natural resource properties), employees, and intellectual property.

Old-economy companies often hold idle physical assets that they choose not to liquidate. These are not contributing to free cash flow—in fact, maintaining them is a cost that shows up on the income statement and reduces valuation on a DCF basis. If this behavior is rational, it would seem that idle assets represent options and that their cost is the maintenance cost. Looked at this way, that maintenance cost would be the sum of out-of-pocket costs *plus* the cost of capital attributable to their liquidation value.

In the petrochemical industry, when pricing is depressed, it is typical to shut down, or mothball, plants when out-of-pocket (cash) costs exceed net revenues. The usual logic is that when the industry has overcapacity, those plants with the highest variable cost will shut down first. But because the industry is subject to pricing cycles, there is a recognition that these plants can be restarted, with a positive contribution to FCF, when conditions improve. Analyzing this situation is a classic example of real option theory: Is it time to scrap this old plant, or should we hang on waiting for the cycle to turn? The answer will depend on both the volatility of the market and the salvage value.

Natural resource companies face similar issues. They understand the marginal cost of producing gas, oil, gold, copper, or diamonds from a particular site. Do they accept the production costs, allow the assets to lie fallow, or liquidate their properties?

A few companies, such as Enron, are beginning to pursue this logic quite aggressively. They have begun investing in *inefficient* electrical generating plants, which are not cost competitive with the industry as a whole, with the intention of turning them on only when spot prices justify it. In a deregulated environment, these "peaker" plants represent real options, and real options valuation methods are being used to determine at what price the investment is attractive.

Another example of proactive investment in idle physical plant is the investment that cable companies are making in placing up to three unused fiber optic lines in new cable. Their reasoning is that while the potential bandwidth is not needed today to cover existing television channels, it may be sold very profitably as new Internet-driven services are developed in the future. A mile of optical fiber is cheap compared to the labor cost of installing the underground cable in which it is embedded.

The real option to sell this capacity has been recognized by Wall Street and has become a factor in the valuation of cable service providers.[3]

The human and intellectual assets in the plans loop have analogous characteristics. Those that are embedded in a viable plan contribute to strategic value; those that are not contributing to plans should not be retained because they destroy value.

Employees first. The San Francisco 49ers long carried two outstanding quarterbacks, Joe Montana and Steve Young, when the customs of the game allowed only one on the field. Either player could have been traded for an outstanding athlete in another position or simply for a financial gain. Clearly, the 49ers had idle, and expensive, human capital. Most of their competitors solved the value equation with a star quarterback and a journeyman backup. The 49ers' logic must have related to options theory. With Montana starting, Young was outstanding backup. In certain situations, his running skills provided tactical advantage. And retaining his services provided a hedge against the day when Montana hung up his cleats (or their modern-day equivalents) and new talent had to be drafted.

The third type of idle assets comprises intellectual property. A typical R&D-intensive manufacturing company may generate a patent for every $1 million to 3 million of R&D effort. For a company with an R&D budget of $100 million, this level of intellectual productivity can mean up to a hundred patents per year; for a larger company with a $1 billion R&D budget, it can mean a thousand patents. Very few of these patents are likely to produce significant value, but all incur costs: the initial cost of filing and prosecuting the application in a variety of jurisdictions and the subsequent costs of annual maintenance. Unfortunately, the owners initially face considerable uncertainty as to which patents will prove valuable and which will prove worthless. (In its internal prioritization process, the company has already rejected prosecuting those patent disclosures that seem economically marginal.) But as time goes on, likely winners stand out, likely losers become more evident, and options can be framed. In the patent field, the options on such idle assets are typically to license, to swap, to donate to a charitable institution, or to abandon.

■ SIX STEPS TO TOTAL VALUE

With these general ideas as a framework, it is time to introduce a practical method for valuation using the Total Value Model. As a working example, we will revisit our friend Peggy Sue.

➤ Step 1. Calculating the Economic Value of the Enterprise

This step is traditional MBA stuff and most valuation books focus on it. For example, I have used Copeland's *Valuation*[4] for this purpose in my classroom at Yale University. The general method is to compute the free cash flow of the enterprise from its business plans out to a horizon year. After the horizon year, a terminal value for the enterprise is calculated. There are many ways to estimate terminal value, but a standard method is to assume a realistic growth rate in perpetuity starting with the FCF in the horizon year. The DCF method is then applied to calculate the present value of the forecast FCF up to the horizon year plus the terminal value. The result, of course, depends on the imputed cost of capital.

Double counting must be avoided. If a promising program is already included in the company's cash flow projection, it cannot be included in steps 2 through 6.

We worked through this problem for Peggy Sue back in Chapter 3. Because her business was growing steadily at 6 percent per year, we were able to use the current year as the horizon year for the calculation. Her FCF of $60,000 per year, her opportunity cost of capital of 12 percent, and equation 4 (Economic

Value = FCF/[Cost of Capital – Growth Rate]) gave us an economic value for her business of $1 million.

> ### ➤ Step 2. Framing the Basic Business Option:
> ### The Peggy Sue Scenario, Part II

Doing this step well will certify you as a master strategist! After all, it is largely skill at framing options that separates top chief executive officers (CEOs) from also-rans. However, investors can also play the game of identifying options by analyzing what executives tell investors about their plans. For start-ups, which need to reveal a lot to attract financing, much of the information will be available, sometimes even in the very useful form of pro forma business plans—the key input for valuing a real option. For old-economy companies, the chairman's letter in the annual report or the story line prepared for institutional investors provides important clues about the options under consideration—whether to divest unprofitable businesses, to make strategic acquisitions, or to implement cost-savings programs.

For insiders, who are addressing a value-creating decision such as funding an R&D program, framing the option is not a problem because it is already on the table and the numbers are in the corporate data bank.

Let's frame a strategic option for Peggy Sue. We last saw her running a thriving dry cleaning business in Lubbock that we valued at $1 million.

Peggy Sue's brother Travis, who lives in Midland, Texas, visits Peggy Sue over the holidays. Over the (proverbial) kitchen table, he mentions that a new shopping center will be built near his home and that the neighborhood badly needs a dry cleaner. He believes Ben, the developer of the center, would be delighted to take on someone like Peggy Sue as a tenant. There seems to be no reason why a successful shop in Midland would operate any differently than her proven formula in Lubbock.

The next week, Peggy Sue meets Ben, and he offers to lease her space if she makes a $50,000 payment. Ben recognizes this sum as the opportunity cost of not committing the space to another party. He also agrees that he will lease to no competitor while Peggy Sue is his tenant.

Peggy Sue's business plan is simple enough: She will need to invest an additional $500,000 two years hence when the shopping center is ready for occupancy, and she expects to enjoy initial FCF of $60,000, which can be expected to grow at 6 percent. She will again finance the venture with equity—from her savings plus contributions from Travis and Ben.

Once she has made the deposit, this business plan becomes an option. We will calculate its value in Step 4.

➤ Step 3. Determining the Option Premium

The cost of a real option, corresponding to the premium one pays for a financial option, will be the expenditures required to make the plan actionable. The easiest case is the situation in which all the needed assets—technology, people, strategic partners, and financing—are in hand. This is a zero-cost option. For R&D projects, the option's cost is the cost of supporting the research team.

We made this step easy for the reader in the Peggy Sue Scenario. This option cost $50,000, as negotiated between Ben and Peggy Sue.

➤ Step 4. Determining the Value of the Pro Forma Business Plan

The most important step in determining the value of the option is the creation of a pro forma business plan. The methodology is exactly as in Step 1 and the output is the plan's net present value (NPV). The key difference is that we are dealing with a plan to which we are not fully committed rather than with a business that already exists. The NPV represents the value of the *underlying security* of a call option. It is directly analogous to a financial call option, where the underlying security of a call option on Exxon stock would be shares of Exxon stock and the value of the underlying security is the market price of Exxon stock.

An internal analyst usually has an advantage in this step because she has access to the numbers that support the business plan and a better appreciation of business risks. Professional securities analysts, who make a living by understanding the dynamics of markets, manufacturing costs, industry margins, and risk, also regularly make pro forma projections for the companies they track. Serious amateurs can set up model calculations on a spreadsheet[5] and use reasonable estimates of the key business parameters to determine a range of values for the basic business plan.

The NPV exercise, in itself, may give an early clue as to whether a security is seriously under- or overvalued. We have again made the math easy for the reader. The value of the underlying security for Peggy Sue's Midland business plan is identical to that of the existing Lubbock business, $1 million.

➤ Step 5. Calculating the Option Value

Because the Midland project is a plan, an options method must be applied to its valuation. A Nobel prize winning (1997) algorithm, the Black-Scholes formula, is our tool of choice. However, because the immediate objective of this chapter is to illustrate the mechanics of the total value model, a broader discussion of Black-Scholes and options theory will be deferred to the next chapter. For now we will treat Black-Scholes as a "black box."

To apply the Black-Scholes formula, five numbers are needed:

(1) the value of the underlying security, (2) the strike or exercise price, (3) the time period of the option, (4) the volatility, and (5) the risk-free rate. The first three numbers are already in hand. The underlying security is valued at $1,000,000. The exercise price is $500,000. The duration is 2 years—at which time Peggy Sue can invest the strike price or walk away. More technically, this option is a 2-year European call option.[6]

Also, the *Wall Street Journal*'s web site states that Treasury Bills currently yield 5 percent—we'll use that as the risk-free rate.

What do we use for volatility? That's sometimes the rub. We need some kind of proxy for a very unique business that is not publicly traded. Here is one approach: A basket of stable retail establishments (McDonald's, Sears, etc.) can easily be created that may arguably be subject to the same economic forces as a dry cleaner. The historical monthly volatilities of listed stocks are available under "Trader's Tools" at the Chicago Board of Option Exchange (CBOE) web site, *www.cboe.com*. Let us assume 30 percent is the average for the basket we select. An option calculator is available at the CBOE web site or from many other sources.[7] Using an option calculator with these parameters, we value the option at $549,894.

It is clear that the option is worth more than its cost ($50,000), so it should be purchased. Peggy Sue writes Ben a check.

Note that the option value for this case is, as would be expected, higher than the DCF value. The DCF approach would consider the situation to be the ownership of an asset with an NPV 2 years hence of $500,000 ($1,000,000 enterprise value minus the $500,000 investment). Discounting $500,000 at 12 percent for 2 years gives $398,597.

The volatility factor relates to basic business conditions. If those conditions are poor, Peggy Sue can back out and forfeit her $50,000. If they are as good or better than projected, she is likely to exercise and move forward to open the Midland store.

Finally, the value of the business plan must be corrected for unique risk. Peggy Sue feels that the main source of risk, a small one, is that Ben will go bankrupt. She does some quiet research, is reassured, and concludes that the risk is less than 5 percent. She reduces her expectation for the value of the option accordingly: $0.95 \times \$549,894 = \$522,399$.

> ### Step 6. Calculating Total Value

Total value is economic value (from Step 1) plus the difference between option cost (from Step 3) and option value (from Step 4). Only options whose value exceeds their cost need be considered.

For the Peggy Sue Scenario, Total Value is $1,000,000 + ($522,399 – $50,000), or $1,472,399.

> ### Further Steps: Capturing Additional Option Values

Applying a straightforward method to a complex business situation will still result in a complex problem. The issue every analyst must face is whether adding the complexities and nuances is worth the effort. Option theory is powerful in this regard because each additional option (or element of managerial flexibility) creates value. In theory, at least, it is only possible to *underestimate* total value.

The essence of this step is to identify each possible source of cash flow available to the enterprise. For a movie producer contemplating a script, the basic option may be to make the film and capture domestic box office revenues. Other cash flow streams, though, may include overseas rights; TV and cable reruns; the CD soundtrack; VHS tapes and DVDs; toys, books, clothes, and like licensing opportunities; a Broadway production; and theme park rides.

Additional option values come in two varieties: (1) independent and (2) dependent. If exercising the second option is a matter entirely independent of exercising the first, one just needs to repeat Steps 4 and 5 for each independent option. For example, a major drug company could be reasonably assumed to be capable of independently exercising options to launch a new cold medicine and a new beta-blocker. The values are additive.

Other options are dependent. Within the option to launch a cold remedy may lie options to delay, expand, accelerate or scale down the launch, or to launch closely related products. These are not independent, and each will add value. In Peggy Sue's case, one opportunity she may have is to find a location even better than the one at Ben's shopping center. If she could handle only one new operation (her expansion options are not independent), she could still forfeit the $50,000, which is a sunk cost. The right to do so adds value to her situation.

The values of complex interrelated combinations of options can be calculated using the methods of *compound options*.[8] Be warned that the math is not simple and is beyond the scope of this book.

The practical question is whether the bonus values built into these refinements are critical to the decision at hand or are in the nature of bells and whistles. In some cases, management may have a great deal of flexibility, so capturing all the degrees of freedom will become tedious, while at the same time the added value of each successive option becomes marginal. In other cases, such as the movie producer, the correct packaging of a group of linked options may be the secret to estimating Total Value. My advice is to focus on what is material and be sure to get the basic option(s) right.

■ WHAT WE CAN LEARN FROM PEGGY SUE

The Peggy Sue scenario is designed to show the differences and the similarities between economic and strategic capital. The value of the Lubbock operating business was $1 million. The Midland option created almost 50 percent additional value. Taken together, the enterprise is worth $1,472,399—considerably more than a true *financial* buyer would pay for it. Such a buyer would pay only for the FCF and not for the additional investment opportunity embodied in Peggy Sue's Midland plan. So in this simple case, about two-thirds of the Total Value of the enterprise is in the operation and one-third is in the strategic capital of the option. Any *strategic* buyer, say an entrepreneur seeking to create a chain of cleaning establishments in the Southwest, would expect to pay Peggy Sue not only for her Lubbock facility but also for her position in Midland.

We need to consider whether we have correctly valued the Midland option. We have accounted for a main source of risk—the volatility of retail margins. This volatility represents *market risk* and occurs as a result of the strength of the general economy and the degree of competition. We have seen in Chapter 3 that the value of Peggy Sue's Lubbock business is very sensitive to the return on capital, which in turn is very sensitive to her margins. Margins also significantly affect the value of the Midland option: Lower margins would reduce the value of the underlying security (which was just the time-lagged value of the Lubbock business). Indeed, if margins drop to the point where the cleaning business is not earning its cost of capital, Peggy Sue should not exercise the option and should walk away from her $50,000 deposit. That scenario is built into the value of the option today through the volatility parameter. So is a happier scenario—that margins may actually improve, making both the Midland and the Lubbock locations more valuable.

Unique risk also came into play. There are some unique risks. Ben's solvency and his ability to complete the project were recognized. Peggy Sue's health is another. New environmental regulations on cleaning solvents may be a third, but they were excluded from the scenario.

In constructing our case, we have not identified any opportunities for diversification to offset any of these unique risks, although there may reasonably be some. Perhaps competent management is available in West Texas to replace Peggy Sue if necessary, or life insurance (a form of risk diversification) may be obtained cheaply. There may be other attractive locales for a second shop. In any case, it is prudent to reduce the value of the Midland option by some factor to take these unique risks into account.

The limited opportunities for diversification set Peggy Sue's business apart from large operating companies with many risky projects. A pharmaceutical company can place its R&D bets on tens of thousands of new molecules. An oil company or syndicate can drill a host of exploratory wells. Like mutual fund investors, these larger operators all enjoy some shelter from unique risks through diversification.

It is also worth reflecting that the Lubbock operation and the Midland option can be valued independently or their values can be combined. The Midland option is a perfectly viable start-up. It has a good location, a business plan, and experienced management. (Peggy Sue could even sell Lubbock and focus entirely on Midland.) Travis, Ben, and this author would be more than happy to buy equity in this enterprise! As a stand-alone business, the value of the Midland venture is precisely the value of the option that Peggy Sue and Travis identified at the kitchen table.

The hypothetical small-business scenario we have been developing can be viewed through the lens of our general business model (Figure 4.1). The Lubbock operation is clearly the left side operations loop, generating a stream of FCF. The Midland plans loop is on the right side of the model, representing strategic capital. In terms of the entire enterprise, we have established that the operational side has a value that is about two times the value of the plan side. So the dashed line would be to the right of center—about two-thirds of the way over.

But it may not stay there for long. Peggy Sue, like every businessperson, intends to convert her strategic capital to economic capital. When that happens and the Midland operation is underway, the dashed line will be all the way to the right—unless Peggy Sue has other plans or options. Her business will again be defined by economic capital alone.

But what created this strategic capital in the first place? It was an innovative idea—an informed response to another innovative development in the outside world, namely, Ben's plan to build a shopping center in a Midland neighborhood. The idea was not independently generated by Peggy Sue; it became actionable as a response to other events. The take-home point is that the potential for profit is often contingent on the emergence of possibilities that had not been seen before! In larger companies, those possibilities can be created internally by R&D, but more often are a response to a new circumstance in the marketplace. Such is the nature of innovation.

■ TOTAL VALUE AND THE REAL INVESTOR

Peggy Sue's enterprise is a simple case, but the valuation method we used can be applied to a much more complex company, even when the operating business is not yet profitable. The keys are to disaggregate expenses that are in effect investments (such as R&D) from the ongoing operations, to forecast the operating business so that a cash flow analysis can be made, and to identify and value the options available to management. For Amazon.com, as it began operations in 1998, those options included creating new businesses (in music, toys, and electronics) using their existing business model, auctions, forming strategic alliances with important partners, merging with a traditional retailer, and so forth. As long as a cash flow model can be constructed for each important option and the total financial and managerial capability of the parent organization is not overextended, a valuation can be achieved.

Options theory will work even for complex cases in which the various business options are mutually dependent or mutually exclusive. In these cases, straightforward additivity of options will not apply to the calculation of strategic capital. The mathematics also becomes more formidable than when options are independent; but they have been developed, and a very illuminating example has been published.[9]

There is no magic bullet in options theory: Complex situations are inherently difficult to analyze; and to the degree that the analyst has gaps in his or her knowledge or oversimplifies, the result may be flawed. However, one of the beauties of an option (unlike a money-losing operating business) is that it cannot have a negative value. Therefore, there is little danger of overvaluing a company using a DCF model supplemented with a realistic valuation of the options apparent in its business plan. The larger danger is of overlooking an important option that is available to management and of substantially undervaluing the firm. On the one hand, in a dynamic business environment such as the one created by the Internet, the universe of business strategies may be too large for any analyst to comprehend them all. On the other hand, the best business analysts, just as the best executives, have a way of seeing business combinations that those focused on short-term cash flow projections are bound to miss.

An important valuation problem is that the transition from a company based primarily on strategic value (such as Genentech or Amazon) to one based on economic value is seldom smooth. The problem is manifested when the stock of a "high-flyer" goes down just as it earns its first profit. This event is traumatic and all too frequent. It occurs because analysts and investors just changed yardsticks.

In the absence of positive cash flow, the yardstick is likely to be a comparable company. Consider two biotech start-ups, both without earnings or meaningful revenues. If biotech start-up A has 50 Ph.D.s and is valued at $200 million, then biotech start-up B with 25 Ph.D.s may be valued at about $100 million plus or minus a "quality factor"—a subjective notion as to which firm has the better projects and the better management. Anchoring B's value to A is not very satisfactory—there is just no alternative. There are many other phony yardsticks that have little to do with economics. They are used because there are no others. Besides R&D budgets, price-to-revenue ratios, eyeballs, click-throughs, and even "price-to-vision ratios" have been mentioned. Managements chasing phony metrics to attract financing risk destroying value in the process.

But the day start-up B earns a profit, economic yardsticks can be applied. Investors will then have a great deal of trouble making the transition between future promise and actual financial performance, particularly when there are many expensive projects still in the R&D pipeline.

The problem of valuation is by no means confined to start-ups. A great project or a business buried in a large company will likely be missed by the analysts. Such omissions represent a large universe of potentially lost value because corporate R&D budgets, running over $130 billion per year in the United States,[10] are a much bigger part of the economy than venture-capital–financed start-ups are, and they also far exceed university and government-funded R&D expenditures.

For example, Hughes Electronics has a rapidly growing satellite-based web-access business. That business is buried in giant General Motors, which tends to attract analysts and investors with a value mindset. And the promise of the Palm Pilot in 1999 and 2000 was greatly undervalued as a part of 3Com. There are countless other examples.

The changing yardstick problem is simply a problem in valuation methodology, but an integrated valuation model based on real options offers a sound way to overcome that problem. One way or another, it needs to be overcome—not just so investors can do a better job in stock picking, but also so that top management can make decisions that maximize Total Value.

■ REAL OPTIONS APPLY TO "REAL LIFE"

Finally, it is interesting to see how the Total Value Model reflects real life. Consider a very small organization, a nuclear family. Its principal economic activities can be taken to be the income produced by the breadwinner(s). The costs of maintaining the household are set against this revenue. Any surplus goes into a capital account, as a source of additional income and as a shield against illness or old age. Absent a surplus, the family is likely to devolve—to lower its standard of living. These are the dynamics of a very small operations loop.

The most prevalent strategic option of a family is to educate its children. Education may pay off in the long term in increasing living standards and upward mobility, but it comes at short-term cost: both the direct cost of education and the imputed costs of not employing the children in generating short-term cash flow. There are significant market and unique risks in educating children: Their skills may not be demanded by the marketplace when they complete the educational process, or they may fail to meet the requirements of their chosen profession. These forces reflect the dynamics of the plans loop.

The family will constantly weigh the merits of increasing its economic capital at the expense of its strategic position, and vice versa.

This basic equation can be affected positively by the outside world through gifts, inheritance, subsidies, and scholarships or negatively through taxation, conscription, and happenstance.

Be the oval a family, a hamlet, a city, or a nation; a shop, a young corporation, a mature corporation; a university, a charity, or a church, the principles of Total Value will apply.

Enter the Options Dragon

The introduction of options thinking to valuation is a very new thing. It recognizes that uncertainty provides managers with investment opportunities—something that traditional valuation methods have seldom acknowledged.[1] Yet we live in an extremely turbulent world, and the flexibility that options afford to investors is an increasingly important part of value creation. It is safe to say that investors who weigh options will outperform those who do not. Options are the dragon that changes the game.

This assertion was taking on the nature of hard fact even as this book was written. Companies that have used real options aggressively in pricing and capital budgeting, such as Dynegy and Calpine, have profited, while utilities in California that did not properly understand the nature of risk were declaring bankruptcy.

Traditional thinking about options has focused on their usefulness in hedging risk, their potential for highly leveraged speculation, and their role as a tool for motivating and compensating key employees. The potential of options for creating competitive advantage in the ordinary course of business is innovative, and it is something exciting. Now options are being considered as a valuation tool—for quantitative decision making—in situations where strategic considerations are important. For many high-risk business investments, including young companies and innovative research-and-development (R&D) projects, options may prove to be the *most* important valuation tool.

Three books[2] and several dozen papers on real options appeared during the period 1998 to 2001, and a number of regular professional conferences on the subject have sprung up. Representatives of petroleum, pharmaceutical, and energy firms are conspicuous among the presenters, and other industries are beginning to take an interest. Clearly, conference attendees aim to apply real option techniques to the real problems faced by their companies.

Because many readers may find the subject of options to be a bit exotic, this chapter is organized to review the implications of options thinking in some relatively familiar situations and then to move progressively into less-charted territory. The chapter will also discuss some of the philosophic underpinnings of real options theory, since the intellectual issues are far from settled. At the end of the chapter we will introduce an example that illustrates why options theory can predict very high valuations in situations characterized by high growth and high volatility—the very essence of high-risk investing.

■ THE REVENGE OF THE QUANTS

An *option* is the right to carry out a transaction without the obligation to do so. Some options are extremely valuable, and some are practically worthless. But holding an option is *never* a liability. In general, the more options one has, the more valuable one's position is.

An option is a capital asset. This fact is obvious for a financial option that can be sold on a public option exchange or for a vested employee incentive option that can be exercised. Liquidity makes the value obvious. In these cases, we are dealing with tangible capital. However, the value is less obvious for the much less liquid options in real life where we are largely dealing with information, strategy, and virtual capital.

In the business world, options capture the value of managerial flexibility. Trigeorgis[3] has described a business plan in which the investor holds five identifiable options. These are mostly options to abandon, to defer, or to change the scope of the project (expand or contract). In combination, they are called *compound options*. Such complex combinations of compound options exist in many real business situations. Trigeorgis first examines the value of each option taken individually, some being much more valuable than others, but any and all being more valuable than having no options. "No options" means being fully committed to the base case plan, which happens to have a negative net present value (NPV) in his example. Several of the single options are valuable enough to change NPV from negative to positive. Then he calculates the value of all combinations of two options, of three options, up to all five options. And, as must be, the combination of all five is the most valuable of all because it includes all the others. It turns out these five options add about six times the value of the (negative) NPV to the positive side of the equation! However, the complexity of the calculations also increases dramatically as multiple interacting compound options are included, and so possibly does distance from business reality. Hence, it might be illusional to conclude that rigorous options analysis is a substitute for managerial skill.

The take-away point of this discussion is to confirm quantitatively what business executives are increasingly recognizing: that many business plans that seem to create no value on a pro forma cash flow basis are actually very attractive once the full value of all management options is recognized! This recognition is a huge source of competitive advantage for those who understand the value of strategy versus an older generation of "quants," who were content to grind NPV and IRR (internal rate of return) numbers based on the most probable scenario.

This revolution in thinking is an especially important fact to high-risk investors, which, as a former R&D executive, I consider myself to be. My colleagues and I had long been frustrated by our inability to create business plans that were both credible and economically viable around risky projects with long-term horizons. Yet there was abundant evidence, from hindsight, that great industrial fortunes were being created by just this process. Our intuition as experienced professionals was that we were on the right track. Options theory provided the confirmation.

I would hardly be the first to observe that clever business strategists have often turned the tables on shortsighted "numbers men"—you saw in Chapter 2 how the Japanese were able to use the rigidity of Detroit's financial planners against them in gaining nearly 30 percent of the U.S. car market. But I suspect Japan's success was based on intuition. In the next rounds of competition a new generation of quants will have an opportunity for revenge by bringing in the heavy guns of options theory.

■ OPTIONS, TIME, AND INFORMATION

"Time transforms risk, especially when decisions are irreversible."[4] This statement succinctly summarizes the essence of options. Options buy time. Time produces information. Information will eventually validate or invalidate the plan. And information is virtual.

For publicly traded options, where uncertainty equates to market risk, the closer one gets in time to the decision point, the more certain it will be whether the option should be exercised. In this case, the information comes to you. Financial options are priced by professionals and can be bought and sold at fair value. This price is referred to as the *premium*.[5] You can win at this game consistently only if you have better business information than most professionals do or superior trading skills.

For situations largely determined by unique risk, whether

they are performing R&D or drilling for petroleum, the information does not come to you. On the contrary, you usually pay to get information. Changes in value tend to be highly irreversible. You rely on your own expertise for a competitive advantage—and you must use that expertise to determine whether the value of the information you want is worth its cost.

It is important to remember that options expire and that they constantly lose value as the clock ticks down to the expiration date. This fact means that a company whose options value is very high today cannot expect to maintain that valuation two years into the future; the option must either be exercised or renewed! Internet investors learned this reality to their sorrow.

■ OPTIONS ON COMMON STOCK

Financial options based on common stocks are traded every day on licensed exchanges such as the Chicago Board of Options Exchange (CBOE).[6] They are classified as puts and calls. A *call option* is the right to purchase the underlying security at the strike price. A *put option* is the right to sell it. The holder of a call will benefit when the share price rises. The holder of a put will benefit if the share price drops. The value of such puts and calls is driven by market risk.

Let us say that I hold a call option to buy 100 shares of Acme Chemical stock at a strike price of $100 that expires nine months hence. Today, Acme stock is trading at $105. My call option has an *intrinsic value* today of $5 per share ($105 – $100). I have the right to buy the stock at $100 from the individual who sold me the option contract (actually from someone randomly selected from the pool of persons who wrote this class of call). I can immediately turn around and sell this contract for a $500 gain ($5 × 100).[7] Of course, if Acme were selling below $100, I would not exercise because I could buy the shares more cheaply on the stock exchange. I have the right, not the obligation, to buy.

However, I would be foolish to exercise and take the $500 profit. This option could be traded on the CBOE for, say, $22 per share,[8] netting a gain of $2,200 ($22 × 100). Why does this option sell for $22? A small part of the reason is that it has an intrinsic value of $5, but the main reason is because the upsides in the next nine months far outweigh the downsides. Acme might, in nine months or at any time in between, reach $120 or $140 or perhaps $160. There is also a possibility that it could drop to $80, but I need not worry too much about that. The $22 is a weighted average of all the upside possibilities from here and the possibility of dropping to zero, but none of the negatives.

The weightings themselves are determined by the estimates of traders, some of whom buy or sell based on their business judgments about the future of Acme and the broad stock market. Others are guided by mathematical formulas, which would take into account the historic volatility of Acme stock. And it is predictable that at the hour this option expires, when the upsides have nearly evaporated, its quoted price will have fallen to the intrinsic value.

■ RANDOM WALK THEORY, THE NORMAL DISTRIBUTION, AND BLACK-SCHOLES

How did we come to value this option at $22? We used the Black-Scholes formula (already mentioned in Chapter 4), which usually tracks quoted option prices closely. Richard Brealey and Stewart Myers[9] describe this mathematical formula as "unpleasant-looking" but one that on "closer acquaintance [the user] will find exceptionally elegant and useful." Reviewing the formula itself serves little purpose, but exploring the underlying concepts is worthwhile. And in the next section, we will describe enough of its characteristics to get the reader started.

There is nothing really magic about Black-Scholes: Option values may also be calculated using the older binomial method[10]—and as a practical matter the binomial results usually track the Black-Scholes values closely and are based on similar assumptions. Some real options specialists argue for the risk-neutral method. But in engineering parlance, the beauty of Black-Scholes is "plug and chug"—a close-ended calculation.

There are two basic assumptions in the Black-Scholes formula. One is that securities prices perform a random walk around mean values; the other is that the distribution of values around the mean can be accurately represented by what is disarmingly called a "normal distribution," or a bell curve. Many statistically random phenomena, such as a series of coin flips, are normally distributed.

The term *random walk* derives from the path said to be followed by an inebriated person. There is no pattern to this path, and nothing in past movements is predictive of future movements. Per the definition in *Barron's Dictionary of Finance and Investment Terms*: "Random walk: Theory about the movement of stock and commodity futures prices hypothesizing that past prices are of no use in forecasting future price movements. According to the theory, stock prices reflect reactions to information coming to the market in random fashion, so they are no more predictable than the walking pattern of a drunken person."

A true random walk also implies that markets handle information efficiently. This assumption appears to be reasonable when working with large capitalization stocks whose price movements are tracked by many thousands of investors. It is much less true for situations where only a few individuals have information about the security.

Everyone knows that, on average, 100 coin flips will yield 50 heads. But the odds of getting *exactly* 50 heads in a single 100-coin trial are, in fact, not very good. And the chances of getting 51 heads are almost as good as getting 50. The chances of getting 60 heads are considerably lower.

The actual odds of getting any specific number of heads can

be calculated using the laws of probability in the mathematical form of the normal distribution. For example, you may use a normal distribution to calculate the chances of getting exactly 55 heads in 100 flips. By extension, you may also use it to calculate the chance of getting 55 heads *or more*: This function is called a *cumulative normal distribution*. Normal distributions and cumulative normal distributions are common in nature; and scientists, statisticians, and expert gamblers are familiar with them.[11] They are standard fare in spreadsheet programs like Excel, as well as in packaged statistics software.

The normal distribution curve is defined by only two parameters: (1) the mean value about which things vary (for example, 50 heads) and (2) the standard deviation, which defines the width of the curve. A handy characteristic of normal distributions is the fact that in 68 percent of trials, the result will fall within one standard deviation of the mean; and in 95 percent, the result will fall within two deviations. For securities, standard deviation is synonymous with *volatility*. Thus, if stocks in the Standard & Poor's (S&P) 500 have an average annual standard deviation of 0.15, on average, a year later, they will be priced within 15 percent of their mean value 68 percent of the time and within 30 percent of their mean value 95 percent of the time.

Random walk theory contains a threatening implication. It implies that the thousands of professionals who make their livings by picking stocks for mutual funds, money management accounts, and financial institutions can do no better than a dartboard or an index fund. Those who have outperformed the market are deemed lucky: In any normal distribution of stock pickers, about half will beat the average and half will lag it. Hence the common disclaimer: "Past performance is no guarantee of future performance." And for just these reasons, the issue has been studied extensively. Professor Burton Malkiel[12] of Princeton University has written a popular book, *A Random Walk Down Wall Street*, on the arguments for the random walk theory, and there is a fine discussion of the theory and of the normal distribution in *Against the Gods*.[13] The author's view is that while the concept has minor flaws, as does the Black-Scholes formula, for the purposes of this book it is more than good enough.

The second assumption behind Black-Scholes valuation is that the shape (width) of the normal distribution will be reasonably constant with time for the decision of interest. This postulate is absolutely true of coin flips and true often enough with securities that the theory can be profitably used to price stocks, bonds, and options in real financial markets. Obviously, the standard deviations of *different classes* of securities are not the same. Utility stocks have (or at least used to have) much less volatility than biotechnology stocks. It is mechanically straightforward to calculate standard deviations for each publicly traded stock (Exxon) or for all stocks in a class of securities (e.g., petroleum companies), and such calculations are widely published.[14]

■ THE BEHAVIOR OF OPTIONS

There are three important rules to remember about how option values behave under changing conditions. Knowing them can be handy for rapid mental calculations in a business situation when one doesn't have a calculator handy.

1. *Options react to the price of the underlying security.* In the earlier Acme example, we discussed a situation where nine-month calls on Acme with a strike price of $100 were valued at $22 when Acme traded at $105. What happens if Acme goes up or down 5 points tomorrow (that is, the intrinsic value goes up or down by 5 points)? To a first approximation the value of the option will go up or down by a smaller but comparable amount— in this case, about $3.25 per share. (The value of this option moves at 65 percent of the rate of the underlying security—3.25 ÷ 5 = 0.65. Traders refer to this relationship as the "option delta.")

What does this behavior mean in the case of a real option? For a real option, the underlying security is the pro forma value of the business plan. If information comes in that expenses will be higher or revenue will be lower, the value of the underlying security will drop. If the reverse is true, the security will be worth more. What is most important is recognizing that its value will fluctuate as new information arrives.

2. *An option's value varies nearly in proportion to the volatility.* For an option that is near the money, double the volatility and you approximately double the value of the option. Halve the volatility and you halve the value.[15]

In valuing a real option, often the biggest decision is what volatility to assign. A stock in a closely analogous business is often chosen. Merck has used volatilities characteristic of the biotechnology industry for high-risk drug research,[16] a judiciously chosen petroleum company stock might be a good "proxy" for an energy project, and so forth.

3. *The value of an option is proportional to the square root of the time over which the option is valid.* An option that has four times the time to run will have double the value. Consider three-year (36-month) Acme at-the-money calls. They should be priced at just about twice the 9-month calls.[17]

In summary, the value of an option is a function of three things: (1) the strike price relative to the current market price of the stock, (2) the volatility of the stock price, and (3) the amount of time left before the option expires. Generally speaking, *the value of the option is directly proportional to the volatility and proportional to the square root of the time to expiration.* Volatility is the standard deviation of the stock price, calculated as a percent.

The values of real options are very sensitive both to changes in business assumptions and to the option parameters of time and volatility. Thus, sensitivity analysis—calculating results for a range of intuitively reasonable values[18]—may be a useful tool.

■ INCENTIVE OPTIONS

In the preface, we noted that many individuals today favor stock options over cash compensation. This preference is particularly true of employees who are investing their human capital in high-risk start-ups. Options have the advantage over cash of both great leverage and deferred (or no) tax consequences.

Consider an R&D scientist named Julia, whose firm granted her an option in year 2000 to buy 1,000 shares of its stock at $50 per share, no matter what its current market price might be. Under the terms of the plan, Julia can exercise this option at any time during the 10-year period ending January 15, 2010.

In the parlance of options trading, $50 is the strike price, January 15, 2010, is the expiration date, and Julia has a "call" option—the right (but not the obligation) to "call" 1,000 shares of stock from the company treasury, at the strike price, any time before the expiration date.

Suppose the stock of Julia's company has dropped by $5 to $45 per share since the options were granted. She is "out of the money" by $5 and the *intrinsic value* of her options is currently zero. But if the stock had a volatility of 50 percent and she applied the Black-Scholes formula,[19] she would estimate her options to be worth $28 per share, or $28,000.

■ OBJECTIONS TO THE RANDOM WALK APPROACH

One of the most provocative and valuable business ideas has been the controversial notion that markets have no memory. As described earlier, this idea is embodied both in the random-walk concept as it is applied to the stock market and in the everyday pricing of financial options. The term *stochastic* is used to describe it.

Yet, as a practical matter, many investors and business people don't believe that history is irrelevant. If the market is truly a random walk, there is no reason to consult charts; yet investors (including myself) almost always do. The other extreme on the spectrum of thought is called "technical analysis," which can take chart watching to a point approaching astrology. For technical analysts, history is everything. Technical analysts act as if certain patterns of prices and/or volumes, such as the "head-and-shoulders" pattern, give excellent predictions about future market behavior.

Yet another group of investors believes in reversion to the mean—the idea that what goes up in unusual measure will inevitably revert to its historical average, and, with equal probability, what goes down will go back up. In other words, companies whose values are depressed compared to historic measures are more than likely to rebound. There is merit in this viewpoint but also peril. The collapse of Long-Term Capital Management (LTCM) in 1998 seems to have been in part caused by misplaced reliance on this idea: "In effect, LTCM had a one-way undiversified bet that credit spreads would narrow"[20] to their historic range.

Just as there were reasons for the credit spreads of 1998, some companies with low price/earnings (P/E) ratios have them for good reason and will continue to devolve, perhaps right into bankruptcy. Others will solve the underlying problem and rejoin the ranks of the financially healthy. So it makes a great deal of difference whether you believe a low P/E ratio is a fair reading of current business cause and effect (to be altered by the next random event) or an aberration that permits investment under circumstances where downside risk is outweighed by upside opportunity.

A certain amount of healthy respect for both viewpoints is wise, because real investors who determine the market dynamics act on both beliefs. Belief in the business cycle is a prime case in point. It is not so important to determine whether cycles exist—there is ample historic evidence for their existence. The core issue would seem to be whether the timing of the cycles is predictable from available metrics. If so, the fountain of riches has been discovered!

There is also a practical problem in using mean-reverting algorithms[21] to value options: The general time frame over which reversion occurs must somehow be determined. Naturally, it makes all the difference to an investor if mean-reversion can be expected in a one-year cycle or a 20-year cycle or if it is truly cyclic at all.[22] In other words, in addition to a volatility parameter, we need to add at least one more parameter to model mean-reversion. Given a database extending over a reasonably long time period, rates of mean-regression that best fit a mean-reverting model can be calculated mathematically. But the answer would be intrinsically questionable because a few decades of security price data would be inadequate to handle long time periods with statistical confidence. A credible response would also be needed to the inevitable question of whether fundamental structural changes in the economy may invalidate the results.

Finally, the mathematician Benoit Mandelbrot[23] has criticized the random walk model by noting that real stock market behavior often involves discontinuous steps that are larger than those that would be predicted by a conventional random walk based on the normal distribution. Mandelbrot's point seems to be valid: The practical issue is whether it materially affects the valuation of options.

■ OPTIONS IN ORDINARY BUSINESS

Options can be built into any business contract and can create value for both buyers and sellers. This value invariably has to do with information about either unique risk or market risk. The financial option examples in the first part of this chapter dealt fundamentally with market risk. Let's now look at options in a situation where the issue is more one of unique risk.

Suppose I am negotiating with a property owner for a building lot in an attractive community. I have already found a more-or-less equivalent building lot available for $200,000. But this new lot has a problem: There is a small spring, which begins to flow in the winter and usually dries up by July. It is possible that the local officials would classify enough of the lot as a wetland that my plans for a dwelling would be precluded; but a definitive survey would be required to establish the facts. Also, a neighbor has reportedly offered $40,000 for the lot, hoping to expand his backyard. His standing offer provides some salvage value to me in the event I buy the land but cannot build.

My real estate agent estimates the chances of *not* receiving a building permit at less than 40 percent, but I am not sure she is a disinterested party. Anyway, I calculate an expectation, or expected value, of (60 percent × $200,000) + (40 percent × $40,000) and consider offering $120,000 + $16,000, or $136,000. The owner agrees the price is fair.

Still, the risk of a major loss keeps me from sleeping well. A hot shower in the morning has many virtues. After reflecting in the steam, I ask the owner for an option to buy the property for $136,000 in the next two months and offer to pay him $10,000 for this option and the right to survey the property. To the owner the $10,000 premium looks like a fine return on his capital; he is simply giving up the still hypothetical opportunity of selling it at a better price for the next two months. For me, for the sure price of $10,000, I will have eliminated a 40 percent or greater chance of losing $96,000 ($136,000 – $40,000). The option is worth at least $38,400. I have made a very good deal and I am sleeping better. In option-speak, I have bought a call, and the owner has written one.

Note that this proposal is characterized with legal certainty about the price of the option and the strike price but with considerable uncertainty about the value of the underlying security (the lot). And in addition to the unique factors in play, market risks, such as the changes in interest rates and local real estate valuations, will be considerations in correctly pricing the option.

But these market factors should be minor in view of the short time needed to resolve the situation.

■ REAL OPTIONS

The groundwork is now laid to make the transition from traditional financial options to real options. As noted in the preface, real options theory is the extension of options thinking to nonfinancial assets. The term *real* is somewhat unfortunate in my opinion, because it connotes a relationship with physical assets. But while options theory applies to the tangible side of business transactions, it can be even more important when applied to the intangible/strategic/virtual side of capital. In fact, the term was originally introduced by Stewart Myers in 1984 as a tool to close the gap between strategy and finance.[24] Real options analysis is certainly effective in this regard. Myers also recognized early that discounted cash flow (DCF) techniques tended to understate the option value attached to growing businesses. And the term "real" is on target in its implication that framing, developing, and exercising real options is what real managers in real companies do to add value, as contrasted to treasury wizards who traffic in the buying and selling of complex financial derivatives representing liquid assets.

The value of most complex financial derivatives can be "marked to market" and thus are tangible, whereas many real options are embedded in opportunities available to the corporation and are blanketed by darkness and fog. There are also important structural differences between real options and financial options, which make real options inherently more complex.

1. Real options may not have a fixed strike price; indeed, the cost of exercise may have its own stochastic pattern.
2. Real options do not expire on a certain date, as financial options do.

3. Exercise of a real option is not necessarily instantaneous.

4. Real options often have very limited liquidity.

5. Transaction costs for real options may be higher than those for financial options.

To illustrate these differences, the cost of building a generating plant may be taken as the strike price for expanding in the power business. But at the time this real option is framed, the cost of construction will often be only an estimate, not backed by a firm contractual commitment. That plant may be built over a two-year time frame, and there will be changes in timing, cost overruns, and possible changes in scope along the way. Some of these uncertainties can be handled as options themselves. Nevertheless, treating the investment as the strike price for an option is still very useful because of the stochastic behavior of gas and electricity prices in unregulated markets.

Despite the complexities, the analogy of real options to financial options has great power. It highlights the value of management flexibility in a financially persuasive way and unlocks the basic attractiveness of business proposals in a way that DCF cannot approach. So, the concept of real options is enjoying its own "boomlet," both among theorists and practitioners; and by the time this book is off the press, real options literature is likely to be expanded very considerably. What companies are using real options today? As I write this chapter, at least 15 operating companies have made public statements regarding their use of real options.

Broadly speaking, there are three groups: (1) Pharmaceutical companies are using real option valuation for R&D decisions. (2) The petroleum industry is using it for decisions regarding exploration and production, and gas and electric utilities are looking at it as a pricing tool. (3) There are at least two aerospace examples.

In pharmaceuticals, the pioneer seems to have been Merck

(1994).[25] Other health care companies that have made presentations at financial conferences include Eli Lilly, Baxter International, Amgen, Genentech, Genzyme, Smith & Nephew, and Endo Pharmaceuticals.

In the oil and gas area, one of the pioneers was Larry Chorn of Mobil, who has founded a consulting firm (Real Options Software Inc.) and is affiliated with Thunderbird University in Phoenix. In addition to Mobil, other petroleum companies that have entered the real options space include Chevron, Petrobras, Texaco, Conoco, and Anadarko Petroleum.

There was a recent conference in Chicago entitled "Valuing Electric Power Assets and Companies" on the uses of real options in the utility industry. Some of the corporate presenters included Dynegy, Amerada Hess, Duke Energy, and Aquila Energy. Quoting the promotional blurb: "*Real Options* is the emerging valuation method to enable energy companies' management to make better decisions within this new dynamic world."

In aerospace, John E. Stonier, airline marketing director for Airbus Industrie North America, said, "Airlines generally commit to a future stream of aircraft deliveries long into the future. In an attempt to capture this uncertainty within the investment decision, airlines tend to use high hurdle rates in comparison to their cost of capital. Over the last few years, by virtue of reduced manufacturing lead times and product standardization, manufacturers now offer significant contractual flexibility to airlines. Option pricing theory can be used to quantify the value of this flexibility, which should reduce the hurdle rate required for airlines to invest."[26]

In addition to operating companies, at least a half-dozen consulting companies are now offering real option valuation services, currently led by PricewaterhouseCoopers and Navigant. It was also recently reported that the buyout firm of Forstmann Little used Black-Scholes to drive a $250 million investment decision in troubled XO Communications.[27]

■ DRILLING FOR OIL: COMBINING UNIQUE RISK AND MARKET RISK

Several companies are using real options today in the decision to explore for petroleum. Let us look at a hypothetical, highly simplified example that demonstrates how real options theory adds value. The corporate geologists have identified a promising geological structure. They have the expertise to estimate the probability of success (not having a dry hole), the probable size of a reservoir if one is discovered (related to the size of the reward), and the investment in facilities needed to develop and produce the field.

Evaluating the financial opportunity involves a sequence of cash flows: (1) an initial investment to secure the mineral rights and to drill an exploratory well, (2) an investment in developing the field, and (3) a cash flow stream from the sale of petroleum until the well is depleted. The cash flow stream will depend on the price of oil at the time it is produced. In a classic DCF analysis, the two investments and the resulting cash flow stream will be aggregated to give an NPV.

Let us assume that NPV is negative and that a traditional manager would turn down the project. However, the price of oil in the DCF model is, at best, an educated guess. The analyst might use the current price, or a "conservative" estimate arrived at by some internal process, or she may be slightly optimistic about price inflation. But options analysis provides a better way. For although future oil prices are entirely unknown, there is extensive data on the volatility of petroleum prices, which allows an option value to be calculated.

A manager using real options thinking would view the first investment in exploration and a lease as the purchase of a call in the form of an option to produce. The strike price—the price at which that option can be exercised—is the cost of the second investment, for the production facility. The value of the underlying security is the revenue stream from the oil to be produced minus the cost of lifting it. A financial value can be assigned to this stream based on the *current* market price of petroleum and its volatility.

The issue is no longer whether the NPV is positive! If in fact the value of this call exceeds its cost, specifically the investment in exploration and mineral rights, it is rational to make the investment. This circumstance can occur, particularly for volatile markets, even when NPV is negative.

The investor may reason thus: "I have no idea of the future price of oil; but if it doesn't get any better than this, I would never produce this well. But if and when it does get better, I have the option to invest in development and start producing. And better yet, I am in a position to calculate whether the value of the option is worth the cost."

Let us put some numbers on this example: Assume that $1 million is the proposed investment for a four-year lease and an exploratory well. This million is the *cost* of the option, or premium. Let us also assume the geologists estimate a one-in-four chance of finding oil whose present value, based on current oil prices minus variable production costs, is $20 million (oil prices are at a cyclic trough). The cost of production facilities is also $20 million, coincidentally just equal to the present value of the revenue stream. Therefore, the investment in development and production facilities is a wash and creates no value even if oil is discovered. The NPV of the entire venture is a negative $1 million.

However, we can still make a case for the investment. First, let us address the market risk in the value of the option to produce. We have a four-year option with a strike price of $20 million. The underlying security, the oil income stream, is "at the money," also $20 million. A look at a table of implied volatilities for commodities suggests oil prices have an annual volatility of about 30 percent. Using a Black-Scholes calculator, we find that this option has a value of $6.35 million. The value is driven entirely by the possibility that oil prices will rise over the next four years.

Second, we must factor in the unique risk. There is a 75 percent chance that the option to produce will be worthless because there is no oil or not enough oil to be found and a 25 percent chance that we will exercise an option worth $6.35 million. Hence the value of the option, after factoring in the unique risk, is 0.25 × $6.35 million, or $1.59 million. The value of the option then exceeds its cost of $1 million by $0.59 million, and the decision to explore is still eminently supportable.

Unique risk diminishes the value of this option, whereas market risk enhances it. Note also that while an estimate of market risk is basically available to all investors, we depend totally on the skills of our geologists in estimating unique risk— such as the possibility of a dry hole and the probable size of the reservoir. The potential for diversifying this risk is discussed in Chapter 9.

■ THE ABANDONMENT OPTION

The option to abandon is probably the most important, but the most poorly understood, option in the management of risk. It is useful precisely because time and information transform risk. And its aggressive use is the keystone of smart R&D management.

Consider this hypothetical case. A custom molder, Palmtree Plastics, is one of two qualified bidders to produce a plastic doll for Marvelous Toys. Marketing estimates the profit from a successful bid to be $180,000 and is quite certain it has a 50 percent chance of getting the order. The problem is that it will cost $50,000 for tooling and another $50,000 to set up the production line; and work must begin immediately to prepare for the Christmas season. The expectation for profit is 50 percent of $180,000, or $90,000. The investment is $100,000; so the value is a negative $10,000, and the proposal is a nonstarter. (We ignore the time value of money in this exercise.)

Now new information arrives! Marketing comes back and says that the status of the bid will be known *before* the line needs to be set up. Unfortunately, the order to make the molds will be noncancelable. There is a 50 percent chance of losing $50,000 and a 50 percent chance of making $80,000. So the expectation is (–$25,000) + $40,000, or a positive $15,000. The value of the option to abandon is the difference between the two cases, or $25,000. It is also the difference between a bad deal and one worth consideration.

Let's look at this example again using options terminology: Structured as a call option, Palmtree would have paid $50,000 for a call (the mold) with a strike price of $50,000 (the production line) and an underlying security worth $90,000. If Palmtree exercises the call (50 percent probability), it will net $180,000 – $100,000, or $80,000. If it does not exercise, it will lose the initial price ($50,000). So the expectation is again 50 percent of $40,000 + 50 percent of (–$25,000), or a positive $15,000.

This proposal can also be structured as a put option.[28] Assume Palmtree pays $100,000 for a put option, with a strike price of $50,000 (the salvage value). If Palmtree does not get the order it recovers the strike price for a net loss of $50,000. If it does get the order, it makes $80,000. The expectation remains $15,000.

This problem was initially evaluated as a simple comparison of decision trees—the terminology of option theory was not needed to think it through. What is important is the ability to quantify the value of converting uncertainty into certainty, that is, the value of timely information, and how identifying and framing the option turned a bad situation into a better one.

In Chapter 11, *Taming the Risk Bogeyman*, we will discuss why serial abandonment options based on the expected flow of information are the key to value creation in high-risk investments, including R&D and the production of movies.

■ THE MARK I MICROCOMPUTER CASE AND THE OPTION TO MAKE FOLLOW-ON INVESTMENTS

Now let us consider how business decisions may be altered by the opportunity to make follow-on investments. Consider the fictional Blitzen Mark I MicroComputer case from the corporate finance textbook of Brealey and Myers.[29] The proposition is as follows: There is a proposal to produce a new computer model, the Mark I, which will require a first-year investment in capital and net start-up costs of $450 million. The business runs for six years and is harvested in the fifth and sixth years.

The chief executive officer (CEO) turns down the project because he has set a hurdle rate of 20 percent; and using that rate as a discount rate, the NPV of the cash flows is a negative $46 million. (This figure implies that the cash flow stream in years 2 through 6 has a present value of $450 million – $46 million, or $404 million.)

The chief financial officer (CFO), however, is a real options advocate. She argues that the Mark I project carries with it an *option* to build the Mark II three years hence. The Mark II is forecast to be no more profitable than the Mark I (!!); but because of the high growth rate of the industry, it will be double the scale of the Mark I—it will require a $900 million investment in year 4 and throw off double the cash flows in years 5 through 9. Therefore, its cash flow stream will be worth $808 million in year 4 or $462 million when discounted back to year 1.

The CFO characterizes the Mark II as a three-year call option on an asset valued at $462 million with a strike price of $900 million. Using the Black-Scholes formula, she finds that this option is worth $55 million, assuming a volatility of 0.35, which is reasonable for a computer stock. This volatility is a proxy for the fact that it will be difficult to forecast Mark II revenues and margins in years 5 through 9, but they might be either better or worse than forecasts for the Mark I. Only if they look better will the decision be made to build the Mark II.

Her argument is that, with the embedded option to build the Mark II, the real value of the Mark I is the sum of the pro forma enterprise value, negative $46 million, and the $55 million option value, or a positive $9 million. Hence, the decision should be to move ahead.

Leaving aside the question of whether a $450 million investment decision to be followed by a $900 million investment decision should hinge on a difference as razor thin as $9 million, it is worth focusing on the point that this analysis depends critically on both the growth rate of the computer industry and the volatility.

Consider the growth rate first. If the growth rate were zero, then the Mark II would be the same size as the Mark I, and the option value would be halved: $55 million ÷ 2 = $27.5 million. This result would not have been enough to offset the negative $46 million enterprise value, so the decision would be made not to build the Mark I.

➤ Options Are Extremely Valuable under Conditions of High Growth and High Volatility

Let us now think of what this decision would look like if the growth rate were at "Internet speed," say a multiple of 10 in three years instead of double. Then the option value would have a value 5 times as large as the double case, or 5 × $55 million = $275 million. This large value swamps the negative $46 million and gives a total value of $229 million. Mark I now looks like a *great* project based on options thinking.

But there is more to come, for we haven't considered volatility. The value of an option is almost directly proportional to the volatility, or annual standard deviation, of the stock; and it has not been unusual for Internet companies to exhibit volatilities of 1 (100 percent) or higher. Let us consider the implications of a volatility of 1.0. Then the value of this option is $275 million ×

(1.0/0.35), or $786 million; and the value of the deal is $786 million – $46 million, or $740 million. In this scenario, the enterprise value is completely overwhelmed by the option value.[30]

All of this reasoning is, of course, entirely orthodox, as long as the circumstances of high growth and volatility are maintained. The textbook story even contains a rather coy (but correct) remark by the CFO—that the Mark II carries with it a call, which she ignores, to build a Mark III, and so on. Hence, the total value could in effect consider a cascade of compound options, which could justify even higher valuations.

> **Implications of the Mark I Case**

The Mark II aside, we can also now recognize that the Mark I may have had embedded in it many other options we now associate with small computers: the potential to chat or shop online, to be a home entertainment center, and to manage a sophisticated suite of office software. Whether those options were recognized or effectively exercised is another matter: In fact, neither Apple nor IBM became a Microsoft or an AOL. However, the positions that allowed coupling small computers with unknown emerging technologies and markets were indisputably present in hindsight. (IBM did attempt to develop its own personal computer (PC) operating system and invested in the pioneering Prodigy online service, but failed in both cases; Apple elected to restrict its excellent operating system for its own use. Looking backward, IBM and Apple shareholders paid a very heavy price for these failures.)

So the lesson of the Mark I case was not just the option to build the Mark II or the more valuable option to build the Mark II, III, IV, and so on. The most important option was to exploit the platform to couple the technology with emerging technologies and markets. This point argues powerfully for assigning a

high strategic premium for developing platforms, like the Mark
I, that have high optionality.

■ THE DOWNSIDE OF TURBOCHARGED VALUATIONS

We have just seen how real options embedded in a high-growth,
highly volatile enterprise can lead to turbocharged valuations.
But these valuations have a dark side, as evidenced by the collapse of many Internet stocks late in 2000 and into 2001. How, in
option terms, did this come to be?

First, in conventional economic terms, the sequence of events
(highly oversimplified) followed this pattern: The phenomenal
early success of e-pioneers such as AOL, Netscape, Yahoo!, Amazon, and eBay created enormous profits for early-stage investors, especially venture capitalists. Reports of these high returns
led a next round of investors to pursue the many remaining
niches in e-space that had yet to be filled. Plausible business
plans were easy to fund, and the 1999 gold rush was on. Under
such circumstances, the law of diminishing returns virtually ensured that the quality of the ideas and management teams that
were being funded would drop steadily. In time, a few spectacular failures made this apparent, and investors and analysts began to balk at the risks. Also, the ease of entry into e-businesses,
driven by abundant financing, low barriers to entry, and the
enormous enthusiasm of talented would-be-entrepreneurs, led
to multiple companies racing to enter each identifiable niche.
Tough competition for limited new markets led to discounting,
heavy promotional costs, unrealistic claims, and inevitably heavy
losses. A shakeout ensued, the weaker companies folded, and
even the stronger ones saw their market capitalizations cut by 50
percent to 90 percent. As I write, their business models are being
restructured to meet a set of conditions in which cheap financing
is *not* available, and careful attention to basics will be required to

achieve profitability and sustainable growth. On the bright side, however, the burden of excessive competition imposed by the "greater fool" conditions of the year 2000 has been removed.

What might this mean in *option* terms? Clearly, the value of the underlying securities—the business plans of the dot-com world—was undermined by inadequate profit margins, even when the projections of revenue growth were being sustained. The executives of the dot-coms argued, sometimes quite plausibly, that a part of their losses was in fact attributable to the costs of exercising their options to enter new businesses.

It is very difficult to separate continuing operating losses from start-up costs (which can be viewed as investments) under circumstances of extraordinary growth. Nonetheless, a decline in the perceived value of the underlying securities put pressure on the stock price and set the stage for a terrible year.

A major issue for any option holder is always the expiration of his or her option. For a financial option, expiration occurs on a date certain. For the real options of the Internet world, the date is not so certain. The term of these options was, in fact, defined by a company's cash position divided by its burn rate. If a dot-com held $30 million in cash and consumed it at a rate of $3 million per month, its options to expand could be considered to have a term, more or less, of 10 months. Absent new cash from investors or effective action to stop the cash flow drain, the company was toast. And when the financing window closed, toast was served.

Finally, we must deal with the issue of whether the underlying security is correctly valued. A skeptic may allege, "If the average business plan based on NPV underperforms, how can you justify hyping its valuation even more using real options?" The question is well taken, but it mixes apples with oranges. The answer will lie in part with honest but erroneous assumptions. If the hidden errors are favorable to the bottom line, the project is likely to move forward; but if the errors are unfavorable, the project may never be considered in an NPV world! But perhaps an even larger pitfall may be an upward bias built into many business plans. A plan assumes many parameters that afford an opportunity to fatten the bottom line: Prices, market share, and rates of market penetration are among them. Because, above all, project champions want funding, they have an incentive to bias their plan parameters upward to meet the hurdle rate required to gain approval. Caveat emptor.

In summary, real options can turbocharge value creation. But their potential for value destruction is equally awesome. When real options thinking is applied without consideration of competitive dynamics and of the volatile nature of the capital markets that serve high-risk investors, the consequences to the unwary can be punishing.

■ THE AMAZON CASE

Amazon.com provides an example of a venture with a host of embedded options. At the height of its valuation, around January 2000, Amazon's growth rate and its volatility were both extraordinarily high. Revenues in the previous four quarters (through the third quarter of 1999) were 288 percent higher than those of the previous four quarters (through the third quarter of 1998), and the Christmas season was looking good. Monthly volatilities for the stock in 1999 had ranged from about 70 percent to as much as 140 percent.

The company was of course losing money at a prodigious rate, which greatly disturbed value investors. But that was said to be explained by costs needed to finance its future expansion into books and into its newer business lines, such as music, toys, and electronics, and perhaps unannounced further strategies. In terms of the Total Value Model, Amazon had negative economic capital but enormous strategic capital. Analysts and investors needed a way to disaggregate the two.

One way to deal with this issue was to estimate gross margins and apply reasonable administrative costs to the base business, thus disaggregating costs relating to current operations from costs related to investments. This process is guesswork, but informed guesswork.

There is a traditional economic approach to just this process. I recall downloading a spreadsheet from the analyst Warren Gump[31] called Internet Bookseller Startup (not identified as Amazon). His approach is interesting, not because it is right or wrong, but because it is typical of conventional valuation methodology for high-risk start-ups. Gump assumed a 20 percent gross margin, rapid sales growth to $1.2 billion (similar to Amazon revenues for 1999), a 15 percent growth rate after this horizon year, and a cost of capital of 25 percent. He obtained a base case present value for this earnings stream of $18.5 billion. This economic value can be compared to Amazon's market capitalization of about $40 billion at the stock's high and of about $5 billion when the stock fell from grace a year later. In essence, Gump built an economic value model for this business, while acknowledging the huge uncertainties in the parameters.

The Total Value approach also addresses the need to disaggregate operating costs from investment costs for the base business. If gross margins were sufficient to earn the cost of capital, an economic value would be created for the book business. The methods in Chapter 3 could be used to calculate it. I question the need to apply a cost of capital as high as 25 percent for long-term future earnings because an established business should be able to raise capital for far less. I also question a long-term growth rate of 15 percent because this presumes an infinity of attractive but unidentified investment opportunities of whose existence I am uncertain. The more logical model is fast initial penetration in identified markets, followed by moderate growth as competition reacts.

The economic value of Amazon's book-selling operations could hardly be close to $40 billion because the totality of available U.S. book revenues are only about $15 billion annually and Amazon will capture and hold only a fraction of that. But there was and is enormous strategic value in its options to expand into other retail goods using its business model. Music, toys, electronics, auctions, "Z-shops," pets, and so on, could each be developed into a pro forma business plan similar to the one created for books. Each plan had the potential to generate a present value driven by the size of the business, the margins characteristic of that business, and Amazon's rate of market penetration. Each plan represented the "underlying security" for an option. The existence of these many options, sensed intuitively rather than quantitatively, largely drove the stock price in the heady days of late 1999. Since then, Amazon has made some progress in exercising its options in books, music, and toys, but it has been less successful elsewhere. It abandoned its investment in Pets.com when it became apparent that going forward required more cash than the financial markets were willing to extend to it.

What happened thereafter? The window of opportunity to raise cash closed. Competent competitors, such as eBay and Barnesandnoble.com, successfully defended turf that Amazon targeted. Resource constraints barred the door to other opportunities. Talent was in short supply in the first half of 2000, and financing for dot-coms was even scarcer in the second half. The resources, both human and financial, needed to simultaneously execute a host of business plans could not be mustered. In options parlance, some once-valuable options expired. CEO Jeff Bezos's decision to step back from pets may have saved the company; it certainly bought time in option space.

What is Amazon worth today? Things have surely changed and will continue to change in the year ahead. But there is a general answer. To get that answer, one must first calculate the economic value of the individual businesses in which Amazon has established itself. There may be considerable remaining strategic value in the businesses it is trying to enter, particularly because of the difficulties in which its competitors find themselves. And there is the strategic potential of merging its business model with a large traditional retailer to create a clicks-and-mortar powerhouse. There is a good case that Amazon's $5 billion market cap is too low.

What have we learned from the roller coaster ride? First, we learned that most of the price fluctuation relates to perceptions of strategic value: Amazon's operations have grown fairly smoothly and predictably. Second, we learned that options expire. And third, we know options will be overvalued if the underlying business plans are not realistic.

■ THE eTOYS CASE

Let's turn to a parallel tale[32] with a less-than-happy ending. eToys was the number-one seller of toys on the Internet in 1999, with rapidly growing revenues. It put in place an aggressive operating and marketing plan for year 2000, including Christmas 2000. It had enough capital to support operations and growth though Christmas 2000, but not beyond

Early in 2000, while the capital markets were open and the Nasdaq was still high, some people inside the company and some investors urged management to raise more capital, to give it more than one season's cushion. Management, and especially the founder/CEO with a large stake, did not want to take the dilution.

This one decision gave management a situation with no flexibility and no options; for at that point, three things needed to happen in series: (1) not exceeding planned spending in year 2000, (2) demonstrating a successful Christmas 2000 as measured by revenues, and (3) immediately thereafter raising substantially more capital.

Here's what happened: The company hit all its operating targets in 2000, so it had a success in that dimension. But, in the interim, the capital markets changed. eToys was unable to raise capital in January 2001, which the plan of spring 2000 required. The company went out of business in March 2001.

■ COMPETITIVE POWER

Competitor reaction to an innovative new development is always uncertain, but it is to be expected. Competitors have the power to obviate the assumptions in a business plan. Ignoring this power can lead to overvaluation of the option. We have seen this factor in the Amazon case.

Prior to the innovation, some competitor reaction is already built into the economic base case; after all, the existing price structure and market share has been established in a competitive environment. Changes tend to be incremental. But a new development typically may elicit an exceptional response.

Consider a hypothetical situation. Today's catalytic converters on automobiles must meet government-mandated emissions specifications regarding performance and durability. They require expensive noble metals, such as platinum, palladium, and rhodium. Assume that Aardvark Catalyst Co. invents and patents a new formulation that replaces more than half the noble metals with nickel and can thereby reduce its cost of goods sold by a full 50 percent. It offers the customers, automobile manufacturers, the new product at a 25 percent discount. This discount reflects half the cost savings, thereby giving the customer a compelling value proposition, while adding the other half of the savings to Aardvark's bottom line.

Its competitor, Warthog Catalyst, must now react. Warthog now knows that a major technical breakthrough is possible. It may even have a good idea of how to do it through a reading of Aardvark's patent or by analyzing converters obtained in the marketplace. To save its highly endangered business, Warthog will consider:

- Cutting its price to match Aardvark's.

- Seeking to invent around, or to otherwise invalidate, the Aardvark patent.

- Assuring its customers that it will soon offer technology that is even better than Aardvark's.

These actions may seem reprehensible, but they are hardly uncommon among desperate businesspeople. In the computer business, such phantom products are referred to as "vaporware." Very likely, though, the competitor reaction will have an immediate negative impact on Aardvark's value proposition.

In options parlance, Aardvark purchased a call on great new technology, which, when exercised, increased the strategic value of the firm. Not only will its profits rise through the cost savings involved, but also it may have a chance of forcing Warthog out of the business. However, Aardvark's planners may well have ignored the possibility that, in so doing, they were simultaneously selling (or at least issuing) *a call* on the technology. They invigorated an aggressive program by Warthog to protect its market share and even created some risk that in time Warthog will leapfrog their invention. They may have also created sufficient concern among the purchasing managers of the customers that they would take steps to prevent Warthog from being forced out of the market. The customers may insist Aardvark license the technology to Warthog to assure independent sources of supply. Or Aardvark may have unintentionally created an auction whereby the customers will use Warthog's defense tactics to force Aardvark's price even lower.

Such contingent liabilities are often created by technical and commercial success. These liabilities must be factored into the decision, either through a more conservative model of the business plan or as separate options reflecting the real uncertainty as to how competition will respond. Without considering them, overvaluation can be a trap for the unwary.

Game theory has been taught for some time in business schools to simulate competitor dynamics. Real options theory is relatively new, and game theory enters only in the framing of the option and the assumptions in the pro forma business plan. But as real companies use real options in decision making, the rules of the game will themselves change! It makes sense to integrate options valuation with competition models; this exercise is the next frontier in business thinking.[33]

■ CHANGING VOLATILITY

In businesses where the value of the option is the major source of overall, or total, value, businesses will be worth more to the degree that the market is more volatile and worth less as it is less volatile. But the volatility of a stock is not a universal constant; it is itself subject to change as market conditions change.

If option value is a major source of an enterprise's total value, then increased volatility will increase the value of the business. Therefore, uncertainty is "good" in the sense that it increases value. The conventional wisdom in business is that volatility is axiomatically bad and that it reduces value. For an old-economy company with few options, this principle is certainly valid. But for a fast-growing company with many options, such as one in a new field of technology, volatility will increase its valuation. As long as the market is new, unknown, uncertain, and thus volatile, "turbo valuations" may have a rational basis (which is not to deny that many businesses were valued in 1999 far beyond what even aggressive option-derived models could sustain). In such circumstances, risk drives wealth creation.

But circumstances change. By the beginning of the year 2000, the Internet was no longer a new frontier. That year was the culmination of three full years of vigorous—extremely vigorous!—marketing of a dizzying array of services to consumers and businesses. If Christmas 1998 was the first year the Internet became a mainstream way for millions to shop, then the entire year of 1999 was a chance to see how thousands of Internet businesses fared in a maturing, stabilizing marketplace. An enormous amount was learned about how consumers behaved, how business users behaved, which business models met consumer needs, and which services saved businesses money. In short, the environment created market knowledge and reduced uncertainty.[34] Valuations that had been rational in a highly uncertain, volatile market were now questionable. With much less uncertainty, option mathematics would show valuations dropping sharply—and option value still comprised the vast majority of the total value of the new Internet businesses.

Thus, the Total Value approach tells us that in businesses where the majority of value is in the option—where current DCF value is low or negative—volatility is a boost to valuation. But the situation may not prevail. Increased knowledge of the market and reduced volatility are a prescription for option-based valuations to fall. That is what happened in the steep March–April 2000 decline in many companies' stock prices. Investors digested the marketplace data from 1999 and reached a number of conclusions about what would and wouldn't work on the Internet. And then, quite rationally, the stock market responded by driving down valuations.

Chapter

6

Why Plans
Are Options

F. Peter Boer and Ranch C. Kimball*

When companies announce their plans, stocks soar or swoon. Millions or billions of market capitalization are created or destroyed. These reactions prove that there can be no more compelling evidence that plans are a form of strategic capital. So Genentech's stock soared on its plans to market Activase—its recombinant tissue plasminogen activator—and swooned when the Food and Drug Administration (FDA) put speed blocks in the way. Boeing's stock soared when it canceled plans to develop a superjumbo transport, the 747-X. The stock market obviously valued the option to market Activase very highly but harbored grave doubts about the value of the 747-X.

Announcements of merger plans elicit the same reactions. When investors see the option to create valuable synergies by bringing two companies together, they reward the planners with higher stock prices. When they refuse to acknowledge that the synergies outweigh the risks, the stock of the acquiring company drops.

---

*Ranch C. Kimball, Managing Director, Tiger Scientific, Inc.

Of course, the deal is not done when it is announced—it is only a plan, and there is a real risk of it falling through. But value is created (or destroyed) nonetheless when the plan becomes visible.

In this chapter we explore the nature of plans and why they are essentially identical to options. Plans typically have a cost, an exercise price, and a time frame. Above all, they convey the ability to take an action, but usually not the obligation to do so. Optionality creates value and is the crucial distinction between a plan and an income-producing asset.

■ PLANS AS COSTS

Webster defines a *plan* as "a method or scheme of action." A plan identifies and communicates intent with regard to resources, schedules, and the outputs that people need to organize their own activities. The discipline of the planning process helps management identify future problems, such as a shortage of resources or a scheduling conflict. A plan may have useful byproducts, such as control documents intended to ensure that events are taking place as anticipated.

A pilot flying on instruments is required to file a flight plan. That process will ensure that she checks the weather and the winds and calculates her arrival time at key waypoints. If she is missing at arrival time, an emergency is assumed. Similarly, an operating department is asked to submit an annual budget plan. This document ensures that its cash needs are anticipated by the corporate treasurers and that deviations from the plan can be recognized and corrected early.

Because of such simple but useful features, we have all learned to accept that planning is an important part of the job, and we accept the cost of putting in the time to do it. This cost is an *opportunity cost*: We find some of our time is better spent planning the job than actually performing it. We have also learned that we can buy plans or planning services (house plans, financial plans, tax plans, even cookbooks and sewing patterns) and that we unconsciously apply a value measure to them—we look carefully at their cost before buying.

The evidence that organizations regard plans as a cost is the common practice of sacking planners whenever overhead needs pruning, reckoning that operating and financial managers can get the necessary work done in the short term.

So much for the obvious.

■ PLANS AS ASSETS

The accounting mentality in business culture obscures the potential value of plans as assets. After all, the work of the planners is almost immediately written off as an expense. And some of the plans produced more often than not sit in loose-leaf binders to be safely discarded a few years hence as casually as I discard my daily "to do list." Because of their intrinsic impermanence, plans do not look like valuable documents.

But let's consider a contrary view. First, most companies would be apoplectic if a competitor (or even a customer) were able to get hold of its five-year-plan document; the plan tells too much about its strengths and weaknesses and how it creates and maintains its value chain.

Second, the plan and its review may well have engaged the best minds in the company for many days or even weeks. Business plan reviews before a phalanx of top management are an annual ritual in many large companies. This exercise would not be justified if minimizing planning costs were a sure way to boost profits.

Third, a credible business plan is one of the two key criteria for obtaining project funding from venture capitalists (the other one is capable management). In essence, venture capitalists buy a plan, often for large sums of money. They look for an innovative idea or technology, and they look even more closely for a clear understanding of the market, the customers, the competitors, the distribution channel, the financial reward, and risks. Currently, this structural description is being called a "business model." The dialogue that takes place between entrepreneurs and venture capitalists over funding is, at heart, a dialogue over valuation of a plan.

Thus, a business plan is much more than a document. It is the epitome of strategic capital, linking the experience and the talents of individuals and their intellectual property to the creation of future rewards. (Financial and physical capital will soon be required to realize those rewards.) The plan's value is determined by the robustness of its fundamental concepts and by the capabilities of the management team to execute.

My central thesis, then, is that *the strategic capital of a firm is captured in its business plans.*

As we have noted, an innovative business plan does not have the characteristics of an operating business. It has the characteristics of an option. Creating or purchasing the option has a cost (the premium). Much of this cost is associated with identifying the team, gathering information, and organizing the details. Exercising the option likewise involves a cost (the strike price)— a commitment of additional financial, physical, and human resources to execute the plan. And the revenue stream obtained when the option is exercised becomes the underlying security. This stream is subject to the volatility of the market place. Realizing value from the option requires management activity.

I have seen many hundreds of business plans in the course of my career. Most contained a calculation of return on capital, and many included a calculation of net present value (NPV). Very few were evaluated as options. We are in new territory.

■ PLANS: THE SPECTRUM OF VALUE

We saw in Chapter 5 that very valuable additional options may be embedded in a business plan. It is because of these options that the business is far more valuable than accountants can measure.

Because this point may still seem radical to some, most of this chapter will be dedicated to justifying it. We will progress from the simplest case, where risk is nominal, to the moderate risks involved in most manufacturing businesses, and finally to the very high risks involved in bringing new products and services to the marketplace. At one extreme of the spectrum, total value is synonymous with economic value. It is defined entirely by discounted free cash flow. At the other end of the spectrum, economic value may be zero or negative; but a high total value may be justified by a large strategic premium derived from a dynamite business concept and plan. In time, of course, that strategic capital must be transformed into economic capital.

Figure 6.1 indicates some of the possibilities. A start-up company with a great business plan may begin in the upper-left quadrant. But it cannot stay there—it must prove its economic viability to attract capital on a sustained basis. If it transforms its plan into successful operations, it will end up on the right side of the chart. When Charles Hall invented his process to make aluminum in 1888, he could not foresee the possibilities, nor could his customers. But within a century, his process led to Alcoa's established, profitable commodity business.

The upper-right quadrant is a desirable location; high profitability and high opportunity coexist. There is nothing wrong with being in the lower-right quadrant, making good money but with somewhat limited opportunities. However, it is possible in time to slip into the lower-left quadrant from any position in the chart. But one can't stay there either; low returns inexorably

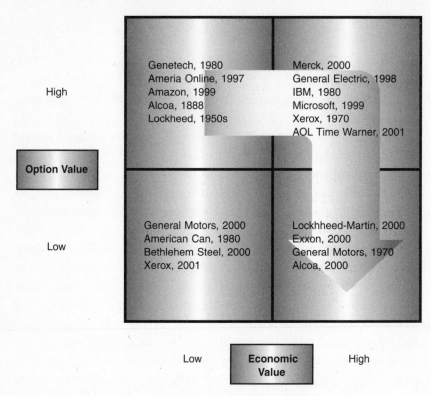

Figure 6.1 Strategic Position of Selected Firms

destroy value, and the firm must escape to another quadrant or perish.

Young vigorous companies begin in the upper-left. As their markets grow and mature, over time, a successful management team will guide the company through the path shown by the arrow, while attempting to stay in the upper-right quadrant as long as possible. The format and the prescription are similar to BCG's growth/share matrix; the labels for the boxes could be identical ("Question Mark," "Star," "Cash Cow," and "Dog"), but the analysis is driven by mode of value creation rather than by market position.

■ PLANS AS FORECASTS: NO VALUE

A forecast is not a plan. A forecast has no strategic component. Those real-life plans that are forecasts in disguise are immune to our thesis that total value equals economic value plus strategic value. They are trivial but not uncommon examples of my general thesis and occur when operating the existing business *is* the sum and whole of the business plan. Looking at this circumstance is useful because the distinction between economic value and strategic value becomes very evident.

An example may be helpful. General Power has sales of $4 billion, employs $2 billion in capital, and earns $400 million. It has grown revenues and income over the past five years at a steady 5 percent per annum. Its business plan for the coming year projects revenues of $4.2 billion on a capital base of $2.1 billion with profits of $420 million. Such a plan is merely a forecast. The whole world expects this result. In this event, the business can be valued solely by the discounted sum of its future free cash flow (FCF) growing at 5 percent per annum. Any valuation above that number would not be justified because there are no plans to enter new businesses or to change the business strategy. General Power's free cash flow would ultimately be used to buy back stock, or it would be distributed as dividends to shareholders because the company has, by our definition, no interest in investing the cash for any other purpose.

This condition does not mean that the company will not grow and prosper; only that it is organized to grow at the rate the marketplace already anticipates. Although it would not invest any portion of its FCF in attempting to develop new investment opportunities, it would continue to invest capital within the existing business as long as those investments covered its cost of capital. In a stable, growing market, this company would likely grow with the market. Like every other company, it will be subject to the effects of market volatility, but its cost of capital will take this factor into account.

The company, of course, creates economic value by continuing to operate, but its plans add no value above the value of its anticipated operating cash flow. Its cash flow is fully monetized: An investor could safely sell it and buy an equivalent security of equal risk. A regulated utility fits this general description.

In the world of Wall Street, the valuation of this enterprise is straightforward. An analyst asks management to make a short-term projection of its profits for its planning horizon (say 3 or 5 years) and then projects the FCF "into perpetuity," assuming some growth rate in perpetuity. (More detail was given in Chapter 3.) The cash flow forecast might be adjusted downward if the analyst suspects undue optimism; the growth rate is likely to be consistent with past long-term-growth rates. While a level of competence is certainly required to execute this plan, an investor knows it adds no value.

What about human and intellectual capital? Does this proposition mean that knowledge assets are not important? No! These assets will be critical to the company. But they are fully valued in the operating results. If the employees develop new and creative ideas, there is no interest in them. A utility chartered to sell electricity in Kansas, for example, may have no mechanism to reward shareholders for a risky, innovative idea for building Internet-capable wireless electric meters.

Looked at in option terms, the best feature of the business-as-usual plan is that it costs nothing to purchase this option. In effect the option premium has been paid. So the option of doing no more than operating the business is free, and it is worthless. As for risk, no new risk is added; existing risk is also built into the valuation though the risk premium paid to equity investors. Again, note that we are precluding all novel value-added activities—new product lines, investments in new processes, mergers and acquisitions, divestments of unwanted operations. Any such activities would, by the definition used here, involve plans and would be valued on the plans loop-side of the model (Figure 4.1).

▪ PLANS FOR CAPITAL INVESTMENTS: MODERATE VALUE

Business executives and board members are very familiar with plans to invest in new facilities—for moderate-risk capital projects. Moderate risk implies moderate value, at least in relative terms. An example might be the decision of a chemical company to invest in a new ethylene cracker to supply raw material for its growing product line. These investments begin as options and are transformed into operations as the options are exercised, that is, as intellectual and financial capital is committed and converted into physical capital. It is interesting that the leading application of real options analysis today seems to be precisely in this area—resolving issues and facilitating decisions in capital budgeting.

Building a new plant to expand in an existing business is typical. Because the market is familiar and the technology is understood, there should be few deep risks. But there are many small, nagging risks. There may be a cost overrun, or a start-up delay—unique risks to which a probability and an expectation of loss can be assigned. Some upsides, such as expansion options, may also become apparent; for example, that the plant's nameplate capacity may be increased at a relatively small cost.

And there is always some element of market risk—the available market for the physical goods may grow more slowly than anticipated, prices may drop, or construction labor may be more expensive than initially projected. There are systematic risks from financial factors as well; for example, interest-rate changes can affect the value of the project. But these risks reflect nothing more than the normal volatility of a security.

The request for capital authorization that the moderate-risk project sponsor takes to top management, and perhaps for board approval as well, contains a business plan that is built on a "base case"—a best estimate of revenues, operating costs, and fixed capital. Risk in the fixed-capital projection may be explicitly recognized by adding a "contingency" of 10 percent to 20 percent, that is, a budgeted allowance for unknown problems encountered in design and construction. We will leave aside the common cultural issue as to whether the proposal is to be biased conservatively for self-protection and the glory of beating the projections or biased aggressively to ensure approval. In addition, the plan will typically include an analysis of the sensitivity of the base case to downward, and upward, changes in the assumptions.

The value of that plan has two pieces, one readily calculable and the second hidden. The nominal value is the NPV, the discounted value of the base-case cash flow net of the initial investment. This number should be reliable if the project analyst has done a good job in averaging the upside and the downside variations. But the second part can be of considerable importance, recognizing the value of management flexibility. There will be opportunities to modify the plan during the course of the project to more closely meet market conditions as they change. If business conditions prove weaker than originally forecast, management can defer some planned expenditures or reduce their scale. If they are better than forecast, construction might be accelerated or the scale of the plant increased.

Valuable additional options can be embedded in an investment plan. One of these was described in the Chapter 5—the option to build the Mark II microcomputer, an option to make a follow-on investment. Commonly, a successful manufacturer will recognize that it has options to expand its business into other parts of the world. Toyota exercised this option in the United States. A successful consumer franchise can also be globalized. Much of the value of McDonald's relates to its ability to exercise expansion options in foreign markets whose needs are incompletely served by local restaurateurs. There may be dozens of other options. Some options add much more value than others, whereas some are valuable only under very unlikely conditions. But the very existence of any options means that the project is *certain* to be more valuable than discounted cash flow (DCF) analysis can show!

The real issue is whether the option values are great enough to *materially* impact the project decision. Parts of the energy industry have decided the answer is yes in volatile markets and view options analysis as a source of competitive advantage over those using only traditional financial tools to evaluate capital projects.

■ PLANS FOR NEW-TO-THE-WORLD PRODUCTS AND SERVICES: HIGH VALUE

The introduction of new-to-the-world products and services involves the highest level of risk; yet conversely it is the most potent creator of wealth. Research-and-development (R&D)-based companies, venture capitalists, and entrepreneurs alike have created enormous wealth through this route.

In the world of R&D, the chances of a new raw idea being successfully commercialized have been characterized as one in three thousand.[1] In the narrower world of pharmaceuticals, the odds of a new molecule becoming a commercially successful prescription drug have been quoted as one in ten thousand; and the fully loaded cost of its development is said to be in the vicinity of half a billion dollars. How can one make money against these enormous odds?

The key difference in managing such high-risk investments and a moderate-risk investment is that one must focus on ways to place the larger part of the total investment after most of the risks have been removed. An important principle is doing the intellectual part of the work before making large, irreversible physical and contractual commitments.

In Chapter 10, we use options theory to discuss how the very high risks involved in early-stage research can be managed to create great value—namely through efficient gathering of critical information, early identification of potentially fatal flaws, and aggressive abandonment of less-promising leads. What is worth recognizing here is that the value that financial analysts place on the quality of the R&D "pipeline" is itself telling evidence that plans play a major role in the valuation of pharmaceutical companies. Indeed, pharma giants prowl relentlessly for acquisitions when their pipelines are empty.

It is also worth going back a step to ask how a research pipeline could be empty in the first place. Bad luck may explain it, because chance plays a major role when there are many unique risks. A merger of two pharma companies can reduce the element of chance and can create value by diversifying the unique risk over a bigger project pool. The other reason for an empty pipeline may be that the company is less skilled in the performance or the management of R&D than its leading competitors are—it has accumulated less strategic capital with which to fight the competitive wars. It is unlikely to succeed in a business where strategic capital heavily outweighs economic capital.

A second category of high-risk investors, venture capitalists, also deals primarily with plans and the options they imply. Indeed, venture capitalists would do well to analyze their portfolios using a real options approach, though there is little evidence any yet do so explicitly. Let's look at their situation.

Consider a fictional venture capitalist who has raised money from investors for a new fund in which he will also carry an interest and to which he will charge management fees. His first task will be to screen many business plans that seem to fit the objectives of his fund. The term for this activity is "deal flow."

He may think along the following lines: Some of the plans will appear worthy of investment because the "story" (or business model) is compelling, the management team is proven, and the potential revenue stream is sizeable. The founders will present some kind of business plan on which a valuation can be, and probably has been, performed. However, he will not accept that valuation outright, but will do his own analysis.

For example, his experience may tell him that there is a one-in-ten chance of meeting or beating the optimistic plans of the founders, doing an IPO (initial public offering), and hitting a "home run." He may estimate that there are *three* chances in ten of a total failure, *three* more chances in ten of a partial failure where the company is acquired by a competitor, and a remaining *three* chances in ten that the company survives but produces average business results—a "single." He can then assign an expectation to each of these possibilities and weight his portfolio according to the probabilities. His valuation for the investment will be the weighted average of these small and large expectations. If that value meets his rate-of-return criterion (which may be very high, perhaps 30 percent to 50 percent, because of the risk) on his initial investment, he will take the next step.

In principle, he can improve his expectation by negotiating for a bigger piece of the company; but he then runs the risk that the founders will balk and do business elsewhere.

The process followed by the venture capitalist can be adequately performed by creating a pro forma cash flow model for each of the four types of business cases. However, there is an options approach to the same problem. Here the venture capitalist's initial investment becomes the cost of the option. The underlying security is the expectation value of the enterprise (which will go up and down based on its fortunes). The strike price is the amount of money to be raised at the next liquidity event. The amount of money needed can be calculated from "burn rates" before the company is profitable or from an estimate of the cash required before the company is able to achieve positive cash flow. Looked at another way, the term of the option will be defined by the cash available divided by the burn rate. The share of ownership the investors are given in the current financing round becomes the variable and depends on the expectation of value at that time. Market risk is very much in play; for it is well known that at times IPOs can be very hot, and at other times the capital window can be closed to all but gilt-edged deals.

Thus, by financing the entrepreneurs, the venture capitalist is buying options from them. These options can be sold at a profit to later-stage investors.

There is another good reason to believe that venture capitalists are thinking, consciously or not, in terms of options. When a venture fund is created, not all the money will be invested at the outset in the most promising young firms. Instead, as much as half the money may be held in reserve for subsequent rounds of financing, especially for mezzanine financing, a name for the round that precedes the IPO. This practice creates a situation in which the start-up does not have enough funds on hand to make it to the IPO, while the venture capital firm has a pre-ferred position to make a follow-up investment on advanta-geous terms. The venture firm will be in a position to channel the mezzanine money to what appear to be the most attractive investments and to withhold financing for the likely losers in the portfolio. This behavior is exactly analogous to astute research managers who create go/no-go decision points in their research programs (Chapter 10).

In fact, in the summer of 2001, this strategy characterized the activities of the leading venture firms in Silicon Valley and Boston. Not only were they investing in fewer deals, a condition well-reported in the financial press, but they have systematically reviewed their portfolio of companies and identified the likely winners in their portfolios. These winners receive additional funds from venture capital funds, while the likely losers are on their own. This behind-closed-doors process is as opaque as financial options on the Chicago Board of Option Exchange (CBOE) are transparent, but the underlying options behavior is the same. The example of management flexibility in the ethylene cracker in the preceding section is replaced with investor flexibility: The cost of each option is the capital require-ments of the corresponding portfolio company, and the venture firm is deciding which firms are worth buying, based on track record, management team, business prospects, and exit-strategy considerations.

Venture capitalists differ from conventional investors in two ways, which relate to their intentions. First, venture capitalists do not intend to tie up their capital as investors in operating businesses. Operations do not fit their expertise or their risk/ reward profile. So they intend to sell their option down the line to less risk-tolerant investors, at a price that is substantially higher than the one they paid for it. To achieve this result, they may reserve the right to sell their shares as part of the IPO in so-called "piggy-back rights."

Often they will do as well or better by selling the option to a strategic investor; for example, a pharmaceutical company may buy a start-up biotechnology company because it views the purchased technology as highly synergistic with its own new product-development program. That pharmaceutical company may not have had the risk tolerance to invest in the original ideas behind the start-up; but now that these ideas seem proven, the investment makes business sense. For just this reason, Big Pharma mostly played a waiting game when the first biotech start-ups appeared in the late 1970s, but began to make substantial, though selective, investments as the uncertainty diminished.

Second, venture capitalists will be looking to add value *actively* to their investments. This skill can create a competitive advantage over rivals who are passive investors. They know that a business plan document is not really an executable plan unless there is money in place to finance it and resources available to execute it. Of course, the venture capital firm helps bring the option to life by bringing financing capacity to the business. In fact, without financial capacity the founders effectively lack an option.

But the venture capitalists will be concerned that the founders have the other resources to have an optimum chance of executing their plan. A primary resource is competent management. If the founding team does not seem to have management skills, the venture capitalists may press to bring in associates or acquaintances as chief executive officer (CEO), marketing vice president (VP), and the like. Some large venture capital firms actually retain promising executives for these roles, sometimes calling them "entrepreneurs-in-residence."

Because successful venture capitalists have close relationships with a previous generation of successful enterprises and because they also know the newer players via their deal flow, they are well positioned to create strategic alliances that are a further source of value to the start-up. Hence an informal network of allied firms can circle about the orbit of a major venture capital firm. Kleiner, Perkins, Caufield & Byers (KP), for example, has had in its orbit America Online (AOL), Sun Microsystems, Oracle, @home, Excite, Netscape, and Amazon.com, plus many smaller firms. When Netscape was threatened by goliath Microsoft, KP helped engineer its rescue by AOL. KP actually speaks of itself as a *keiretsu*, an analogy with the loosely linked conglomerates that have dominated Japanese industry and finance.

■ THE VALUE OF MANAGEMENT FLEXIBILITY

If management flexibility, represented by real options, is the key to value creation, logic would seem to tell us that losing flexibility can destroy value. This section will illustrate this point.

The first example occurs under command-and-control conditions. In a planned economy, a plant manager may be rewarded only for producing his quota, which he will attempt to produce whether it is needed or not. This condition alone guarantees that market economies will outperform centrally planned economies. Such "plans" destroy value, at least in comparison to plans that allow for flexibility.

Comrade Zhukov's plan is to produce one million liters of

black paint and to deliver it to the Lada factory. He is given one hundred thousand 10-liter cans, one-half million liters of solvent, and the required amount of polymer base and carbon black. He has no incentive, nor access to resources, to produce more. If Lada doesn't want the paint, it's not his problem. And if there is a fire in the carbon black factory, well, that would not be his fault. So in principle he has no options. His Western counterpart, Ms. Jones, with a similar business plan, might trim production and inventory to adjust to a current shortage of cans, prebuy to take advantage of low prices for polymers, and attempt to exploit a new market trend toward red sports cars. She may perceive options to recycle cans, inventory an emergency supply of polymer, and purchase red pigments. All of these options add value.

The same phenomenon can occur, of course, in a market economy, but then the wounds are self-inflicted. One form is the fixed-price, or "take-or-pay," contract. This arrangement is seemingly riskless to the buying party and may seem desirable for that reason. Ironically, the buying party may pay the selling party dearly for accepting the downside risk and yet give up all of the upsides if market changes are favorable. For example, a new steel mill may require an oxygen plant "across the fence." The management of Big Steel contracts with Big Air to build the oxygen unit for a fixed price and a fixed time, while Big Steel focuses on the steel mill. Fixing this contract may initially buy some peace of mind. But assume the steel company soon learns that its start-up will be delayed at least three months because another vendor is unable to deliver a rolling mill on the date planned. Under this form of contract, the steel company has needlessly given away the option to defer the oxygen plant for three months.

A case history from the Boston Consulting Group is a tale of how loss of flexibility (or options) can destroy value even while NPV is being dutifully pursued. One of this chapter's authors was consulting in the auto components industry in the mid- and late-1980s, a period when U.S. automakers and their major component suppliers were generally at a cost disadvantage to their Japanese counterparts.

The client was a major producer of forged auto components—products such as connecting rods, ring gears, camshafts, and axles. By the middle 1980s, five major forging technologies were available to component makers, each with its own specialized equipment: hammer, hot forge, hot form, warm form, and cold form. This component company's plants typically had only one or two technologies in place. Management had concluded that the appropriate overall strategy for solving their cost disadvantage was to install all the new technologies in each plant. On paper, and analyzed in isolation, the decision seemed sensible. The newer technologies were, on a direct cost basis, lower-labor and therefore apparently lower-cost than the older technologies. We can assume the projected savings were mirrored in a positive NPV for each capital investment.

But management embarked on a five-year capital spending plan, adding new equipment to the plants, taking the typical plant from two technologies in place to all five. And despite a five-year capital expenditure that was several times higher than their historical level and several times higher than that of their Japanese competitors, their costs actually rose. In fact, they rose enough that it was possible to demonstrate that the capital expenditure had actually produced a negative return—not a return below the cost of capital, but a negative return!

How was this possible? The main cause was the loss of all options for operating improvement. The plant had a limited number of engineers, and the new equipment was very engineering intensive, requiring experienced technical talent to analyze, acquire, install, and operate.

As each new piece of technology came into the plant, engineering resources were pulled away from the existing technologies' equipment. The result was that quality fell, rejects increased, and uptime fell dramatically on the existing machinery. Indeed, the increased costs in the existing equipment actually were greater than the cost savings brought about by the new technology. The situation had become so dire that on the plant's four hot formers uptime had fallen to 28 percent; Toyota's forge division, running exactly the same make of machine, was achieving 85 percent.

Management's emphasis on capital spending and its specific decree to acquire and install the latest forging technologies thus precluded a great number of other options, such as incremental operating improvements, modifications to the existing technologies, refinements in tool- and die-making, product-line restructuring, and materials technology. In fact, the Japanese competitors pursued a successful strategy emphasizing operational improvement. Beguiled by the technical advantages to be gained by this large capital project, management unintentionally chose a course that foreclosed other options and greatly reduced its flexibility in pursuing other avenues to achieve cost parity.[2]

■ PLANS VERSUS DREAMS: THE IMPORTANCE OF POSITION

Although many plans begin as dreams, a dream is not a plan. The crucial distinction is that a plan deploys resources against an objective. Until the resources are in place, we are dealing merely with a dream.

The corollary of this statement is that plans do not need to be captured in writing. A strategic position itself is the source of flexibility, and a smart leader can build flexibility into his or her plans. We shall explore the view that position is a necessary, but not a sufficient, condition for the generation of a plan. The option may exist in principle, but it typically requires intelligence, information, and creativity to frame it and analytical skills to value it. These steps are the prerequisite to an actionable real option: namely, (1) frame, (2) analyze, (3) act.

To put it more simply, to make the distinction between plans and dreams, just ask if the plan is currently actionable. If so, you own a real option. The financial analogy is that to exercise a financial option, you first have to own it. To own it entails a cost or a premium. In the end, your profit will be the value of the option minus the cost of the option.

Real options derive from plans. But a real option is ambiguous in regard to the moment of ownership because full ownership may not arise from a single event. Let us explore this point for a hypothetical case.

An old-economy company such as Anheuser-Busch (AB) decides to build a new brewery and bottling plant in the Southwest. This decision is tantamount to exercising an expansion option. When the decision to proceed is made, AB clearly owns the option. Why? Because AB has the financial capability to borrow money to finance the plant. It has the technical know-how to design breweries and to construct and operate bottling lines. It has experienced engineers and executives to review the plans and to put in place the many contracts with suppliers and customers needed to make the plant run and to distribute the beer.

Now consider two college roommates whose objective is to build a microbrewery in Austin, Texas. They sit at the kitchen table and review what is needed to make their project a success. They identify a number of trendy bars, restaurants, and liquor stores that are possible customers. They estimate the initial production capacity needed to match the potential demand; the capital investment needed to get started; the numbers of employees needed to brew, bottle, and deliver the product; and the permits required to brew beer commercially in Texas. Their next step will be to integrate their estimates into a business plan and seek seed financing.

The roommates have a plan of sorts, but they have not yet purchased (and do not yet fully own) the option to create a microbrewery business. They will need a distinctive recipe and a reliable brewing process, an eye-catching label, some commitments to purchase product (which no doubt will require some samples), and the promise of enough capital to carry them through the first stage of their financial plan.

During the next three months, they find a retired brew master who agrees to act as a technical adviser. They brew small batches under his tutelage in the kitchen and garage, develop the Hook M Horns brand name and logo, and take samples to bars and restaurants on the edge of the University of Texas campus. When it turns out that several bars popular with students are interested enough to buy a few "commercial" batches, four seed-round investors (a dad, one of the bar owners, a business school professor, and a real estate broker) each agree to invest $10,000 for 5 percent of the company. Shares are distributed to the founders, the four angels, and the brew master.

What has happened? This company now has an implied market valuation of $200,000 because 20 percent of it was valued at $40,000. The option to execute the pro forma business plan has been purchased with cash, promises, and sweat equity. The future is fraught with high risk and seemingly unlimited opportunity. The value of the option will now fluctuate with the fortunes of the business.

A real example of a start-up that fully exploited the possibilities of a small position was Microsoft, which was in a position to offer IBM a personal computer (PC) operating system when IBM needed one badly. The terms under which DOS (disk operating system) was licensed were part of a masterful business plan that led to Microsoft's hegemony in PC software instead of the more common outcome of the minnow being swallowed by the whale.

■ EXPLOITING POSITION

The importance of position in framing plans (and creating value) is evident in the more complex strategies employed by the entertainment industry.

An entertainment industry myth is that owning a hit television show or movie is the key to a winning strategy. "Content is king" is an old catchphrase of the media and the entertainment world. At the extreme, it is true—but it is more a truism, no more a guide to strategy than is advice to only buy stocks that are about to rise. The largest value is derived not from ownership of any one media property, but from aggregating them (or, in the argot of the industry, "packaging" them). The package and the supporting infrastructure create the strategic position from which individual options (or plans) can be framed.

Owning rights to one future Disney movie or one Steven Spielberg movie is itself no guarantee of economic wealth. In fact, most of Disney's animated movies and most of Spielberg's movies have lost money when costs were measured narrowly against box office receipts.[3] Why, then, have these films been creators of great corporate and personal wealth?

With the hit movie *The Lion King*, Disney made about a billion dollars for its shareholders. But only a small part of the earnings came from showing the movie in U.S. theaters. In other words, when the movie is evaluated as a single project, most of the value is missed. Instead, Disney earned its total profit from *The Lion King* because the movie was part of a much broader aggregation of talent and plans: Disney people had the transformational capabilities to convert this piece of strategic capital, with vigor and skill, into a wide variety of cash streams. Merchandising plans for toys and other licensed products and corporate tie-ins (with fast-food chains and the like) were developed two years before the movie was released. Asian manufacturing of the toys was begun nine months before release date, and production was increased substantially when early versions of the movie tested well. The European release of the movie was highlighted and promoted. The mere ownership of the movie would have created but a fraction of this value. The options had been framed and enabled at the time of the film's production, but the decisions to execute many of them were made *after* the movie's success was visible to management. Many management teams are capable of investing when success is staring them in the face. Disney's management creates additional value by being strikingly skilled at framing options early on.

On an even larger scale, the importance of position is illustrated by Ted Turner's purchase of the MGM/United Artists movie library, containing over 3,000 movies, for slightly over $1 billion in 1990. The library did contain some hits, and a few true blockbusters; but the real value was in the strategic options that the library created. By aggregating the content, in a few years Turner was able to raise the ratings of his existing cable superstation "TBS" by showing, and promoting, the hits by launching a new network, TNT, which showed several *thousand* hours a year of programming out of the library and created the Turner Classic Movie (TCM) channel. This increased product line and viewership leveraged Turner's revenues and gave him better negotiating positions with cable operators, enabling him to restructure and pay off some debt in the mid-1990s. Then a financially strong Turner Network Group merged with Time Warner—earning Turner several billions of dollars. The option value of the entire aggregated portfolio of movies was the key that unlocked this financial treasure chest.

A colleague asked me to describe "the one that got away." For me, this big fish was the failure to frame an option when the position was in hand. It occurred in the Dow Chemical Company's Texas Division in 1973–1974, when one of my staff members had become very excited about the potential of microprocessors, which were in their infancy. Indeed, he programmed microprocessors using "machine language" for portable applications in a manufacturing environment and for personal applications in his spare time. Coincidentally, the previous year I had my own "personal computer," an IBM 1130. This clunky machine still took up half a laboratory, had no monitor, and communicated with me with a typewriter and punch cards. But it was lovable nonetheless because it did what I wanted when I wanted it done. I had programmed it in FORTRAN and BASIC for crystallographic applications that previously ran on mainframes. A key part of the system was a BASIC compiler, which translated BASIC source code to machine language. Microsoft got its start by shoehorning a BASIC compiler onto a microprocessor! All the skills were in my hands to exercise this same option; and if I had seen it, I don't doubt Dow would have financed the first stage of the venture, as they had recently done for another of my projects, ion chromatography. But I never framed this option, nor did countless others in the technical community who were at least as well positioned.

■ REAL OPTIONS AND FATAL FLAWS

In the R&D world, when a new idea is proposed, it is standard practice to look for the fatal flaw. A *fatal flaw* is a condition that is certain to preclude, or that has a high likelihood of precluding, exercise of the option. Its existence in effect negates ownership of the option. That flaw can be technological; it can be in the revenue model; and it might be a health, legal, or environmental issue. In essence a plan with a fatal flaw is no more an option than a call on a worthless security, such as the stock of a defunct company. The absence of a fatal flaw does not imply business success—every business has known risks.

The converse of the situation may also be that *a real option comes into being when the last fatal flaw is eliminated*. In the case of Hook M Horns, our fictional brewer, lack of financing was the last fatal flaw to be overcome—a common occurrence. Here, financing hinged on customer commitments. Customer commitments hinged on production of samples. And production of samples hinged on gaining the services of the master brewer. Any failure in this chain would have been lethal to the project.

It happens that the proponents of an idea may miss the fatal flaw, which can become obvious only when the option begins to be exercised. The Anglo-French Concorde aircraft had a near-fatal flaw long before its first literally fatal crash in the year 2000. That flaw was the sonic boom, which precluded the Concorde's access to most commercial airports and overland routes. When the problem of gaining landing rights became apparent, the production run was capped at 20 aircraft, and its flights were restricted to the transatlantic route, to a small number of other routes over oceans, and to charter flights for the curious. Supersonic operations are not even permitted until the plane is over water. With such a small production run, it was obvious that the development costs of the Concorde could never be recouped and that the investment would have to be written off, an elegant symbol of technical risk and national prestige.

In options language, an enormous price was paid in development and tooling for the call option to produce hundreds of Concordes and the possibility of dominating commercial aviation through the critical attribute of speed. That option was partly exercised with the initial production run. But the value of the underlying security—the business of manufacturing and selling Concordes—dropped to zero; and the manufacturing facilities, and even some of the aircraft, were consigned to salvage.

■ REAL OPTIONS AND MERGERS AND ACQUISITIONS

We have postulated that a real option comes into being when the last fatal flaw is eliminated. In the case of a merger, the fatal flaw may be the willingness of two companies to merge: In principle, any two companies can announce a plan to merge at any time; but in practice the stock market only values these options when they have substance, because for the most part they are not under active consideration and may well be resisted by management. There is little strategic premium under normal circumstances.

There are three important ways in which the fatal flaw to an acquisition can be eliminated and a real option (and with it a strategic premium) created. First, the announcement of a seemingly viable merger plan begins to break the management resistance barrier. Second, the firm may be undervalued in the marketplace. A real option to be acquired comes into being when the stock price falls below the company's value as a leveraged buyout (LBO). At that point a large universe of financial buyers begins to take an interest. Third, a company becomes an acquisition target by actions that put itself into "play," that is, actions that label it as vulnerable. In any of these situations, professional investors will begin to buy on anticipation that an offer to acquire is likely—in other words they frame the option and speculate on it.[4]

A failure to gain regulatory approval—as happened to telecommunications giants Sprint and Worldcom in 2000—represents a risk that revealed a fatal flaw. The initial announcement in the Sprint case (and to GE and Honeywell in 2001)—the option to merge—created value that was built into the price of the stock. The value of this option seemed to decrease as regulators demanded more and more value-destroying divestments. In time Worldcom voluntarily chose not to exercise, and its stock subsequently rose, indicating that investors agreed with management's analysis.

■ SUMMARY

In this chapter, we have shown that plans are options and that they are especially valuable assets under high-risk conditions. Plans derive a great deal of their power from management flexibility. One prerequisite for a plan is framing it, as in the case of Disney, Turner, Microsoft, and the fictional Hook M Horns.

Once the option is framed, the second step is establishing an actionable position and exploiting it, a feature of all of the named cases. Bill Gates, Michael Eisner, and Ted Turner have been masters at exploiting the optionality of position. The third step is ensuring that the plan is not subject to a fatal flaw, as were Worldcom, Sprint, and the Concorde. Position is a necessary but not a sufficient condition to having a high-value plan.

The Source of Wealth: Mastering Risk, Innovation, and the Law of Diminishing Returns

Chapter

Diminishing Returns: The Dusty Road to Devolution

Economics is called the dismal science, and the law of diminishing returns is responsible for its bad name. That law is no law at all—we shall see in this chapter that there are sweet spots in economic life where one can obtain increasing returns. In a later chapter we will see that the law can be, and often is, overcome by innovation. But by and large we must expect and reckon with the law's consequences, which apply to both visible and virtual economic activity.

We thus far have assumed economics is a virtuous process, where economic capital can be continuously amassed in the "operations loop," while strategic capital in the "plans loop" can catalyze and accelerate the process (see Figure 4.1). We turn now to the three forces that influence these processes: (1) diminishing returns, (2) risk, and (3) innovation. These forces are, in a sense, those of darkness and light.

On the dark side, we know that wealth can be squandered gradually through unchecked devolution (according to Webster, "the disappearance or simplification of structure or function in the course of evolution"). Or wealth can disappear suddenly and catastrophically through a single event. We need to look at this dark side to understand why risk taking and innovation are the foundations of prosperity. First, we do so from a historical perspective, and then we look at the same issues as they confront modern businesses.

■ DOWN ON THE FARM: DIMINISHING RETURNS IN A PRIMITIVE OPERATING SYSTEM

Consider a primitive economic system where villagers raise grain in a fertile valley. The village initially prospers and grows because the resources required to grow grain are less valuable than the grain produced. The farmers and their families can easily produce more grain than they consume. But as the village grows, new fields must be added. Because these fields are farther from the river and higher above the water table, they produce less. These fields can be irrigated, but doing so would require considerable additional resources. Expansion up and down the river is the easier approach to increasing production, but that course is limited by how far a villager can walk in a day and still have time to tend to the crops. It may also be limited by the land claims of the neighboring village.

Given these basic constraints, growing the next bushel of grain can only become increasingly difficult. Farmers learn, by trial and error, that some plots are more productive than others, and they utilize these. The less-productive plots create frustration and relative poverty for those who work them.

At some level of population the village can no longer add value by expanding its farming enterprises. In an economy where value is measured in grain production, this level is reached when the first farmer finds that he cannot produce more grain than his family eats. At this point, the village is better off urging its people to try to use the upland meadows as pasturage for live-stock or to learn crafts that could earn an economic surplus and be traded for food. At a higher level of population, the village will not even be self-sufficient in food—when, on average, the farmers and their families who produce more than they eat are outnumbered by those who eat more than they produce.

A primitive village cannot measure the point when farming ceases to create value. First, rudimentary accounting systems cannot track resource consumption. Neither the mathematical skills nor the knowledge of how to account for resource inputs is present, even if production records are kept.

Second, the productivity of the land is affected by familiar agricultural risk factors, such as weather and pests. Depletion of nutrients in the soil is another confounding factor; the impor-tance of the Nile flood to ancient Egypt exemplifies it. Human productivity is impacted by other risk factors, such as disease and accident. Modern societies usually view such risks as statis-tically predictable and invest intellectual energy in forecasting them. Primitive societies, in contrast, ascribe the consequences of risk to supernatural causes. For them, appeasing the gods through sacrifice was an early, persistent, and conspicuously unsuccessful form of risk management.

Nevertheless, villages learn, and embody their learning in tradition, a form of intellectual capital. In time the logical bound-aries for grain farming become well established. And the village understands that with a reliable grain surplus, it can support a certain number of specialists who make life better—scribes, priests, and constables, for example. It may have opportunities to make periodic capital improvements: a water system, roads, irrigation, and public and religious buildings that will in time transform the community.

Cultural factors can also affect how a village behaves. Cul-tural traditions may never have worked very well, or perhaps no longer work, but they are always present. The economic his-torian Angus Maddison has concluded that the persistent poverty of villages in the Indian subcontinent is due to a tradition that allows population to rise to a level where no economic surplus can be earned.[1] In effect, this means persisting in agriculture well past the point of diminishing returns, thus precluding capital formation and ensuring economic stagnation. A similar hypothesis has been applied to the rise and decline of the Anasazi culture at Chaco Canyon in northwestern New Mexico. "The Anasazi prosperity of the ninth and tenth centuries crashed to an end with serious droughts that began about 1090," Adler wrote. "Within a few generations, the great houses of Chaco's social experiment were left to crumble as the ancestral Pueblo people moved to upland areas."[2] If the hypothesis is correct, excessive investments were made based on a temporary surplus, without fully accounting for the risks.

The conclusion from these societal disasters might be that, although it is easy to talk about value creation, knowing the point at which diminishing returns set in, and evaluating the level of risk, is far less obvious. Primitive societies learned by trial and error and incorporated their experience, for better or worse, into durable traditions. Modern societies are considerably better at microeconomics, but they face an even more formidable problem of measurement as their economies become increasingly virtual. Skill at exiting unpromising businesses has become a driver of corporate performance and value creation.

■ DEVOLUTION DOES HAPPEN: ANCIENT MEXICO, ANCIENT ZIMBABWE, AND MODERN RUSSIA

Persisting in economic behavior that no longer adds value may be a result of human nature. As individuals, we invest in our skills, and the fact that some of these skills are no longer needed is hard to accept. If farming is all we know, then farm we seemingly must.

Second, it is easy to ascribe economic failure to outside causes, such as the inevitable droughts, insect infestations, petty thefts, and the diseases to which a peasant is subject. The gods were propitiated in an attempt to control the noncontrollable. But a society has three long-term choices: (1) continue to evolve by building capital, (2) begin to devolve by destroying value, or (3) find an elusive sustainable equilibrium where value is neither created nor destroyed.

The readers of this book mostly live in times and societies where the first happy alternative is the reality. The societies of North America and Western Europe have been building capital for so long that its inevitability is assumed. Nevertheless, human history has been a rocky road, and devolution is one of its features. Jane Jacobs tells of an ultraprimitive tribe living in a remote jungle habitat in the Philippines that had no toolmaking capabilities whatsoever.[3] It is self-evident that the tribe's ancestors had such capabilities because they are known to have migrated by sea from Southeast Asia. Building a seaworthy boat requires a fairly high level of both engineering expertise and toolmaking skills, knowledge developed independently by prehistoric societies in several parts of the world.

Lest this example seem remote, Jacobs also documents the devolution of a bypassed hamlet in western North Carolina, which by the 1930s had been reduced almost to a subsistence economy, having lost most of its traditional practices and skills and nearly having lost its contacts with the outside world.[4] Clearly, the founders of the hamlet had skills in trade and handicraft, but the community's remoteness eroded the value of these assets. Therefore it focused on those activities that would enable self-sufficiency in a difficult rural environment and allowed the earlier skills to erode.

Mayan civilization likewise appears to have devolved from very promising beginnings in the first millennium, apparently peaking about A.D. 600 to 900. The classical-era Mayans developed sophisticated irrigation systems and created enough of a surplus to spend heavily on stone pyramids, temples, observatories, and municipal edifices. Yet farming in the Yucatan had returned to near subsistence levels by the time the Spanish arrived early in the sixteenth century. The reasons for devolution have been a matter of speculation (protein deficiency, deforestation, internal social stress, the rise of Aztec power, and other causes have been named), but it was clear that the Mayans had developed a very regimented and ritualized society. If so, diminishing returns in agriculture and persistence in continuing value-destroying enterprises might have sufficed to bankrupt their great cities and precipitate decline.

The Great Zimbabwe is another case in point. This stone city was apparently built by the Monomotopa empire, ancestors of today's Shona tribe, in southern Zimbabwe during the period A.D. 1200–1500. Its ruins give evidence of elegant granite buildings and ritual purposes. Archeological estimates of the peak population there run to 20,000 people, making it a large city for that time in any part of the world. But by the time the Portuguese arrived in the mid-1500s, it was already the ghost town we visit today.

What was the cause of the devolution of the Great Zimbabwe? The answer may relate to wood. Wood must have been a critical resource, needed both as fuel and as a construction material (the roof structures of both the stone buildings and the thatched hut dwellings clearly required wood). Wood is a renewable resource, but even in the tropics it requires a 20- or 30-year growing cycle.

The labor required to cut this amount of wood should have been no problem. In principle a certain percentage of the labor available to a Shona community was already devoted to cutting trees and gathering wood; this fraction would just supply the annual per capita wood consumption in a Shona village. That percentage might be somewhat higher in a large town because of the number of public buildings, but no matter. However, transport would be another issue, and that is where diminishing returns were inevitable. As the population of the town grew, the diameter of the wood-gathering area needed to sustain the population would necessarily grow. Southern Africa had no draught or pack animals,[5] and the wheel was not in use. In fact, the distance to haul a piece of wood from the outer radius of the gathering area would necessarily increase as the square root of the population at the center. Longer and longer treks were inevitable, consuming an increasing portion of the town's resources. At some level of population, diminishing returns were inevitable. If in fact (as seems likely) the expended woodland resources within the existing circle were not renewed through good forestry practices, the decline would be much faster, and wood would become extremely expensive. Bringing wood from distant reaches over seas and rivers was not an option because the Great Zimbabwe was surrounded by large plains and was a substantial distance from the great Limpopo and Zambezi rivers. The diminishing returns implied by such negative economies of scale fit the hypothesis of near catastrophic abandonment.

The threat of devolution has not been extinguished by modernity. Russia, whose engineers put the first man in space in our lifetime, is on a downhill slide. It decapitalized in the 1980s to a level where it was unable to support the Soviet Union. The growth of its gross national product (GNP) was mostly negative through the 1990s, and both birth rates and life spans are now in serious decline. The reasons for Russia's great leap backward appear to derive from a grossly inefficient system of internal transactions, which is a by-product of a command-and-control economy. The country's problems were aggravated for a time by excessive diversion of resources to a military establishment committed to maintaining parity with richer competitors. To use the terminology of our book, Russia had a high level of human capital, particularly in science and engineering, and a great store of natural resources. But a cultural inability to create flexible business plans ensured that its capital could not be translated into value creation. Until Russia as a whole learns to operate under conditions where it earns the cost of capital, devolution will continue; the fact that capital flight continues suggests that that point has not been reached.

■ DEVOLUTION IN BUSINESS ORGANIZATIONS: AUTOMOBILES

Businesspeople are supposed to be smart, but they are hardly immune to diminishing returns. They, too, fall into the value traps from time to time.

During its growth phase, a new organization will enlist a considerable amount of strategic capital. And as long as new investments earn more than their cost of capital, growth increases the value of the enterprise, often dramatically so. At the outset, this strategic capital is largely human: engineers, market development specialists, planners, and research scientists. They are the people charged with opening new markets and building the facilities that will supply goods and services to them. In a rapidly growing company, they form a large portion of the corporate staff.

Just as an agricultural village reaches its limits, a firm will inevitably encounter diminishing returns. The available market becomes saturated and competitors emerge to challenge each new sale and to exploit the remaining opportunities. The U.S. automobile industry provides a familiar example. Its growth in the first half of the twentieth century was phenomenal; that growth slowed in the third quarter of the century, and maturity characterized the fourth quarter. The industrial leader, General Motors (GM), which inherited the legacy of Alfred P. Sloan, was widely viewed as the paragon of industrial management excellence. In more recent years it has been pilloried (with some reason) for being among the largest value destroyers in the Fortune 100. In other words, its automobile business has in recent years chronically earned less than the cost of capital, forcing GM to shed assets. This circumstance has something to do with market saturation. With many families already owning several vehicles, the capacity of the market to absorb additional vehicles or more expensive vehicles cannot grow significantly faster than the economy as a whole; indeed, it may grow more slowly if a larger portion of the economy is diverted to other goods or services.

The economics of the auto market, and its inevitable diminishing returns, are beyond the control of GM management; and its being among the least skillful of the major carmakers in managing change hasn't helped. GM has devolved strategically as well as economically. For example, its market share, which is closely related to its image in the minds of consumers, has dropped from over 50 percent to less than 30 percent over several decades, and signs of a turnaround are few.

What do rational companies do as growth slows and devolution begins? The first step is to attempt to cut costs without unduly losing revenues. If this works, returns can move from below the cost of capital to above it, giving the firm time to establish more effective strategies. One of the first cost-reduction targets is the staff engaged to support growth that no longer exists. Market developers, central engineering, the technical center, and corporate strategic planners become partially or wholly expendable. Chrysler, in desperate need of a turnaround in the 1980s, adopted a strategy of minimizing internal research and development (R&D) and outsourced most of its needs to vendors; meanwhile GM and Ford continue to maintain formidable staff groups.

The consequence of cost-cutting is to convert strategic capital to economic capital—to move resources across the dashed line in Figure 4.1. At the end of the process, there should be more operating capital and less strategic capital in the structure. If laying off an engineer saves $100,000 on the net income line and if the marketplace values GM at a price-to-earnings (P/E) ratio of 10, then GM's market capitalization should increase by $1 million. If a thousand engineers are laid off, the gain is $1 billion. And the stock market often responds in just this manner when a mature company cuts apparently redundant staff. Nonetheless, a tremendous loss of human capital is involved, and management and investors must be convinced that the layoff cuts only to the level at which the remaining engineers and outside consultants can fill the gap. If the quality of cars from an assembly plant plummets because there are too few supervising engineers in the plant or if mandated fuel efficiency standards cannot be met because the engine designers are on the beach, then the move may bite back.

In defense of General Motors, it should be noted that the company made an investment in Hughes Electronics, a high-tech company whose valuation as a GM subsidiary has grown to the point where it is estimated to be comparable to the market capitalization of General Motors and far exceeds its book value. In other words, this portion of GM's capital, comprised mostly of strategic capital, has become as valuable as the entire automotive operation, which represents mostly operating capital. Thus a buyer of GM stock can be thought to get the automotive operation for free! This outcome may be entirely appropriate if the value-destroying carmaker has no prospect of turning the corner; but it indicates that management did exercise at least one strategically sound option in the face of diminishing returns.

■ DIMINISHING RETURNS FROM TECHNOLOGY

Technology executives have long understood that when a new technology emerges, technology progress can be very rapid but it will slow in time. Successive improvements become smaller and more expensive as the fundamental limitations of physical laws or of materials are reached. In some cases the limits are absolute, while under other circumstances unexpected opportunities to move to new, higher limits are discovered. Consider an absolute case, that of burning gas to produce heat. Very likely the first gas burner was created by a person who found a source of swamp gas and managed to ignite it. Swamp gas, one of several natural sources of methane, is produced by bacteria under anaerobic conditions, as may exist on the bottom of a marsh, where microorganisms quietly digest dead wood, reeds, fish, and other organic debris. Chemists know that pure methane has a theoretical heat of combustion of about one million British thermal units (Btus) per 1,000 standard cubic feet.

The first gas burner no doubt produced a sooty, low-efficiency flame. Why? The methane was far from pure, and its mixing with oxygen was far short of ideal. Combustion was undoubtedly incomplete because some of the methane didn't burn at all but escaped from the edges of the flame into the atmosphere. Other portions of the methane burned incompletely, forming carbon (soot) or carbon monoxide, an everpresent impurity in combustion gases. So our pioneer's yield of energy would have been substantially less than theoretical—let us assume it was 10 percent.

The pioneer's successor operating during the early Industrial Revolution would have designed a much more efficient burner where gas and air were thoroughly mixed in close-to-ideal proportions and where flame temperatures were much higher to ensure more complete combustion. Perhaps these combustion yields were 70 percent of theoretical. But incomplete combustion would still occur at the walls of the furnace and elsewhere.

A contemporary designer would have access to complex fluid dynamic modeling programs, better mixing technologies, and advanced materials. Perhaps, with the use of these expensive tools, 99 percent of the available carbon would be completely combusted in the burner, and almost all of the remaining carbon monoxide combusted in a catalytic converter to give a yield of 99.99 percent.

But the yield can never be more than 100 percent. And at some point the efficiency-raising additions—the fancy burner tips, the ceramic linings, the heat exchangers, and the catalytic converter—cease to add value and extract an economic penalty.

The art and science of sailing provides another instructive example of diminishing returns from technology. Enormous intellectual capital has been expended on sailing faster. One of the value drivers is obvious and visible: capital productivity. A ship that sails 10 percent faster can haul 10 percent more cargo in a year than an equally costly but slower ship can.

But in the age of sail, there were even more important value drivers, which related more to strategic capital than to economic capital. The first ship home to port from the fishing grounds or the spice harvest would reap the highest prices at market. (This first-to-market advantage is still a critical advantage in modern commerce.) The owners of the first ship home with news of an overseas military victory or a financial collapse stood to benefit in the securities market. It brought the near equivalent of inside information. And an East Indiaman or a clipper that could outsail a typical pirate, if even by 1 percent, would be at far less risk than a ship that was 2 percent slower than the marauder. Likewise, a frigate that could outsail most enemy vessels would gain the enormously valuable real option of engaging or declining combat.

So, in terms of strategic capital, in the age of sail, small improvements in technology often meant great value, and shipowners invested in obtaining them.

Physical limits, though, play an important role in sailing. The concept of "hull speed" is virtually an axiom. It implies a maximum speed for any sailing vessel whose hull displaces water (the typical situation, but not so for a hydrofoil) that is proportional to the square root of the length—longer vessels sail faster. Using this rule, a vessel that is twice as long (and thus perhaps eight times as large in mass) will not sail twice as fast but only 41 percent faster. These facts imply an intrinsic law of diminishing returns on speed with mass (and therefore cost).

Of course, for a given length, there are many ways to more closely approach theoretical hull speed. These included developing improved rigging design, adding more square feet of sail, developing more efficient hull design, and careening or otherwise modifying the surface friction of the hull. Small craft can escape this limitation by planing, but the amount of power required for the transition to a planing mode is beyond practicality for conventional ships.

The apparent limitations of sailing have been challenged time and time again by countless innovations large and small: the centerline rudder; the development of advanced keels, which produce hydrodynamic lift to windward; the clipper ship with its incredible spread of sail; the Marconi rig, the modern yachtsman's standard; the catamaran; and special low-friction surfaces. These innovations have all propelled sailing technology forward—enough to win races, but with zero chance to match breakthrough technology such as the hydrofoil or the airplane.

■ DIMINISHING RETURNS FROM PLUNDER

This book introduced an enterprise that started as an innovative plunder business, the conquest of the New World by Spanish treasure hunters. Its principals found other opportunities and created options, and the enterprise evolved into much more. But that is another story. Here, we will focus on the unique role of plunder in the devolution of societies and businesses.

Ironically, plundering other organizations or societies may be one of the oldest businesses, much in the sense that prostitution is said to be the oldest profession. When we disapprove of plunder, we call it crime and worse, much as there are worse words for prostitution. But plunder played an undeniable role in our past history; successful plunderers have been honored as national heroes, and the business is alive and flourishing in many parts of the world today.

Plunder has all the dynamics of a business model—free cash flow, value creation, value destruction, planning, risk, innovation, and diminishing returns. It also has important effects on those who are plundered.

The beginnings of plunder are the ability to earn an exceptional return on seemingly little capital. Usually, however, the risks are high. In civilized societies we contrive to make them so high that the risk/reward ratio discourages plunder severely.

However, there are times when individuals, organizations, or nations develop enticing wealth, which they are in a poor position to secure. Viking seafarers exploited vulnerable communities from Russia to Britain and France and as far south as Sicily. The Mongols found rich cities along the trade routes of Asia and Eastern Europe that could not defend themselves against their innovative cavalry tactics. The rich Incas and Aztecs proved amazingly vulnerable to small groups of conquistadors, inviting systematic plunder. More recently, the oil rich and militarily weak states of Kuwait and Saudi Arabia proved a temptation to a regional military power, Iraq. Iraq's failure is only a testament to the risks involved.

The plunder business is severely subject to diminishing returns. Once the gold and the gems are gone, it will be many generations before they are replenished. Plundering expeditions to more-distant places suffer from another form of diminishing returns—that of operating over long lines of supply and difficult communications. Alexander the Great figuratively ran out of gas in the Hindu Kush; Attila the Hun did so in France; and Napoleon found his tank empty once in Egypt and again in Russia. The Vikings are thought to have found the profitless combination of minimal treasure and formidable resistance when they encountered indigenous North Americans.

One option open to successful plunderers is to become colonizers and to attempt to continuously extract wealth from conquered civilizations. The dynasties founded by Alexander's successors Ptolemy and Seleucus lasted a few centuries in Egypt and Syria, as did those of Genghis's successors Kublai in China and the Golden Horde in Russia. The Spanish colonies in the Americas lasted three hundred years or more. However, all of these systems eventually devolved and were replaced by more vigorous successors.

In modern times, there has been a temptation to plunder and exploit industrial economies. Germany's capture of Belgium and Luxembourg during World War I and of nearly all of Europe during World War II, France's seizure of the Ruhr in 1923 and 1924, the Japanese Empire from 1910 to 1945, and Soviet hegemony over Eastern Europe from 1945 to 1989 have been cited.[6] Modern societies are vulnerable to coercion and repression. Hence, determined conquerors can use police methods to compel collaboration and to suppress resistance.

However, the critical question is not whether the conquering state can extract value from the conquered. In the short run the answer is always yes. The real question is *whether the entity comprising the conqueror and the conquered creates value.* If it does not, the forcefully unified entity cannot be sustained and will devolve. The process can be rapid if there is no effort to renew the capital of the conquered territory, if its inhabitants are demoralized, or both. In the later stages of devolution, political and military control will deteriorate, and any fragments that appear to have the capability of creating value will attempt to do so independently. This sequence of events happened to the Soviet Union and its satellites. It now appears that a few states (Poland, the Czech Republic, Hungary, and Estonia) have learned to earn the cost of capital, whereas most have not. Russia, Ukraine, and other states have been unable so far to tame the plundering activities of their mafias and kleptocracies, contributing to the continuing destruction of value in those societies.

There have been a few examples where unification has created value: Germany was so successful economically after Bismarck unified it that few question its viability or recall that the many previous attempts to subjugate and rule this territory had all resulted in failure. Similarly, the territories that the United States seized from Mexico—places like California—soon became value adding, and the conquests were quickly stabilized.

■ PLUNDERING STRATEGIC CAPITAL

Usually, economic capital is the first target for plunder. But strategic capital in the form of human and intellectual property can be the target as well. It has long been so. Its destruction has even more profound effects on the process of devolution.

When great trading cities along the Silk Road resisted Genghis Khan, he slaughtered the inhabitants and piled up their skulls. Cities such as Gaochang, near Turfan in Western China, have been uninhabited ever since, and their ghostly remains are a frightening testimony to organized predation. As the process has been described:

> Organization, discipline, mobility, and ruthlessness of purpose were the fundamental factors in his [Genghis's] military successes. Massacres of defeated populations, with the resultant terror, were weapons he regularly used. His practice of summoning cities to surrender and of organizing the methodical slaughter of those who did not submit has been described as psychological warfare; but, although it was undoubtedly policy to sap resistance by fostering terror, massacre was used for its own sake. Mongol practice, especially in the war against Khwarezm, was to send agents to demoralize and divide the garrison and populace of an enemy city, mixing threats with promises. The Mongols' reputation for frightfulness often para-

lyzed their captives, who allowed themselves to be killed when resistance or flight was not possible. Indeed, the Mongols were unaccountable. Resistance brought certain destruction, but at Balkh, now in Afghanistan, the population was slaughtered in spite of a prompt surrender, for tactical reasons.[7]

Clearly, these tactics involved the wholesale destruction of strategic capital—the trading, agricultural, and industrial skills of the conquered people. In this case, the human capital was not temporarily appropriated and converted to treasure; it was utterly destroyed.

In addition, human capital was also a frequent objective of plunder in the form of slaves. Slavery was common practice in the classical world and in large manner amounted to the appropriation of women for agricultural and household servitude, including concubinage. It was the principal return from numerous military expeditions.

This human capital was not necessarily exploited at just the lowest levels; one of the most productive historians of ancient times was the Greek slave Polybius, who wrote a definitive history of Rome during his detention under Scipio Africanus about 150 B.C. The strategic capital of Greece was thus systematically plundered by the Romans, often resulting in a large discount to its inherent value.

In modern times, the United States and the Soviet Union competed for one of the prime spoils of World War II—Germany's expertise in rocketry. U.S. intellectual property in nuclear weapons was also targeted for espionage, another mechanism of plunder that targets only intellectual capital.

The same phenomena take place among commercial firms. Industrial spies have targeted their competitors' secrets employing legal or illegal methods. In the 1970s, Hitachi agents were apprehended in IBM facilities looking for clues about IBM's new product offerings.

There is, however, a profound weakness to obtaining intellectual capital through espionage. The spy is generally targeting information that is more or less old. It exists in prototypes, drawings, and business documents. Meanwhile, the "target" is thinking about new and innovative ideas, many of which are embodied in scattered reports or even merely in the minds of the pacesetters. Such options for future action are the product of the plans loop. When they are implemented, the organization that relies on espionage for innovative technology will find itself behind by one or two generations of technology and perhaps quite unable to use its plunder to create new value.

■ DEVOLUTION AND THE LEVERAGED BUYOUT

Barbarians at the Gate[8] was one of the great business reads, capturing the excesses of corporate greed and vanity in the 1980s. The book focused on several business groups that competed to effect a leveraged buyout (LBO) of RJR Nabisco. It took place in an era when businessmen characterized as "corporate raiders," such as T. Boone Pickens and Carl Icahn, took advantage of undervalued stocks to take over, or to threaten to take over, operating companies by exploiting the LBO concept, which was introduced in Chapter 2. Even unsuccessful raids could net profits for these raiders, so the term "greenmail" was coined for the practice of threatening a raid and calling it off for a price. Another popular book about that era was aptly titled *The Predator's Ball*.[9]

"Corporate raiding" was greatly facilitated by the innovative application of high-yield/high-risk financing developed by Drexel Burnham under Michael Milken's leadership. Because the raids disrupted the jobs of thousands of employees, the activities of Milken and the raiders were widely deplored. Milken eventually paid a huge fine and served a jail term for securities violations and was banned from the securities industry. His downfall seems a combination of the resentments he generated and of a personal blind spot regarding the ethics of his methods and associates. But the subject of buyouts remains fascinating because it has aspects of both plunder and value creation.

The preconditions for LBOs typically emerge when companies begin to devolve—to destroy value—when they can no longer earn their cost of capital. Indeed, the process of devolution can occur within a business unit of a company even as the rest of the company experiences profitable growth.

Although there are several other solutions to the problem of a devolving business, the buyout has become one of the most prevalent. It is a strategy of creating value (but not necessarily maximizing value) by converting all strategic capital to economic capital. In its classic form, those planning an LBO attempt to determine the pretax cash flow of the unit as if it had no debt or taxes.[10] They then calculate what costs the business is incurring that are not needed to generate that cash flow. They recalculate pretax cash flow including these economies. Next they determine the size of the loan that could be paid off in a reasonable period of time (with interest and principal) using the projected pretax cash flow when unneeded costs are eliminated. This loan will surely bear a high interest rate (a.k.a. "junk bond") because the company is essentially debt financed. Why pretax? Taxes will initially be minimal because reported operating profits would be offset by the huge interest payments. And note that the LBO is now covering the direct cost of capital (essentially its debt) because its cash flow more than covers its interest payments.

If the numbers work out, the buyout team obtains financial backing for the loan and offers the owners that price, in cash, for the business. If some of the leaders of the planning group are managers of the business (often needed to assure the bankers that the plan is sound), then the transaction is called an MBO (management-led buyout). The amount of the initial financing requirement can also be reduced if the planners can identify nonperforming assets that can be converted to cash.

If all goes well, the loan should be paid off in a few years or refinanced through conventional (and cheaper) debt instruments. The new owners are left with a sound operating company, a somewhat tired physical plant, and presumably a more-than-tidy paper profit. Note that in the absence of any unanticipated interruptions in cash flow, the LBO is a financial transaction in which the owners cannot lose if their cash flow calculations are correct. The additional risks of leveraging are built in to the negotiated interest rate.

To get to this point, the business will sell some of its accoutrements of image and prestige, such as corporate jets and its handsome headquarters building on prime real estate. To the degree it can, the company will attempt to serve its customers using existing assets. Most important, the company will generally forsake that part of its organization that is intended to promote profitable future investments—R&D, engineering, market research, and so forth. In other words, it will convert its strategic capital into cash. Since the LBO's primary objective is to pay down debt, it is likely to forego opportunities to earn more than the cost of capital on new long-term investments. So it is, in principle at least, not maximizing long-term shareholder value.

LBOs are facilitated by situations in which the stock market gives no credit, or negative credit, to a company's strategic capital. In these cases, it is a "no-brainer" to buy the company for less than the amount for which it can be mortgaged and to quickly pay down the debt. The threat of an LBO can be a tragedy for a company that is investing in long-term plans that will revitalize its earnings and growth if its stock is depressed because of these costs. But this same threat has been excellent medicine for complacent managers who were not watching value creation in their day-to-day decision making.

In option terms, in the presence of respectable pretax earnings, the ability to plan and execute an LBO or one of its variants is itself a business option and should be included in any valuation exercise.

In hindsight, managements and employees learned that rigorous attention to value creation was the best defense against corporate plunder. Whether by coincidence or not, the stock market has performed extremely well since that era. To some, Milken, surely a high-risk investor and an innovator, was one of the creators of our current prosperity and a business hero; to others, he was the consummate barbarian.

■ INCREASING RETURNS: THE LAW CHALLENGED

Advocates of the "New Economy" concept occasionally boast that technology has defeated the law of diminishing returns and that we have entered an era of "increasing returns." The thesis is based on the notion that knowledge products have different economics than physical products. A frequently mentioned example is software. There is a large one-time cost involved in writing a useful piece of software. Once it is completed, however, the cost of distributing it to customers is low. Let's say it is an application that cost $1 million to write and test. It is sold to retail shops for $110 per copy. Assume that the box, the manual, and the CD-ROM cost $10, leaving a gross profit of $100. Breakeven is reached when 10,000 copies are sold. Each additional copy is virtually pure profit. After selling the second 10,000 copies, the developer will have doubled his money on his initial investment, and after 110,000 copies are sold he will have a 1,000 percent profit (again, on a gross basis). Later, the developer may charge for downloads from a web site, in which case each additional copy may have a cost of goods of just a few cents! While this popular application is in its growth phase, the developer's financial statements will show increasing returns—his costs are behind him and the profits roll in. Most likely, the developer may attempt to repeat this success with another "killer ap" and keep his revenues from the original software rolling in by issuing version 2.0, 3.0, 4.0, ...

In principle, though, there is little that is different between this software example and old-economy models, except perhaps the accounting treatment of the most important assets (investments in software development and R&D are usually expensed, whereas physical investments are depreciated) and a more extreme ratio between selling prices and variable costs. A drug manufacturer invests in R&D, protects its investment with patents, receives Food and Drug Administration (FDA) approval, and invests capital in a production facility. The initial investment, especially for R&D, is large; but the firm recoups it quickly with high gross margins. As the drug takes off, the firm will appear to have increasing returns as well. The effect is far more visible if this product is the company's first or second success, such as Epogen for Amgen, and less spectacular when it is just another successful drug from an established manufacturer, such as Mevacor for Merck.

There is a second aspect to increasing returns, which is not really new either. It is that market leaders get more than their fair share of the high-quality opportunities that a new technology unleashes. They are in a position to enjoy economies of scale, to earn higher margins as a result, and thus to have more financial capacity to make new investments. Monopoly power may be within their reach. In a high-growth environment, the results can be dramatic. New Economy leaders such as Microsoft and America Online (AOL) have benefited from this effect. But a reading of the early career of John D. Rockefeller shows the same phenomenon; Rockefeller adroitly used the power of scale to force weaker competitors to consolidate within his Standard Oil trust.[11]

Do increasing returns invalidate the concept of diminishing returns? Not at all. Increasing returns are a characteristic of the earlier part of an S-curve—illustrated in Figure 12.1 and to be discussed in more detail when we review innovation processes in Chapter 12. But increasing returns are never sustainable. Common sense tells us that no business can grow *indefinitely* at a rate that is faster than the economy as a whole, for the simple reason that it will eventually be larger than the economy as a whole—an impossibility.

The faster any segment grows, the sooner it will begin to bump up against a limit. In fact, the classic S-curve[12] (sometimes called a logistics curve) has an inflexion point at which the rate of growth begins to slow (although the growth may still be tremendous). At the inflexion point, the growth rate is halfway to the limit and into the zone of diminishing returns. Absent innovation—a new S-curve—the law of diminishing returns prevails in the end.

There are investment considerations to these insights. It makes a great deal of difference to high-risk investors whether the law of diminishing returns sets in sooner or later. The most obvious indicator of its onset is the slowing of reported growth rates. However, this information may come too late to cut losses, since it is obvious to all. A more sophisticated method,[13] which should allow a decision earlier in time, is to estimate the upper limit of the S-curve, take any two representative historical points, and calculate the point of inflexion. For example, for an Internet bookseller, the limit may be the available book market, and the two representative points could be book sales at two points in time. For as long as reported growth rates are increasing, the stocks of participants in the innovation are likely to continue to rise. Thus, those who understand a nonlinear phenomenon and see the inflexion point coming will get to the exits faster than the mass of linear thinkers deploying the growth-in-perpetuity formula and plugging in the most recent estimate of the growth rate.

There are also practical considerations in using such a forecasting technique. The first is that almost every reported data point will be affected by special circumstances, for example, whether the economy is booming or in recession. So the S-curve will be "noisy," and as a consequence, the inflexion cannot be predicted with mathematical precision. Second, it is safe to bet that the leaders of the business are well aware of the threat of maturity and will invest in the types of innovation that seek to transcend the current S-curve. In the end, informed judgments must be made about how representative the available data is and whether efforts to overcome the law of diminishing returns through innovation have a realistic chance to succeed.

As noted, the only real difference between the software case and the drug case is that manufacturing investments must be made and depreciated for a pharmaceutical product, thereby reducing reported profits. But on a cash flow basis there is not much difference at all. Merck, like Microsoft, will reinvest its profits to find follow-on products. Other old-economy industries work with lower gross margins, but the principles remain the same.

Chapter

8

Five Millennia of Value Destruction

We live in times of incredible wealth creation. Few wonder how the good times came about, but many more wonder whether they will continue. And there is good reason to wonder. Prosperity is a rare thing. Are we deluding ourselves in our expectations of future return?

It is perplexing why so many of civilization's physical and intellectual monuments were constructed during very brief periods, often in small pockets of the world, and why the world is so poor, relative to the wealth it might have possessed today if the capital of early ages had been invested at a return that would be viewed as pitiable underperformance by modern investors. Consider this quotation: "If the rich Medici family in Italy just six hundred years ago had set aside at 5 percent compounded interest an investment fund equal to $100,000, its 1933 value would be $517,000,000,000,000,000 (517 quadrillions)."[1] The world's wealth, at about $100 trillion, falls short of that number by a factor of 5,000 and, of course, was built off a much larger capital base.

The answer appears to be massive and prevalent value destruction. Much of it stems from a flawed understanding of risk, innovation, and value, the elements of the real options solution.

This chapter sets out to reexamine the situations that societies have encountered over the history of civilization in light of management concepts now being applied to decision making in the business world, especially those relating to the management of risk and the management of innovation. This perspective provides new insights into the behavior of leaders and of nations and a way to differentiate between strategies with a chance of success and those doomed from the start to fail.

■ HISTORICAL GROWTH RATES

Over some 5,000 years of recorded history it is astounding to reflect that more than 99 percent of the wealth creation has occurred in the past 250 years. In fact, economic progress was astonishingly slow for the first 4,750 years. True, there were a number of wealthy and brilliant civilizations in the intervening period—Athens, Rome, Byzantium, Babylon, Thebes, Xian, and Baghdad come to mind—but all of these subsequently devolved. And there were a few great cities that helped to build the foundations of modern prosperity but could not sustain their economic leadership—among them Venice, Genoa, Antwerp, and Amsterdam.

Though we lack good estimates of population, income, and wealth during the earlier periods—economic statistics are also for the most part a new thing—the time scales are so long that there is surprisingly little uncertainty about the magnitudes of growth rates.

As long as economies were dominated by agriculture, growth in wealth was largely determined by growth in population. There were, of course, important productivity enhancements in agriculture during the first 4,750 years of civilization. Better grains were developed by plant breeders; the yoke was invented in the

Middle Ages, enabling the effective harnessing of draught animals; better designs for farm implements such as plows, crop rotation, and fertilization with manure were adopted. The painstaking research of Fernand Braudel resulted in the following data regarding the steadily improving technology for growing wheat developed in Europe, using as the metric "yield of wheat per bushel of seed":[2]

Before 1200–1249	England, France	3.0–3.7
1250–1500	England, France	4.3–4.7
1500–1700	England, Netherlands	7.0
1750–1820	England, Ireland, Netherlands	10.6

But the limiting factor for many years was population itself, which grew remarkably slowly during this long interval. One estimate of world population begins with 14 million people in 3000 B.C., rising to 170 million in A.D. 1, growing very slowly through the Dark Ages to reach 265 million in A.D. 1000 and reaching 720 million in A.D. 1750. World population crossed the 6 billion mark just before the end of the second millennium.

What growth rates can we infer? For the first 3,000 years, to the year 1, population grew at less than 0.1 percent per year! This rate of progress was low indeed. For the next 1,750 years the growth rate was also under 0.1 percent. And for the past 250 years, in which population has grown almost 10-fold, the rate is just under 1 percent. During the past 50 years it has been considerably higher than the 250-year average, approaching 2 percent.

It is considerably more difficult to find scholarly figures on the history of global wealth, but we can attempt to get into the ballpark. The present is a little easier. Global economic data usually focus on gross domestic product (GDP) as a measure of wealth. For the United States in the year 2000, this sum was about $9 trillion; for the world,[3] it was perhaps $30 trillion.

But GDP does not mean wealth (assets); it means revenues,

which are two different things. It is perfectly possible to be wealthy and yet run a deficit or to be profitable but broke. In the long run, of course, there is a relationship between these two things. The total assets in the United States appear to be a factor of three to four times its GDP.[4] If assets-to-GDP for the rest of the world is about the same as that of the United States (and most of the wealth is in developed countries), the total wealth on earth would be at least $90 trillion.

Going back in time to 1750 and beyond to find measures of wealth is much more problematic. However, we do know that per capita annual income today in nonmechanized agricultural communities around the world tends to fall in the $100-to-$300 range. It is likely that inhabitants of cities and towns were substantially richer; they represented perhaps 5 percent to 10 percent of the population and had per capita incomes of $500 or more. So to make a gross estimate of world income in 1750, I would assume 650 million rural people earning $200 per capita and 70 million urban people earning $500. That translates into $130 billion + $35 billion, or $165 billion. If global wealth were 3 times this number, it would be about $500 billion, or $0.5 trillion.

As an economic growth rate, this estimate works out at 2 percent during a time period when populations were growing at 1 percent. (This crude estimate could easily be a factor of 2 high or low, but the nature of exponential mathematics is such that even so the growth rate for wealth would round to 2 percent.) Using the same approach for the earlier period from 3000 B.C. to the take-off point at around A.D. 1750, assuming a per capita income of $100 in 3000 B.C., the economic growth rate would be less than 0.1 percent, just slightly higher than the growth rate for population. Today any money manager offering a real 0.1 percent or even a real 2 percent after-tax return on investment would soon be out of a job. (Real means corrected for inflation.)

The Medicis could not sustain a 5 percent compounded real return: To be fair, it would have been extraordinarily tough to achieve. It is remarkable that today, it no longer sounds so un-reasonable.

■ WHY WEALTH CREATION WAS NOT SUSTAINED

Over shorter bursts of time, real wealth creation must have reached levels of at least 5 percent or much higher; there is no other way to account for the glories of New Kingdom Egypt, second-century Rome, the Ming Dynasty, or the Italian Renaissance. The monuments and the works of art they left behind are clear indicators of significant wealth creation and impressive economic surpluses. None of these, however, were sustained; and the following sections, particularly in terms of the three primary influences built into our model—diminishing returns, risk, and innovation—will examine five possible causes for that.

1. Destruction of capital.
2. Diminishing returns.
3. Failure to understand value.
4. Poor management of risk.
5. Failure to innovate.

➤ The Wanton Destruction of Capital

It is tempting to reach for an easy answer to why wealth creation has not been sustained. Perhaps all that potential wealth was lost because of the devastation of war and other cataclysms, natural and social. In medieval symbolism, these were the four horsemen of the apocalypse: famine, plague, war, and death.

This easy answer seems less plausible now that we have witnessed the devastatation of war in some of the richest parts of the world, such as Germany and Japan, and have seen wealth rebound to new highs in a matter of a few decades. What is much more plausible is that the strategic capital of those countries, the ability of its businesspeople and engineers to develop and execute recovery plans, was only modestly diminished by war. The immediate destruction of physical capital was enormous, but most buildings and equipment destroyed by war had a useful life of only a few decades anyway. And the abundance of high-return investment opportunities in a rebuilding situation virtually assured that financial capital would be found. In addition, the victors, through the Marshall Plan and other aid programs, provided the seed capital needed to jump-start the process. Growth rates approaching or exceeding double digits were quickly established.

It is interesting to observe how poorly other economies that never had the strategic capital of Germany and Japan fared by comparison. There were no economic miracles in Ireland or Portugal, which had lost little in the way of either tangible or strategic capital during the war. Nor were there economic miracles in the Balkans, Latin America, the Indian subcontinent, or Africa.

Of course, war and revolution can decimate strategic capital. We have written about Genghis Khan. Another important example is the bitter religious conflict called the Thirty Years War, in which as much as half the population of Germany perished and from which recovery took almost a century. The enslavement of much of the Greek intelligentsia by the Romans, to serve as tutors and servants, ended the glorious tradition of the classical and Hellenistic civilizations and a promising beginning in the sciences. And the losses of human capital in the French Revolution, the Holocaust, and the purges of Stalin and Mao— basically the wholesale murder of the intellectual and business classes—represented deliberate attempts to destroy the human capital of perceived or potential enemies.

War and plunder can destroy enormous capital in a short period of time but cannot account for the dismal net economic growth of only 0.1 percent. Moreover, the resiliency of an economy appears to be more firmly rooted in its strategic/human capital than in its economic capital. We will focus on other causes.

➤ Losing the Battle Against Diminishing Returns

The second potential cause is failure to make significant headway against diminishing returns. In ancient Egypt, the land under cultivation was essentially the floodplain plus areas that could be effectively irrigated. But irrigation of desert land inevitably produced diminishing returns that were related to the distance from the source of water. When the point of diminishing returns with existing technology was reached, growth must necessarily have halted. In so far as we are concerned with Egypt's agricultural economy, it must remain forever true. Even with the Aswan dam, electrification, and improved agricultural technology, there are limits to what can be grown in Egypt and to the number of people who can be supported from the waters of the Nile.

Similar considerations must have applied to all agricultural economies—past and present. Farming marginal lands produces marginal returns. No value can be created by doing so. And if the risks are underestimated (see the chapter on risk management) and if adequate surplus food is not stored, periodic famine is a likely result. Under these conditions no economic growth can be expected.

Improvements in agricultural technology did occur, albeit slowly, over the course of history.[5] These advances had the effect of both improving yields on existing land and enabling cultivation on land that was previously marginal. Still, every gain soon runs up against a new barrier of diminishing returns.

The attempted exploitation of marginal land continues tragically today, where slash-and-burn farmers destroy tropical rain forests and natural habitat in Brazil, Borneo, and Africa, while creating little or no economic value.

The law of diminishing returns applies equally to natural resources. There has been a steady increase in the number of linear feet of oil well that have to be drilled to produce a million barrels of oil. As time passes, new reservoirs will in general be found, but mostly at greater depths and with smaller volumes. The rich gold beds have also largely been discovered and exploited: Today huge quantities of marginal ores must be processed chemically to meet demand. There will never be a shortage of gold, but absent technological change, gold's real price must inexorably rise as the ore concentrations drop at the margin and as extraction technologies mature. As always, innovative technologies have potential to offset such effects, which we will discuss later.

Commercial activities are governed by the same laws. In the absence of change, markets are subject to saturation. In conventional economics, the next customer is likely to be less profitable than the previous one because the value proposition to this next customer is not as strong. Selling a second car to a family whose breadwinner can walk or ride a train to work is harder than selling it to a family whose breadwinner is employed at a distant site not served by public transportation. The value proposition for the New York or Tokyo commuter is weaker than for the factory worker living in rural Michigan; it takes a lot more to convince the city dweller that she needs a car and an expensive parking place. For the carmaker, selling additional cars at a profit gets progressively more difficult as the best prospects are identified and their needs are satisfied. As the value proposition for the consumer weakens at the margin, the carmaker's return will drop inexorably to the cost of capital, and there can be no further value creation.

As business firms exhaust their opportunities for earning real profits, investment spending declines. And as growth rates decline, economic values diminish, wealth is destroyed, and recession or worse is in the air. Under the conditions of a closed system, diminishing returns are a perfectly plausible explanation for the failure to create wealth.

Peter Bernstein summarized the pathos of diminishing returns elegantly by quoting a song popular during the Great Depression, "Brother can you spare a dime? Once I built a building, now it's done. Once I built a railroad, made it run."[6]

➤ Failure to Understand Value

A third explanation for humanity's history of rotten economic performance may be failure to understand value. Modern economic theory has conclusively shown that value cannot be created when the returns of economic endeavor fail to exceed the cost of capital. This knowledge has been derived from efficient capital markets linked by rapid communications. Under these circumstances, the cost of capital is usually measurable, and economic anomalies are quickly identified and arbitraged. The rule applies equally to modern corporations and ancient kingdoms.

It is interesting to reflect that if mastery of these rules is difficult for businesses and investors equipped with thousands of accountants, mainframe computers, and mathematicians-for-hire, with the clarity of knowing that money is the goal, how difficult it is to run an organization, say an empire, where money is only one goal. For in the end, if an empire is not an economic success, it will fall as surely as if it were militarily weak.

This perspective was basically unavailable to our ancestors. It is tempting to speculate that many ancient leaders made huge policy mistakes as a result of not grasping the concept and that others succeeded brilliantly because their intuition or tradition incorporated it. But it would make no difference whether the laws of value creation were consciously understood: They would as surely apply to the kingdom's treasury as the laws of physics controlled the flight of the king's arrows.

Certainly, the Middle Ages were not a time famous for economic progress. The Christian church taught that the taking of interest for loans of money was income without true work and, therefore, sinful and prohibited. No allowance for the cost of capital there!

The age of exploration created enormous wealth—at first. Then, overexpansion of the empires into low-return investments began to create rot and devolution at home. Portugal and Spain began to devolve in the seventeenth century, although they unwisely clung to their empires much longer. Clearly, they found few opportunities for value-added investments during the intervening period before their colonies achieved independence.

The damage of value-destroying commitments may be hidden for years, if the damage is covered by high returns from other sources. The British Empire at its peak had many marginal colonies, but it also had some very profitable ones. In addition, the imperative of not ceding strategic military positions to competitors must have weighed heavily on British decision makers. But when it was clear after 1945 that returns from India could no longer match costs, the entire empire was essentially dissolved, and appropriately so.

The losers may then have been the countries least able to create value on their own—countries that derived more benefits from the infrastructure and governance of their colonial masters than they returned. Newly independent, developing countries are risky. Investments in them require high returns if the cost of capital is to be covered. Few projects in these countries meet the cost-of-capital test. Investors tend to focus on very high return activities, like the extraction of diamonds, gold, and oil, while ignoring opportunities in the local economy. This situation supplanted a healthier one where the credit of a Britain or a France stood behind the colony and created value if only by reducing the cost of capital.

The World Bank has attempted to rebalance this equation by providing lower cost capital, but it has been criticized for directing that capital to large low-return projects that are poorly integrated with the local economies: dams, airports, highways, and other large infrastructure investments. These centrally planned projects offered little flexibility and were poorly matched to the existing local economy. And the local economy often lacked the ability to generate capital for the anticipated high-value, follow-on investments.[7] In addition, the highest return opportunities in small, poor nations are often in small niches that only locals can identify. In effect, the World Bank may have squandered the advantages of cheaper capital by not tapping the power of market forces to improve returns. To be fair, such an option may never have been available to it, given the cultural and political conditions.

➤ Bungling Risk Management

The fourth source of poor economic performance may derive from failures, often based on ignorance, in the management of risk. It involves concepts equally as sophisticated and complex as the economic concept of value.

Bernstein begins his book on risk with the provocative question, "Why is the mastery of risk such a uniquely modern concept?" He views risk as the concept that defines the boundary between modern times and the past.[8] Prosperity, like risk management, is a new thing. So is it just a coincidence that wealth creation began about the time that the tools to manage risk began to take form?

It is an intriguing hypothesis, but it is clouded by the fact that many other types of progress accelerated at the same time. Nevertheless, a likely suspect for past economic stagnation might have been a general failure to manage risk. Clearly, there was no way prior to 1500, or likely prior to 1750, to develop scientific risk-management techniques. The mathematical tools were not there, the concept of probability was just evolving, and the notion of statistical sampling had not been developed. Risk management was still heavily tied into theology—pray for rain.

We know today that a premium must be earned on capital to account for risk—otherwise devolution is inevitable. Could early societies have recognized this fact intuitively? Did they know when to walk away from an investment, even if it earned a nominal profit?

The answer seems to be yes and no. The wealth of Venice, Antwerp, and Amsterdam developed through good business practices over a sustained period of time. None benefited from serious plunder, but all concentrated on operating profitable ventures, using colonial and military instruments as needed to support their enterprises. And although Venice and Amsterdam lost their global leadership, they never seriously devolved. Antwerp was a special case—its conquest by the Spanish in the sixteenth century (a risk) ended its prosperity, which in large measure was transferred north to Amsterdam by the migration of human capital. Thus, none of these successful cities managed their affairs with world conquest on their minds—they were looking for profitable business where they could find it.

But these cities are an exception. In fact, it seems that the periods of greatest prosperity in the past came when strong governments were able to reduce the risk premium—turning marginal investments into profitable ones. There seems no other way to account for the flowering of the New Kingdom of Egypt under Queen Hatshepsut and Thutmose III, and a second time under the Ramseses. There were no important innovations during those periods, and any booty from the successful wars in Palestine was likely meager in the scale of things. But these governments defended the borders effectively and imposed the rule of law.

Pax Romana represents a similar case. After the defeat of the Carthaginians, Roman fleets ruled the Mediterranean and piracy was suppressed, especially in the time of Augustus and again under Hadrian. It is always surprising that the large percentage of the impressive Roman monuments we see—whether in Italy, Asia Minor, France, Spain, or Palestine—bear inscriptions to one of these two emperors. As historian M. P. Charlesworth wrote: "Our own war-torn generation can appreciate what this solid Augustan peace meant. Occasional outbreaks there might be—a rising in Britain or Gaul—a vendetta in Spain or a chieftain giving trouble in Africa—but they were ripples on a placid surface. War had vanished from the experience of men."[9]

The U.S. naval historian Admiral Thomas Mahan makes a strong case for the concept that Roman domination of the Mediterranean world rested primarily on its naval strength.[10] Mahan was an advocate of naval power, of course, but his general argument that prosperity followed when the seas were cleared of marauders is plausible. The Roman peace, Roman roads, and the empire's administrative and legal systems provided an environment in which many of the risks of the ancient world became manageable.

Several other intervals of prosperity fit the same pattern: Greek prosperity after the Persian threat was overcome, the establishment of the Ming dynasty after the Mongols were overthrown, the Pax Britannica that followed the defeat of Napoleon, and the ability of the United States and its allies to maintain a reasonable degree of peace in the second half of the twentieth century may have had the same beneficial effect.

The downside of the cycle also seems to support the argument—the weak pharaohs that followed Ramses III proved unable to resist the sea peoples effectively, ending strong Egyptian government thereafter. The Greeks fell victim to internecine strife and bred the preconditions for Roman domination. Roman governments became increasingly corrupt and undisciplined and, in time, could no longer resist barbarians. After each of these happy periods, there was political fragmentation, and monument building ceased (indicating that economic surpluses were no longer

earned). Supporting historical accounts suggest that social devolution was severe. In other words, risk levels rose once again,
and capital could not earn a fair return.

Our current times are intriguing in this context. We continue
to enjoy the Pax Americana. Risk premiums associated with war
and plunder are low, and risk-management tools are being deployed on a global scale. Bright people are testing and refining
these tools in the aftermath of each new economic or political
event. And the information age is generating data in unprecedented quantities and making it available on a near instantaneous basis. If better risk management is a key to wealth creation, the best may be yet to come.

➤ Failure to Innovate

The fifth potential cause of economic stagnation is failure to
innovate. The innovation process, the subject of Chapter 12, is
even less completely understood than risk and value; when
viewed in economic terms, innovation is tied closely to the framing and the exercise of real options.

Rational economic behavior tends to force returns from activities of equal risk to a common level. Thus, business textbooks
prescribe that the responsible manager should "seize all investment opportunities that have a positive net present value."[11] To
put it more specifically, if a firm with a 12 percent cost of capital
perceives an opportunity to build a polystyrene plant that earns
a 13 percent return, it should build it. The presence of supply
from this new plant will reduce returns for all participants in the
market; however, few plants will be built if returns drop below
the cost of capital for the industry.

The reader must sense by now that I do not entirely share the
textbook prescription. However, it is agreed that when returns
drop to the cost of capital, no further value creation is possible—
absent innovation. This condition implies that investing for

"value" will not be sufficient to sustain long-term value creation; eventually, the investment opportunities will no longer be there.

When innovation occurs, the innovator is rewarded with bountiful returns. Soon, however, imitators and competitors emulate the innovation, the initial high returns cannot be sustained, and returns fall to a lower level. The economic fire and value creation fostered by innovation dies down, and stagnation or decline follows until or unless a new innovative cycle is begun. In the language of modern business, returns become commoditized in the absence of innovation.

Many of the innovations that gave rise to twentieth-century prosperity are technological. Technological advance is often a precondition of wealth, but it is not a guarantee. The realization of value does not proceed by invention alone. An organizational or business model must be created for the new technology, and it is within this entity that wealth is actually created. This condition explains why so many inventors fail to reap the benefits of their new technologies—others are more successful in incorporating them into business models.

Other innovations are not at heart technological, but they are powerful nonetheless. These include innovative military tactics (the Roman legion), new forms of religious organization (Islam), new financial vehicles (common stock, the credit card), and improved legal systems (the U.S. Constitution). Like technological innovations, these structural innovations must be embedded in a new organizational or business model if there is to be hope of success.

It is only when innovators recognized and exploited situations where rewards exceeded risk that progress occurred. Some, like the great religious and political innovators, defied the system. Others, such as Christopher Columbus and Thomas Edison, worked within it. Those who emigrated to America in earlier centuries saw so little to lose in their current misery that pioneering in the unknown was a rational option.

Why has innovation failed so frequently during 5,000 years of recorded history? The answer is surely a profound but misguided human instinct to avoid or to minimize risk. This instinct carries over not only into the economic sphere, but also to matters of law, religion, security, and many other sectors of life. Ironically, risk cannot be avoided—the uncertainty of weather is a threat to crops, disease is a threat to all families, and the world has always contained individuals whose antisocial behavior cannot be controlled. Yet social systems from ancient Egypt to medieval Europe to the modern Soviet Union discouraged economic or intellectual risk taking, thus delaying the onset of the very institutions and technologies that could mitigate many of the ancient forms of risk.

A visitor to Egypt cannot but be struck by the incredible resemblance of the structures and arts of its early antiquity to those of Cleopatra's time, almost 3,000 years later—a time frame slightly longer than that between classical Greece and modern New York. During this period Egypt was often a rich society, but after a flowering during the New Kingdom, it preserved little of its wealth.

Egypt has been described as an insular society. It was protected from the more dynamic societies of the Middle East and Europe by seas and deserts. And while the Nubian cultures to its south and the Libyans to the west occasionally threatened it, they mostly lacked the strategic and physical capital needed for effective domination. Egypt was also a rich land, offering fertile soils deriving from the Nile flood. Historians agree that it was not innovative and often turned inward to focus on the afterlife.

Egypt had ample opportunities for innovation. The country depended for wood and ore on Mediterranean lands, such as those in Lebanon and Cyprus. Indeed, under Thutmose III, Egypt extended her hegemony as far north as Northern Syria but chose not to rule directly outside the Nile Valley.

Commercial contact with the Mediterranean was continuous. Egyptians were fine sailors. Naval and merchant ships were abundant on the Nile during all of recorded history, and impressive ancient craft were buried in tombs. The fore-and-aft lateen rig developed in Egypt had outstanding sailing qualities and was a technological predecessor of the Portuguese caravel and the modern Marconi rig. So it is difficult to understand why Egyptians left the exploration and colonization of the Mediterranean to the Greeks and the Phoenicians. Egyptians also neglected opportunities to build roads to the Red Sea and the Indian Ocean and to open up sea routes to India and China.

Other forms of innovation were apparently simply rejected. Egyptian hieroglyphics were a dead end, and cuneiform tablets have been found in Egypt. Yet Egypt persisted with hieroglyphic writing long after phonetic systems became available. Egyptian arithmetic was also primitive compared to that of Mesopotamia, whose mathematicians were reputedly able to solve quadratic equations and calculate interest rates. Nevertheless, contact with better foreign technology did not drive innovation or even adoption.

There was a similar reaction to religious innovation. The violent response of the priests of Aton to the innovative monotheistic cult sponsored by the pharaoh Ikhnaton suggests the true power of tradition in Middle Kingdom Egypt. Clearly, the deliberate stifling of innovation by entrenched interests has a long and dishonorable history.

China exhibited many of the same negative characteristics as Egypt with regard to innovation. It was a somewhat younger civilization, with its origins in the second millennium B.C. rather than the third. But at the time of the Ch'in emperor, 220 B.C., it became a mighty power. Under talented leaders, it has regularly reestablished its power quickly—only to fall back into decline.

China was obviously capable of technical innovation: Witness the invention of paper, the discovery of gunpowder, and the impressive capabilities of its medieval navy. But China revered and perpetuated the old ways, whether in painting or agriculture. It regularly closed its borders to outsiders, and built and frequently rebuilt the Great Wall with that purpose in mind. Nineteenth-century Chinese look little different in paintings from their counterparts 2,000 years earlier. (Indeed, I visited the site of a Neolithic village at Banpo, near Xian, and found it remarkably similar to riverside villages I had observed along the Li River a few weeks earlier.) As in Egypt, a hieroglyphic language was perpetuated, which today has to be a tremendous impediment to intellectual productivity.

Mesopotamian civilization arose largely in parallel with that of Egypt and made great contributions by domesticating wild grasses into grain crops and by irrigating the Tigris-Euphrates watershed, a remarkable engineering achievement. Its impacts on mathematics, language, and engineering were enormous.

The Greeks, in contrast to these other great cultures, formed an intellectually curious society. They raised the technology of navigation to new standards and were the first to innovate at colonization. The Greek model for colonization is remarkably similar to Britain's approach to North America and Australia and very unlike the Spanish model, which relied on subjugating local peoples. The Greeks exported *human capital* to new locales. It was a brilliant strategy. Their more successful sites, such as Syracuse, rivaled the cities that had initiated colonization. In economic terms, they did not waste human capital trying to extract agricultural value from marginal land; instead, they moved the locus of population growth to sites where resources were in greater abundance. In this unprecedented way, they used innovation to gain a major advantage over the law of diminishing returns.

The Greek political structure, based on city-states, afforded some protection from the habitual intellectual paranoia of empires and fostered innovative thought. It would not be recapitulated until the Italian Renaissance when innovative cities were reborn. The Greeks pursued philosophy, mathematics, and natural science. Their spirit of inquisitiveness, dating to Thales of Miletus (circa 600 B.C.), represents the earliest beginnings of scientific inquiry. Greek science culminated in the works of Aristotle, which became the standard biology text for the next 2,000 years; the physics of Archimedes; and the mathematics of Pythagoras and Euclid. Translating science to technology was more problematical. Hero of Alexandria may have developed the first steam engine, but the engineering and material science of that day were not sufficient to transform it into a value-creating innovation.

The ascendancy of Rome was both a triumph and a disaster for innovation. The Romans admired Greek science but did little to perpetuate it. There are few records of Roman academies or centers of higher learning, and those few were largely tutored by Greeks. But the Romans were great engineers—adept at converting knowledge to economic value. To my mind, the greatest of their achievements was sanitation—the ability to deliver abundant potable water from distant hillsides to great cities like Rome and Pergamum by aqueducts and the ability to remove wastes with sewers. Sanitation has a negative effect on death rates and, hence, is an extremely positive force in increasing human capital.

Fast communications via road systems, the ability to free the Mediterranean Sea from pirates, and excellent city planning were other technological achievements of the Romans. But having translated the knowledge of the times to technology, Rome hadn't a clue about fostering the next steps in innovation.

The Middle Ages was a curious period. There is ample evidence of technological innovation, but the pursuit of science was virtually shut down. Indeed, an academic institution pursuing science was not seen in the West between the Alexandrian library and the Italian Renaissance. Here, the finger of blame may point toward the medieval Church, the most influential institution of the age, which was receptive to neither capital formation (lending was equated with the sin of usury) nor intellectual innovation.

Universities flourished during the late Middle Ages, but they focused on theology and the training of theologians. Natural philosophy (as science was first called) did not even appear until Renaissance times, and there was no link between university learning and the technological innovation taking place in the towns and villages. If there was a relationship, it was hostile. Roger Bacon's idea of experimentation, espoused in the thirteenth century, earned him several years in prison, thanks to the suspicions of Pope Clement IV. Several centuries later, Copernicus and Galileo likewise tasted the wrath of a Church that actively opposed scientific thoughts.

Yet despite the hostile intellectual climate, some of the technological innovations of the Middle Ages were significant. Progress was especially impressive in the development of mechanical devices that created nonanimal sources of power: notably windmills and waterwheels—nonexistent in Roman times. As many as a half million of these operated in Europe before the advent of steam! Water mills (although much improved) powered the industrial revolution that sprouted in Great Britain and North America through the first half of the nineteenth century!

Other technologies that developed impressively in the Middle Ages were metallurgy (witness elegant medieval armor), architecture (Gothic cathedrals and fortifications), agriculture (the yoke, the horseshoe, and the mole-board plow), sailing, and explosives. Most of these innovations, however, developed and diffused gradually and were examples of incremental innovation, often standing on the shoulders of Roman engineering or imitative adaptations of technologies transferred from the Arab world (where science had not died).

Thus, science was not linked to technology, and technology generally advanced by the taking of small risks. Advancements were often made by anonymous craftsmen, not intellectual thought leaders. It was only when the paradigm shifted in the Enlightenment that more radical innovations became feasible. Risks were larger, rewards were larger, and a faster rate of wealth creation finally ensued.

In general, the notion of creating economic value also appears to have been alien to the medieval mind. To the ecclesiastical powers, this world and the next were just as God had ordered them. It was not for mankind to tamper with it or to challenge the ancient authorities, such as Ptolemy and Galen, about how things actually worked.

The outlook of the secular powers was likewise static. For the ruling aristocrats, wealth was bound up with the land—which was fixed and finite. Thus, the only way to acquire greater personal wealth was to take it off someone else's plate through dynastic marriages, political intrigue, or, failing these, through warfare. The idea that new economic wealth could be created through enterprise was understood by few, notably the small class of merchants and traders whose pursuits took them beyond the reach of the medieval church and state.

■ CIVILIZATION'S MISSING ALGORITHM

This chapter has reviewed the remarkable difficulty that human societies have had building wealth over five millennia of recorded history—roughly from predynastic Egypt to the Enlightenment. Five potential causes for that failure were identified, but can these be integrated into a persuasive model? There is a starting point.

Civilization,[12] a game developed by Sid Meier, has been one of the most popular strategy games of the personal computer (PC) era. If you have not tried it, I recommend it, both for sheer entertainment and for the ability to explore its algorithms. The secret of any strategy game is to discover by a combination of experimentation and study of the game information what algorithms are built into the computer model and then to outplay the AI (artificial intelligence).

The human player begins with a tiny population and an empty world filled with resources. The objective is to build a great civilization by increasing wealth, knowledge, and territory. The computer establishes several of its own Gardens of Eden and builds competing civilizations in remote niches of the world. In time your civilization will interact with computer players.

This game is about value added. You have a value-creating machine in your population and the various economic structures you can build or buy, such as roads, farms, mines, factories, markets, and trade routes. Each requires an investment of labor, resources, or cash, while access to the appropriate intellectual property (technology) is a prerequisite. The best economic model tends to be situational. Some cities have locations that are better suited than others for agriculture, commerce, or manufacturing. It makes no sense to manufacture where there are few resources or to pursue commerce in the mountains.

In addition there are a complex series of costs for maintaining your economic structure and the necessary infrastructures for defense, government, religion, and entertainment. It is perfectly possible to overbuild and spend a city into devolution.

Intellectual capital is gained by research into new technologies. These tend to come predictably and are expensive to earn. However, they can also be stolen, traded, or discovered by chance. The technologies in turn enable more effective economic and military units.

While it can be played as a military game of conquest, the most effective strategies are economic. The plunder business is unprofitable when facing enemies of equal strength, but it gets better if you develop the military superiority and mobility characteristic of the nineteenth and twentieth centuries. But why bother? You can usually use cash to acquire your enemy's resources with far less value destruction than if you bombed them back to the Stone Age. The strategies of corporate raiders tend to win.

The game attempts to simulate how societies developed technology and infrastructure, and it is sufficiently balanced to make these things happen in a time scale that is reasonably close to historical experience. But to account for the remarkable prosperity of modern times, it is necessary to tamper with the clock. Game turns are every 20 years in 3000 B.C., and move from there through several intermediate steps to every year after 1850. This approximation tends to make events happen more or less in the calendar years in which they actually happened. As a player, you can do better or worse depending on your skill and strategies.

But there is an important problem that provides food for thought. The form of time adjustment is extreme, it is crude, and it is artificial; but it had to be imposed to match the milestones of history. Something far more important and powerful has happened in the real world that this complex value-added model does not capture. Progress has become much, much faster than its model predicts. Sure, the simulation is a game, but it is not a stupid one. There is even a provision to induce a population explosion.

The shortcoming must surely be related to the way strategic capital is underestimated in a value-added model that relies primarily on physical capital. The power of networks or of global communication may be the missing algorithm; and a practical solution to the conundrum might be to link progress exponentially to the size of the scientific and business establishments or perhaps even to world population. Not only would the answer to the missing algorithm give a more realistic model; but it also might tell us more about how our societies are evolving.

The missing algorithm may also have to do with risk. Risk is only a negative in this game, and there is not much incentive to take risk—getting overextended is a good way to lose. The main peril comes from enemy forces, who can badly hamper the player's economic performance by occupying the player's agricultural lands and forcing him or her to build walls and defensive units. True, the laws of chance are applied to military encounters and new discoveries. But a popular simulation of a truly volatile environment, with its enormous upside possibilities, is not yet here. This gap brings us to Chapter 9 and an examination of whether risk deserves its bad name.

Chapter

Does Risk Deserve Its Bad Name?

Risk has a bad name. Webster defines it as "hazard; peril; exposure to loss or injury." Early in my career as a research manager, a mentor advised me *never* to use the word in the boardroom. If a project was risky, he suggested the use of the term *long shot*. His advice was sound, for the word *risk* means different things to different people.

What is too often missed in the popular definition is that risk has a huge upside. This assertion is more easily understood when risk is identified with volatility, but the negative connotation is always there. We need to get over the negativity, because risk is absolutely essential to wealth creation. Risk is the flip side of opportunity. Or, as chief executive officer (CEO) Hank Paulson of Goldman Sachs puts it, "Volatility is our friend."

The goal of this chapter is to explore risk—a term that has different connotations for bankers, gamblers, research-and-development (R&D) leaders, and high-risk investors—and then link it to the tangible and strategic sides of wealth creation. Managing risk, a subject with a fascinating history and an intriguing future, is the subject of Chapter 10.

■ UNIQUE RISK AND MARKET RISK

From a valuation viewpoint, the most important thing about risk in business is that there are two kinds, and they can work in opposite directions. One type of risk is *unique* (sometimes called *private*[1] risk). It is risk that is unique to your particular situation and is partially subject to your control. Unique risks can usually be expressed in terms of probabilities. Examples of unique risk are the probability that our R&D project will fail, that we will drill a dry hole, or that the bank in which our savings are deposited will close its doors.

The other form of risk is *market* (or *systematic* risk), which is your exposure to volatility that you cannot control in your current situation. Examples of market risk are the probability that interest rates will increase, that the price of natural gas will rise, that electric power will be deregulated, or that health care will be partially nationalized. An electric utility would be concerned about the first three of these market risks, while a pharmaceutical firm would be concerned about the first and the fourth.

The distinction between these forms of risk is critical because unique risk and market risk affect stock prices in ways that are entirely different from the ways that they affect option prices. Existing operating enterprises will be governed by one set of economic rules, but plans are optionlike in their character and are affected by risk in a fundamentally different way. Sound decision making depends on understanding the difference.

Say you have three classes of assets: a house, a portfolio of bonds, and a portfolio of stocks. You view your biggest risks as the house burning down, interest rates rising, and a crash in the stock market. You can do a lot about the house burning down— install smoke alarms and sprinklers or buy insurance, which diversifies your risk among a pool of policyholders. Each of these is a way to manage unique risk.

However, your bond and stock portfolios are also subject to market risk. While the unique risks of individual securities can be minimized by diversifying, pooling your interest into a bond fund and a stock mutual fund with thousands of other investors would do little or nothing to eliminate your exposure to an interest-rate hike or a market meltdown.

One financial textbook defines unique risk as risk that is diversifiable and market risk as risk that is not diversifiable.[2]

In developing the arguments of this book we come to this important and nonobvious point many times, but it should be stated here. Efficient markets (such as the New York Stock Exchange) assign zero value to unique (diversifiable) risk, whereas exposure to market (undiversifiable) risk increases the cost of capital and thus reduces value. The reason is that stock investors have the opportunity to diversify unique risk; their exposure may be significant if they hold a single stock, but it becomes very manageable in a portfolio of 20 or more securities. For options investors, it is the reverse: Higher market risk increases value.

■ RISK AND VOLATILITY

Much of the literature of risk concerns risk in securities, which many experts measure as volatility. This proposition is debatable, principally because psychologists have shown that there are anomalies, including irrational decisions, in individual behavior regarding risk.[3] However, while the assumption is not perfect, it is good enough for the purposes of this book.

The evidence lies in the extreme difficulty of outperforming volatility-based algorithms (such as Black-Scholes) in valuing stocks and their derivatives. The reader can quickly verify[4] that the Black-Scholes formula, using historical volatility parameters, closely tracks actual option quotes. An investor can either buy or sell options. Options are a risk-management tool. Were the Black-Scholes numbers significantly wrong in either direction, there would be an opportunity for arbitrage, and easy money would be on the table. Of course, in light of the deployment by financial firms of sophisticated computer systems and financial models to detect and exploit pricing anomalies, it is clear that the quoted prices are already adjusted for any known anomalies. Because the differences from theoretical values are small, the case for tying risk to volatility is very strong.

The belief that risk is derived from volatility also lies behind the keen current interest in "value-at-risk" (VaR) methods for calculating the aggregate risk in a financial portfolio as a single number reported to senior managers and investors. One approach is closely tied to modern portfolio theory and expresses VaR as a multiple of the standard deviation of the portfolio's return,[5] a proxy for volatility.

The sources of volatility in securities are many. Investors react to new facts—interest-rate changes, the inflation index, earnings reports, and special industry metrics such as the book-to-bill ratio in personal computers. Professional investors continually reevaluate the probabilities of future events based on small tidbits of information. For example, a Federal Reserve Board (Fed) chairman's speech is scrutinized for nuances regarding interest-rate moves. Investors also change the criteria by which they react to facts—if value stocks have taken a beating, investors may flock to growth stocks, and vice-versa. A report of increased unemployment may be a downer in some markets but an upper in others.

However, investors make other adjustments in their portfolios for reasons unrelated to forecasts of the future. These reasons may be personal or institutional. They average out over time; but in the short run they move the market, and as such they are a source of volatility. Personal events, such as death, divorce, windfall bonuses, tax deadlines, or even a rumor heard at a cocktail party, can cause securities to be bought and sold. So may institutional factors such as guidelines regarding the number of securities in any particular category that may be held, a new report from a star analyst, a money manager's attempt to respond to pressures to improve his performance, or the decisions of the new money manager brought in to replace him.

■ RISK AND TIME

According to Peter Bernstein, "Risk and time are opposite sides of the same coin, for if there were no tomorrow there would be no risk. Time transforms risk, and the nature of risk is shaped by the time horizon: The future is the playing field. Time matters most when decisions are irreversible."[6] This quote states an important point in general terms, but it can be made quantitative. The Black-Scholes formula contains a specific risk parameter; that is, the level of risk in a four-month period is double the level in one month, and both are directly proportional to the volatility.

$$\text{Risk} = \text{Volatility} \times \text{SQRT(Time)}$$

This formula applies to security, currency, and commodity markets, where values change continually and appear to be *reversible*. The factors that propel changes repeat themselves, and movements tend to be self-correcting. They are rooted in the behavior of individual humans and human institutions. A stock can be bought today and sold tomorrow. No one knows whether the Nasdaq will be up or down tomorrow, but the odds on any day are very close to fifty-fifty. After the fact, the commentators will issue a raft of platitudes—the corporate earnings outlook, profit taking, anticipation of the Fed, triple-witching, and so forth. In brief, and although it is an oversimplification, market-based risk is strongly correlated with volatility, and volatility is strongly correlated with reversible factors.

Other risks are irreversible, and we shall see later that they must be evaluated differently. The distinction is particularly important with regard to real options because the manner in which time transforms risk is different. When the option is exercised or has expired, there is no going back. At that point, the strategic value of the option is converted to its economic value. Notable among irreversible risks are commitments and the discovery of what will in time become verifiable facts. But until the commitment is made or the facts are ascertained, judgment (and value!) can only be based on *informed probabilities*. Ascertaining the facts is also likely to cost money.

Here are four examples of high irreversible risks:

1. The probability of a new molecule showing desirable biological activity.
2. The probability that the Patent Office denies your application.
3. The probability that a competitor introduces a new product that outperforms yours.
4. The probability of finding oil under a promising geological formation.

And here are four examples of real, but lower, irreversible risks:

1. The probability that a new aircraft will fail federal noise standards.
2. The probability that a key supplier will suffer a catastrophic plant outage.
3. The probability that a new drug will have dangerous long-term side effects that were not uncovered in the clinical trials.
4. The probability that a key overseas market will be destroyed by political unrest.

These risks are all situational. Once the facts are established, they are established forever, or at least for a long time. And there is no serious question that experts will outperform nonexperts in evaluating and mitigating these types of risk. The situation is unlike one dominated by market risk, where the dartboard has a good chance of beating the pros.

In principle, all of these risks are diversifiable. Consider the high-risk examples first. Pharmaceutical companies diversify by testing thousands of new chemical entities. Patent risk can be mitigated by carefully structuring a host of increasingly narrow, but less aggressive, claims. Producers of consumer products know that a constant stream of new product innovations is needed to protect against competitive innovations. Oil executives form drilling syndicates to diversify their risks—a classical financial solution to unacceptable levels of unique risk.

The lower probability risks are also of great concern because the stakes involved may be high. For aircraft, engineers will attempt to mitigate the risk by incorporating large safety factors into the design and perhaps by including a "fallback" alternative. Diversification is generally possible via personal-injury, business-interruption, and foreign-expropriation insurance. Even so, the first line of defense is having the expertise not to get into a dangerous situation in the first place.

There is a big upside to all of these unique risks—the opportunity to outperform competitors based on superior information, established positions, and personal expertise.

■ THE OIL WELL CASE REVISITED

Let's revisit the risk-management aspects of the oil well case, for which we evaluated a real option in Chapter 5. Suppose that case concerns an independent oilman who is in the business of drilling for oil in the Permian basin of Texas and who proposes to drill in a promising formation. First, he faces several unique risks. The principal risk is that the hole will be dry or that the reservoir when found will be smaller than the geologists' most probable estimate. With regard to these risks, the decision maker is on his own. But he is not without resources. He can estimate the unique risk from the corporate database, government data, technical publications, or industry benchmarking to determine the odds of a dry hole and the probability distribution of reservoir size. The quality of these estimates will greatly affect his success as an independent driller. Obviously, the higher the probability of a dry hole, the lower the value of the venture.

Although he is on his own as regards this one hole, he could reduce his unique risk through diversification. If he thinks there is only a 25 percent chance of finding oil, he may have no appetite for this venture. But he can invest in dozens or in hundreds of exploratory wells by joining drilling syndicates. If he co-invests in 100 wells, which *on average* have a 25 percent chance of striking oil, it is a good bet that the syndicate will divide the profits from 20 to 30 successful trials. Many drilling syndicates exist for just this reason.

The second type of risk involved in this case is market risk. It is the risk that the oil price will be low or high at the time oil is produced. For an oilman, there is no way to avoid this risk. But he can *value* it (just as we did in Chapter 5, and found that this risk was actually an advantage when an option was involved).

■ IS THERE A PREMIUM FOR ASSUMING RISK?

Unique risk can be analyzed by estimating probabilities. Some situations give us abundant data to go on—the actuarial probability of a 55-year-old executive dying next year or the odds of a newly discovered molecule becoming a commercially successful drug can be estimated by experts. Other business risks are truly one of a kind. Who could have given odds on an invasion of Kuwait in 1991? Or who would give odds on an invasion of Taiwan in the next five years? A convenient way to manage *unique* risk is through the concept of an *expectation*, or expected value, which is the sum of the values of each possible outcome multiplied by the probability of that outcome. In complex situations, the possible outcomes may be organized in the form of a decision tree. Consider a lottery in which there is a 10 percent chance of winning a consolation prize of $50, a 1 percent chance of winning the grand prize of $1,000, and an 89 percent chance of winning nothing. The expected value of the ticket would be $(0.10 \times \$50) + (0.01 \times \$1000) + (0.89 \times \$0)$, or $5 + $10 + $0, or $15. This sum would represent the value of the lottery ticket to a risk-neutral purchaser. The same type of reasoning can apply to business cases, where each outcome is the net present value (NPV) of a business scenario to which a probability is assigned.

Of course, although a premium has been identified, a judgment still needs to be made. Some investors would gladly enter that lottery at $10 a ticket and would bet far more if they were able to diversify their risk by buying many such tickets. Others would reason, "Why waste $10 on a negligible chance of making $1,000? I have better uses for my money."

The expected value calculation also tells us that at $20 per ticket the proposition has no premium and is economically untenable and that the lottery is just a form of entertainment.

We have seen that market-based risk can be analyzed by well-known tools of corporate finance, such as the Black-Scholes formula or the binomial approximation. These advanced tools are based on probability theory. Their use depends on the availability of historical volatility data, which indeed are available for stock prices, commodity prices, currencies, and so forth. The formulas are not difficult to apply, even for the mathematically challenged. The underlying ideas are not just theoretical; they are reflected in the very real way in which stock markets and option markets price securities.

The stock market pays no premium for unique risk because investors themselves have the ability to diversify unique risk away. A single company producing ammonia may be harmed by a plant fire, but the impact of that fire may be negligible to an investor holding a diversified portfolio of ammonia producers.

For the obverse reason, the market assigns no special premium to a conglomerate that operates diverse businesses, say airlines and insurance. This economic fact of life is surprising to most, but it arises because an investor can achieve diversification by buying a diversified portfolio of companies in each of these businesses. And if the investor is inclined to doubt that a conglomerate CEO can do a good job of running an airline and selling insurance at the same time, she may impute lower value by applying a "holding company discount." Such investors seek excellence and focus in management and do the diversification themselves.

Conversely, the stock market does pay a premium to investors for market risk. The cost of equity and hence the weighted average cost of capital (WACC) demanded for volatile securities are higher than for more stable securities because their values are apt to decline more sharply in market dips than the value of the average stock will.[7] The company issuing stock would of course view any premium as a penalty. For the options holder, the situation is turned on its head: The more volatile the underlying security, the more valuable the option.

■ THE UNDERLYING NATURE OF TECHNICAL RISK

Because this book is about high-risk investing—with technological innovation at its core—we need to consider why the invention of new technology is an unusually high-risk enterprise. After all, science and engineering are governed by physical laws that are far more precise and absolute than the teachings of economics or the principles of human behavior. In a chapter on risk, it is rewarding to look at this question from both a philosophical and a practical point of view.

From the philosophic viewpoint, it is useful to remember

that in the early twentieth century, before the concept of industrial research was widely practiced,[8] a deterministic view of the universe prevailed. Atoms were thought to be like billiard balls. If we knew where each one was and in what direction and how fast it was going, we could predict where it would be in the future, even after myriad collisions with other atoms. The law of mechanics would determine each atom's future position and velocity. Of course the calculation would be tedious, but it seemed possible, especially with big computers in the offing. Other forms of physical behavior might be determined by the laws of electromagnetism, and so forth. The universe was a giant, very complex clockwork, but it was governed by relatively few laws and would progress to a future that was in principle knowable.

This worldview was shaken by the discovery in the 1920s of the Heisenberg uncertainly principle, which stated that the position and the velocity of a particle could never both be known precisely at the same point in time. Indeed, a probability distribution was really the only way to define a particle's position—physicists referred to that distribution as a quantum wave function. Ditto for velocity.

More recent outgrowths[9] of that perspective are *chaos theory* and *catastrophe theory*—if the action of any particle is somehow probabilistic, then its future effects on any or all the other particles in the universe is equally probabilistic, and at bottom unpredictable. Catastrophe theory has been popularized in the notion that minuscule events may even determine the outcome of large events: The flapping of a butterfly's wings in China may precipitate the sequence of events that leads to a hurricane in the Atlantic.

From a practical viewpoint, the issues are less romantic. It comes down to whether we can expect to use physical laws and mathematics to model the behavior of large and complex systems, such as the earth's weather or a chemical reaction. And virtually all physicists will tell you the same thing: in principle, no, and in practice, only sometimes.

Weather forecasters seek, and attain, greater accuracy by collecting data at more grid points, by applying larger computers to their forecasts, and by "refining" their models by repetitively checking how closely model-based predictions correspond to reality. Despite major flaws in the models, this effort seems to be productive, at least over time scales of a few days.

A model will accurately predict the behavior of many systems to the extent (1) that the physical laws governing a situation are known, (2) that the properties of each component of the system are known, and (3) that there is enough computing power around. These three conditions almost never apply in an absolute sense. For decades, physicists armed with the laws of mechanics, electromagnetism, and quantum mechanics and with access to enormous supercomputers have been attempting to model how just two molecules react with each other. The buzzword among scientists in this field is *ab initio*—from the beginning. So, can you use first principles alone to predict chemical reactions? Although some successes have been scored on straightforward systems, the practical answer is no. No engineer would go to a quantum mechanic to predict what the yield of a reaction might be at 100 degrees Celsius in a one-gallon reactor. He would ask a chemist for the answer.

The chemist might have a pretty good idea, based on experimental data from similar reactions in the "literature" or in her files. The literature is her database and is continually being augmented by new discoveries. The use of combinatorial chemistry and robotics is now rapidly expanding the data set. The skilled chemist would then use physical laws to extrapolate the literature data to the specific target. But the larger the extrapolation, the higher the risk. So in the end she may choose to run an experiment under the conditions the engineer specifies, or one sufficiently similar to make extrapolation safe.

Often, differences in conditions play a surprisingly large role in determining the answer: It may make a difference whether the reactor is lined with glass or steel, whether air is excluded or not, and how fast the mixture is stirred. Differences in conditions magnify technical risks, in much the way that foul weather can affect the odds of a football game. These differences are particularly difficult to model. The real world of chemistry is therefore much, much more complex than two molecules meeting in a vacuum. An *ab initio* model may give a clue as to direction of fruitful research, but it will be quickly discarded in favor of real-time experiments. The models soon run out of gas.

In the real world, early stage R&D more typically begins with a plausible hypothesis. A chemist may guess that running a reaction under certain conditions will produce a desired result. If the extrapolation from the closest data point is not very far, the chemist's risk is much less than if it is from afar. But the most creative ideas are apt to be in the *terra incognita*, and the extrapolation will entail high risk. (With the advent of laboratory robotics, the low cost is increasingly justifying such high risks.) Successful experiments will reduce that risk and point the way to further technical improvements, whereas unsuccessful experiments tend to invalidate the hypothesis. The situation is not unlike what Columbus presented to Isabella in Chapter 1.

So in the real world of R&D risk, the initial issue is too little data about the properties of all the components in a complex system. Paucity of data is often compounded by a lack of basic knowledge of the conditions that govern that system. Both problems apply to the Holy Grail of twenty-first-century R&D—a cure for cancer. Many of the components of the system, such as genes and proteins in the body, have yet to be identified; and the relationships that govern cellular biology—how each gene and protein *functions* in a complex system—are still mostly unknown. The amount of information required is enormous, so any effort to find a cancer cure through discovery research is very high risk. But billions of dollars per year are being spent on gaining the basic knowledge—for example, by sequencing the human genome, and from there linking genes to proteins and proteins to function—which will in time reduce uncertainty and improve the odds of success.

In the meantime, inspired hypotheses and successful experimentation have led to some selective successes in cancer therapy, and a few moderately effective products are in the marketplace.

One cannot resist the analogies between large-scale scientific modeling and large-scale models of the stock market. If anything, the financial modelers have more accurate data in their computers. Unfortunately, there is far less confidence in the financial algorithms (the "laws" that drive the system) than there is in scientific laws. And even more unfortunately for those who seek to predict their behavior, financial systems seem much more easily perturbed by external events than, say, weather systems. Practical weather forecasters can safely ignore Chinese butterflies.

■ FINANCIAL RISK

Compared to the risks of scientific discovery, financial risks seem mundane. A banker would be concerned about a risk of total loss that is worth 10 *basis points*, or 0.1 percent. The R&D director of a pharmaceutical company knows that the chances of commercial success for a new molecule are from 10,000 to 1 to 100,000 to 1. The probabilities of success implied by these risks of total loss are 99.9 percent versus as little as 0.0001 percent. Because the chances of loss are much lower in relative terms, there is a mismatch in vocabulary and in processes among those managing the risk. But the absolute values at risk for the bankers may be very large (for example, billions of dollars of U.S. investments in the Far East), whereas those for the R&D director are relatively small—perhaps writing off a $100,000 project. In brief, R&D managers address risks that are often a thousandfold greater than those addressed by the bankers; the latter in turn deal with investments that are often a thousandfold larger than R&D investments.

The financial community has identified and dealt with a host of transactional risks and has appropriated the term *risk management* to encompass its methods. This term is unfortunate because it masks the ability to turn risk to economic advantage.

Credit risk is the most obvious of the financial risks. Here, an organization or an individual lacks the assets to settle its debt obligations. There is also liquidity risk, exchange-rate risk, market risk, and completion risk. A customer may not have enough cash to pay his bills, or he will pay them in a currency that is worth less than anticipated. There are further risks that a third party to the transaction, such as a bank, may become insolvent. These situations are referred to as settlement or completion risks. The firm itself may be subject to substantial peril if interest rates, currencies, or commodities prices move against it. All of these are included among market risks.

Some of these risks can be managed (though not completely eliminated) through hedging. Others are insurable.

Financial people also worry about what they call *operational risks* (not to be confused with *operating risks*) that arise owing to deficiencies in business systems or controls. The Y2K (year 2000) problem was viewed as a serious potential operational risk, and failures in controls led to huge losses at Barings, Daiwa, and Sumitomo, among many others, during the 1990s.

■ OPERATING RISK

Nonfinancial or operating executives deal with a whole different set of risks with characteristics different from those just described. First, there are industrial accidents of varying severity. Among the worst are explosions and fires. Their consequences can be catastrophic not only if they involve one's plant and employees, but also if a customer's plant or a key supplier's plant is impaired. The latter situation is often called politely a *force majeure* and is a typical exclusion in supply contracts. The distribution system, too, can be disrupted, as occurred for freight shipments when the Union Pacific and Santa Fe railroads merged. In that case, perishable cargoes, such as liquefied industrial gases, literally evaporated on the sidings.

Of course some operating risks involve more than business disruption; they can create enormous injury and liability outside the borders of the enterprise. Chernobyl and Bhopal are synonyms for major industrial disasters.

The safety record of industrial operations is on the whole outstanding; but because there are so many industrial facilities, just as there are so many jets in the air, accidents are inevitable and occur at frequencies that are relatively predictable. In the long term, as in aviation, their frequency is diminishing. Catastrophic losses, whether from personal injury, property damage, or business interruption, are typically insurable in Western countries.

Insurance is the most obvious approach for diversifying unique risk, and it makes a great deal of sense for a company when the level of the risk has the potential to seriously disrupt the enterprise. Smaller risks can be self-insured.

A second set of operating risks attends to unexpected structural changes in the industry. A customer may be lost through no fault of the supplier. The customer may go bankrupt, disappear in a merger, suffer a serious market setback, be closed down by the regulators, or make a major business blunder. The "mad cow" disease, which reduced the consumption of British beef, is one example of this second type of operating risk that is typically uninsurable.

Such risks often seem to start small, say with a scientific report or a news article about a small incident or disgruntled individual, and grow gradually into matters of great importance. The scientific information needed for sound policy is typically lacking, and alarms often prove false. Such crises are inherently random and difficult to predict, though they look less random in hindsight.

The prudent manager typically insures or hedges some of the larger risks. She also builds a certain amount of adversity into her forecast, for example, by creating a reserve for bad debts or future environmental liabilities.

■ LEGAL RISK

Legal risk is an especially important case of unique risk in the United States, affecting companies of all sizes. First, a transaction on which one is relying may prove unenforceable in law. It may be a contract with a supplier, an insurance policy, or a regulation. Long-term supply contracts that seem to lock in a price may be difficult to enforce if the price moves significantly out of line with the market. The copyrights of publishers and musicians may be contested in the courts. Employment agreements can be challenged and often prove unenforceable in practice.

A second set of risks is exposure to lawsuits. There are many classes of suit that arise in the normal course of business. For the vast majority, the stakes are not material and are sometimes insurable. They arise from differences over contracts, auto and truck accidents, complaints against supervisors, and the like. Collectively, these are an element of risk and an ongoing cost of business, but usually not a major concern for investors.

Small companies are subject to suits from shareholders whenever the stock declines. Many of these shareholders (some owning only a few shares) are associated with law firms who seek to gain standing in a class action purportedly on behalf of all shareholders who have lost money. Their likely motivation is to obtain a percentage of the total proceeds of the action, whether it is settled or taken to court. Defendants may consider it a form of legal blackmail; investors should regard it as a cost of business.

Small technology companies are likely to be involved with suits over intellectual property from competitors and former employees.

Larger companies have all of the aforementioned risks but also face substantial risks from product liability actions. Their "deep pockets" attract the interest of torts lawyers who seek to represent sympathetic victims. Litigation over asbestos, tobacco, safety defects in vehicles, silicone breast implants, and intrauterine devices have created multibillion-dollar risks for U.S. corporations. In some cases, such as breast implants and asbestos property damage claims, the complaints eventually proved to have minimal scientific merit. Meanwhile, legal entrepreneurs are seeking to establish yet new classes of complaints, such as the allegation that electromagnetic fields from power lines induce cancer. Massive jury awards have propelled the magnitude of risks like these to the level at which they bankrupt companies and wipe out the savings of small investors.

Tort actions—personal injury and property damage—are also another negative consequence of industrial accidents. They sufficiently weakened Union Carbide after Bhopal that the company became vulnerable to dismemberment.

Finally, legal action by government—typically in the areas of environment, antitrust, fraud, and securities allegations—can create significant risks and costs. The *Exxon Valdez* oil spill and the abandoned nuclear power plant at Shoreham, New York, exemplify multibillion-dollar environmental risks. Over the past decades, industrial stalwarts, such as ATT, IBM, Archer-Daniels-Midland, and most recently Microsoft, have been severely impacted by monopoly or price-fixing allegations. Suppliers of health care services, such as Columbia Healthcare, face periodic accusations of billing fraud. The SEC (Securities and Exchange Commission) may seek fines or even criminal convictions when it believes accounting or disclosure guidelines have been violated.

In many cases, the plaintiffs or the government have good

cause for their complaints. Other situations seem driven by financial or political opportunism. Some torts practices come close to racketeering. In general, material legal risks are not at all rare for U.S. enterprises. They can be amplified by the U.S. system of punitive damages and are a serious, unpredictable cost of doing business and an important contributor to the cost of capital. In many cases, they have been fatal to individual companies and sometimes nearly fatal to an entire industry.

■ NOW FOR THE UPSIDES

Fortunately, there is an upside to all of the different classes of risk described in the preceding sections. First, if adversity does not occur at the forecasted level, performance beats the forecast. This statement does not imply that the forecast is bad; it only recognizes the impact of chance and volatility. Interest rates or customer losses from bankruptcies may move favorably or unfavorably due to changes of course in the economy.

Second, one person's loss is sometimes another person's gain. When beef exports from the United Kingdom to the Continent plummeted, local European beef and beef exports from Australia and Argentina filled the gap, and overseas packaging businesses benefited. And if you risk the loss of a big customer, so do your competitors. Their defectors become your valued new customers.

Third, catastrophes change overall market conditions. Major outages (which may take a plant off line for three to twelve months) are fairly common in the chemical industry, owing to accidents or mechanical failure. Indeed, disruptions seem to be more common when markets are tight because plant superintendents push hard for extra production and defer scheduled maintenance if it involves shutting down a line. The loss of 1 percent or 2 percent of an industry's capacity and the resultant scramble to seek new sources of supply can change the psychology of purchasers and sellers and result in upward movement in prices and profits.

Although upsides can be more quickly captured in terms of economic value, change can affect strategic values. Higher prices for fossil fuel, perhaps triggered by a political event, can only enhance the value of emerging technologies based on renewable resources, such as solar power.

The inescapable conclusion from these facts is that the existence of risk guarantees change, and change creates opportunity. This relationship is reflected in the Total Value Model (Figure 4.1), where risk influences both economic and strategic value.

■ RISK AND UTILITY

A good deal of economic theory assumes investors are *risk neutral*; that is, they seek to maximize their expected profits and are willing to take prudent risks to do so. This assumption makes the mathematics easier. The proposition of risk neutrality is also plausible if the investor views his or her value-at-risk as negligible, but this case is less interesting.

In reality, people are risk averse, owing to the utility curve for money. Risk aversion is highly individual and may be highly situational. It will be affected by age, wealth, experience, and culture. A high-earning 20-some-year-old may accept a financial risk that would terrify an octogenarian pensioner. The generation that grew up in the Great Depression has an outlook that is different from that of subsequent generations who did not experience a depression. A Tokyo businessman will fear bankruptcy much more than his counterpart in Palo Alto because Japanese culture views it as a severe form of disgrace.

That being said, most individuals express a preference for risk that reflects a downward sloping curve when utility is plotted against wealth; that is, each successive dollar earned is worth a little less than the previous one.

Think of a straightforward wager with a coin flip: double or nothing. Most people would entertain a trivial bet for a small sum with these odds, if only for its amusement value. But almost none would risk half of their life savings. What if we made the wager triple or nothing? Most of us would go the casino to make that bet for a series of small sums. But how many would bet half of their life savings? Some would and some would not. Indeed, we might advise the 20-year-old to consider it seriously, but it would be too risky for an octogenarian who depended on her savings.

For we are creatures of economics, and typically each successive use of money, or each successive purchase in a store, has a lower marginal utility. John is a suburban midlevel executive with a wife, teenage children, and good career prospects. If John needs a reliable car to get to work, his first car will be an essential purchase. He buys a car that mixes performance with style, perhaps a BMW. But it would be useful to have two cars, especially two with somewhat different characteristics. A Jeep with four-wheel drive would be great on snowy days and ski trips, and it hauls an impressive amount of furniture—perfect for taking the kids to college. But a third car has a worse cost/benefit equation, and a fourth vehicle in the yard would take on the character of a nuisance because John's garage has space for only three. You could say the utility of each successive vehicle is lower. And for John, this curve drops steeply.

Gerry has made hundreds of millions of dollars in cable television. He feels that collecting cars is a cool hobby, and he has an infatuation with Porsches that dates to his youth. He buys a top-of-the-line two-seater Porsche with a top speed near 200 miles per hour. Gerry's wife Susan says she needs her own car, and the Porsche is not it. So the second car (or maybe the first) is a Jaguar sedan. Gerry builds a 10-car garage at his Palm Desert home and starts shopping for antique Porsches, which he plans to upgrade to prime condition, display at shows, and occasionally use to ferry Susan and himself to dinner at the golf club. However, Gerry will not buy any old Porsche—he knows he can take only one or two to a show. So he wants those with the most élan and in the best condition, and occasionally trades one to make space in the garage for another.

Gerry's utility curve is not as steep as John's, but it trends downward, too.

In 1733, Daniel Bernoulli made the prescient hypothesis that the "utility resulting from any small increase in wealth will be inversely proportional to the quantity of goods previously possessed. . . . Considering the nature of man, it seems to me that the foregoing hypothesis is apt to be valid for many people to whom this sort of comparison can be applied."[10]

Our example measured goods in terms of vehicle units, but this proposition would seem to apply to money in general because money is a proxy for goods of whatever kind.

■ WHY THE RICH GET RICHER

If we accept the basic concept of a utility curve for money, it would appear to support the thesis that high-risk investing is the foundation of prosperity. Bernoulli's concept implies that as investors get richer, they will be more risk tolerant, at least for investments of a given size. In other words, as a population becomes wealthier, it can afford to be more interested in high-risk investments. Because risk and return are correlated, high-risk investments should earn more in the long run. Given many more rolls of the dice, the rich are more likely to accept these risks than those who are not rich and will earn higher average returns. So the rich will get richer. This principle should apply at the level of rich individuals, rich corporations, and rich nations. There is considerable evidence that it happens in fact. The converse is that wiping out concentrations of excess wealth may lower returns for society as a whole.

This hypothesis is politically uncomfortable because it bears directly on the central political issue of trading off policies that make the pie grow larger versus policies that divide the pie more equally.

■ RISK AND CHANGE

We have now talked about enough different forms of risk that the relationships between risk and change should be clearer. In psychological terms, the word *change* tends to have positive connotations, and the word *risk* of course has negative connotations. But they are much the same thing.

Some kinds of change are statistically predictable and hence manageable. People are born, work, retire, and die. Their activities—whether they are inventors or thieves—affect the lives of others. Their presence or absence creates myriad opportunities and threats, and adjusting to these changes creates both opportunities for gain and some dangers. In addition to the activities of individuals, new combinations of circumstance for gain or loss arise constantly owing to the activities of markets and institutions. Each day brings new prices for securities and new values for currencies and commodities. Other events blow through the global economy with some regularity: hurricanes, election surprises and coups, strikes, earthquakes, terrorist attacks, transportation accidents, and so forth. Conventional risk-management tools seek to minimize the hazards and perils; in a global economy with massive financial resources, a lot can be done and a lot *is* done.

An entirely different type of change relates to facts: scientific discoveries, new laws, and irreversible structural changes among institutions, from corporations to nations. New facts also make the world a different place—but in a very different sense than random events do. Penicillin increases life spans, the European Union (EU) changes commerce, cell phones and the Internet transform communication. Of course, new irreversible facts initiate chains of events that affect the kinds of reversible changes that are considered statistically manageable.

The rate at which facts change is predictable to a degree because many societies employ people for the sole purpose of facilitating change: research scientists, mergers-and-acquisition professionals, legislators, regulators, and diplomats.

Some politicians find it convenient to run on a slogan that they will change things. Others find it equally advantageous to vow to stop change in its tracks. But the bottom line is that risk goes hand in hand with change. Progress is achieved when risk is successfully managed to create value.

10

Taming the Risk Bogeyman

"Why is the mastery of risk such a uniquely modern concept?" asked Peter Bernstein.[1] The answer is that the theoretical tools are still being developed, and the data on which they must operate are being assembled at an unprecedented rate. Risk management is being called the most important issue in finance today. Hundreds of books and web sites are devoted to it. No wonder! We have been treated to an amazing string of megadebacles: Orange County, Barings, Sumitomo, Tiger Management, and, most dangerous of all, Long-Term Capital Management (LTCM), where the Federal Reserve itself intervened to avert the risk of a global financial meltdown. Quantifying risk exposure through techniques such as value-at-risk is not only a management tool, but also a regulatory requirement for banks and investment houses. What does all this activity tell us? For one thing, it tells us that, even in finance, risk management is not yet a mature subject.

But for all the controversy about them, the derivatives that are traded on financial or commodity exchanges around the world are only a form of economic capital. The huge risks asso-

ciated with strategic capital arguably comprise a more important and complex subject, whose systematic exploration has barely
begun! Real options have enormous potential for taming this
risk bogeyman. The time seems ripe.

For high-risk technological investors, where the odds of success may be less than 50 percent—and often much, much less
than 50 percent—financial risk-management vehicles such as
insurance are not an option. To manage these risks, our focus
must be on three advanced techniques: (1) technological hedging, (2) the option to abandon, and (3) portfolio diversification.

■ A LITTLE HISTORY

In *Against the Gods*, Bernstein makes an elegant case for why the
ancients had no conception of probability or statistics. He argues
that they simply didn't have the mathematical tools—in particular, they lacked an understanding of the concept of zero, negative numbers, and place value, as we use them in the Arabic
numbering system. Indeed, he asserts that the most famous of
ancient mathematicians, restricted as they were to Roman numerals or their local equivalent, would have had trouble sur-
passing a modern third grader in arithmetic calculations.

Of course, the more successful of the ancients must still have
had intuition about how to manage risk. The tale of Joseph and
the Pharaoh in the Book of Genesis immediately comes to mind.
Joseph's strategy was based on the flimsy fact of Pharaoh's dream
about fat and skinny cows and his own intuitive, but substantial, sense that it would be wise to build more inventory. And he
was right. But today, we would consider any such forecast (seven
years of plenty to be followed by seven years of famine) reckless
in the absence of better data.

The basic concepts of modern arithmetic are thought to have
been invented in India about A.D. 500. These ideas found their

way to Europe during the time of the Crusades, from the end of the eleventh century to the beginning of the thirteenth century, through contacts with Arabic civilizations. The first European coin with a date stamped in Arabic numerals was minted in Sicily in A.D. 1134. This date is virtually coincident with the first really modern economy, which appeared in Venice shortly after the Crusades.

Things began to happen subsequently as additional modern city economies appeared in Antwerp, Amsterdam, Paris, Genoa, and London.[2] The merchants of these cities developed complex trading networks, often discounting bills of exchange. They were exposed to both financial risks and physical risks, and it is plausible to argue that their prosperity derived from mastering high-risk investing.

The second important economic advance took place between about 1650 and 1760. This period was the eve of the Industrial Revolution, which created an explosion of prosperity in England, France, and North America while leaving other parts of the world as agricultural backwaters. Real rates of return were picking up.

The third revolution in thought about risk is still upon us. In 1952, Harry Markowitz developed modern *portfolio theory*,[3] which has been described as the only "free lunch" in the world of finance.[4] It created a quantitative method for reducing risk and thus increasing value through diversification. Portfolio theory is at the heart of many decision support models used by the financial community, from popular systems for rating the performance of mutual funds[5] to complex calculations of value-at-risk. Its power is now abetted by the availability of huge database services, computer-executed trading algorithms, and instant electronic communications.

The evaluation and management of financial risk is much more sophisticated than in the time of Gerald Loeb.[6] And returns seem to be going up.

■ THE MATHEMATICS OF RISK MANAGEMENT

Modern risk management depends absolutely on modern mathematics.[7] In its absence, the ancients were as handicapped as mariners without a compass.

The introduction of modern arithmetic allowed thought pioneers such as Cardano and later Galileo to develop the theory of combinations—essential for figuring the probability of outcomes when rolling dice or drawing cards. Here the modern concept of *probability* was born.

Though useful at the gaming table, probability theory was still not very useful for real world events. The theory of statistics was needed for that, and the first statistician might have been a Londoner, John Graunt, who studied the age distribution and the causes of death from bills of mortality in London parishes. The primitive database (i.e., the church records) from which Graunt derived his study was itself an innovation and was less than 60 years old at the time of Graunt's study, published in 1662. Databases would go on to become a powerful source of wealth and value, but that is another story. The astronomer and mathematician Edmund Halley extended Graunt's work into an analysis of life expectancies, creating in 1693 a scientific basis for the valuation of annuities. Still, it would take nearly another century for a modern life insurance business based on actuarial data to evolve.

From a mathematical viewpoint, the remaining big step was the discovery of the bell-shape curve. Abraham De Moivre in the 1730s, using the binomial theorem,[8] developed the concepts of the normal distribution and the standard deviation, the latter being a measure of the dispersion of the distribution about the mean. In Chapter 5, we relied on his formula, coded as NORMSDIST in the Excel spreadsheet program, to calculate Black-Scholes option values! And how did we calculate volatility? We used De Moivre's formula for the standard deviation.

■ INSURANCE

The first major risk management tool was *insurance*. The insurance industry had its origins in the ancient practice of *bottomry*, in which the owner of a ship borrowed money for equipping the vessel and, for a definite term, pledged the ship as security. If the ship was lost in the specified voyage or period, the lender (insurer) lost his money. Clearly, a rich lender had opportunities for diversification unavailable to the owner of a single ship. Bottomry is virtually extinct today, although the maritime insurance business (which lacks the lending aspect) that replaced it is alive and well. Bottomry was a remarkable development because the risk to the lenders could still be very significant in view of the massive potential losses from a single storm or pirate, whereas the ability to diversify these risks could be limited to the commercial fleet operating out of a single port. Interest rates must have reflected these risks.

The underwriting of accidental risk became an important business in 1771, when 79 underwriters pooled their activities and created the original Members of Lloyd's. They would appear to have intuitively understood the value of diversifying their risks.

Benjamin Franklin set up the first American insurance company in 1752, writing fire insurance. Since then, a massive global insurance industry has developed to handle a host of relatively small risks whose occurrence is statistically predictable: Health and dental insurance, life insurance, fire and flood insurance, and automobile collision and liability insurance are examples. These instruments are familiar because they work their way into most household budgets.

At the business level, insurance carriers have created vehicles that manage larger risks—catastrophe, business interruption, nationalization (political risk), product liability, and so on. Before its more recent troubles, Lloyd's of London developed a reputation for being willing to write a customized insurance policy on almost any form of risk.

Corporate risk managers regularly review whether these policies are cost-effective and decide where to draw the line between purchasing insurance coverage and relying on self-insurance. This analysis may result in buying an insurance policy with a significant deductible per occurrence or, if multiple occurrences seem possible, after some aggregate total has been exceeded. Typically, the line is drawn at a point where the potential loss would not materially affect the organization's financial position.

To the innovator, the potential for a product liability lawsuit may be the most important strategic consideration. It is good to have insurance in this area, but even so there is a risk that insurance coverage may be inadequate or that the carriers will aggressively attempt to deny the claims. Both of these problems have affected manufacturers of products containing asbestos. Certain businesses, such as construction materials, some automotive parts, private aircraft, and medical devices, have high inherent risks of attracting suits. In such businesses, careful analysis of the insurance policies (and the solvency of the carriers) is a necessity, because an innovative product with a defect may risk the company. Alternatively, if adequate insurance is available, the product must earn profit margins that fully cover the premiums.

If adequate insurance is not available, consideration should be given to exiting the business. For a number of years very few light aircraft for general aviation were produced in the United States because personal injury lawsuits based on alleged defects were filed routinely after crashes, even though pilot error was far more commonly the fault. DuPont will no longer sell plastic materials for use in implantable medical devices because of the risk of expensive lawsuits deriving from sales of tiny amounts of plastic. Dow Corning was forced into bankruptcy over similar issues related to breast implants, though the scientific evidence gathered subsequently would suggest the suits had little merit.

■ HEDGING

A second critical tool in risk management is hedging, which is greatly facilitated by the global banking system. In the commercial world, if one wishes to buy a fermentation plant from a Swiss supplier with 10 percent down and 90 percent due on delivery 12 months hence, one considers a currency hedge. If the price is quoted in U.S. dollars, the Swiss manufacturer may buy a forward option on dollars. If it is quoted in Swiss francs, the U.S. customer may buy a forward option on Swiss francs. In either case, for a small price, their business plans are not exposed to currency risk. When I joined W. R. Grace & Co. in 1982, I found just such a contract on a fermentation pilot plant in place. In fact, the dollar strengthened dramatically, so we bought the plant far more cheaply than expected, while being fully protected if the currency had moved in the opposite direction.

The bankers offering these hedges can reduce their risks substantially, for example, by finding a counterparty, perhaps a Swiss firm buying computers from a U.S. supplier in the same time frame. This activity is classic hedging. Note that the hedge is against *market risk*.

In the technological world, the risks are scarier. Who is to predict whether Internet content will enter the home in 2010 predominantly via the ubiquitous twisted pair of phone wires (which have proved with DSL [digital subscriber line] to be far more versatile than first estimates), by cable, by satellite, by microwave, by fiber optics, or over electrical power lines? An accurate forecast would be invaluable to the companies competing in this marketplace and to private investors evaluating telecommunications stocks. But as I write, the outcome of the battle of broadband technologies has not been determined and will yet be influenced by thousands of research-and-development (R&D) programs, investment decisions, regulatory decisions, and other factors that have yet to play out.

Some of those whose financial future is dependent on this outcome have the option of hedging their technological bet by developing knowledge and even products predicated on some or all of these outcomes. Their cash flow will in the short term be reduced owing to the need to finance a portfolio of projects from which there will be some sure losers; but they will have many more options to react if the result is not the same as their most probable forecast.

Some managers are willing to "bet the ranch" on their hunches, and their hunch may be that nothing much is about to change. False confidence is a risk, too, and to counter this risk, companies such as 3M have asked each of their businesses to proactively identify a *pacing project*—one that has the capability of changing the basis of competition—and to fund it. Not only does this policy create the option of reinventing the business to increase returns, but it also creates a mindset where the threat of a competitor doing so is identified and perhaps preempted. In 3M the policy is enforced through a regular three-year cycle of technology audits. In options terms, top management is encouraging (or ordering) division management to frame some real options; it perceives that total value will be created by the process. The presence or the absence of pacing projects, whether mandated or not, is a powerful indicator of the health of the creative process in an R&D organization.

Pacing projects are technological hedges. They come at a cost, but the options they create can be extremely valuable.

■ EXPLOITING THE OPTION TO ABANDON

The systematic use of the option to abandon is an important and relatively new tool in technological risk management. Its power derives from two facts: (1) that the risk of failure in a new project is typically high and (2) that costs rise rapidly as projects progress into advanced development. R&D managers for some time have classified their project portfolio in terms of early-stage (or early-phase), middle-stage, and late-stage projects, because these tend to require different types of resources. More recently, it is being recognized that such classification systems can create a database of costs and probabilities that enable a quantitative measure of risk in technology portfolios.[9]

Robert Cooper is an authority on new product development through his book *Winning at New Products*,[10] which is based on extensive research on new product development efforts in U.S. companies. He popularized what he named the "stage-gate" method. Stage-gates represented logical transitions in a research project, often involving a technology transfer between different teams of players. At each gate, a review takes place in which the management team decides whether to exercise its option to abandon the project or to move to the next stage.

There are no universal guidelines as to what constitutes a stage, but usually it involves a change of both the immediate objectives and the nature of the technical team. The definitions tend to be industry specific, and often company specific. For a pharmaceutical, the first (discovery) stage might be the synthesis of a new molecule and a preliminary screening in laboratory tests; the second (preclinical) stage might be screening in animal tests; the third stage (phase I clinicals) might be preliminary testing in humans; the fourth stage, detailed testing in a much larger human sample (phase II and phase III clinicals); and the fifth stage (new drug application—NDA), the final effort to gain the approval of the Food and Drug Administration (FDA).

Clearly, each stage is aimed at gaining information. Time mediates risk, and the risk in each stage should decrease progressively. At the same time, the costs of moving forward often increase enormously. A 1-in-10,000 chance is currently quoted as the odds that a newly discovered molecule will become a successful new drug. Exceptionally high odds! At the same time the cost of each successful new drug, fully loaded for an expected 9,999 failures, is, according to drug company claims, approaching $500 million. Yet the drug companies manage to be highly profitable.

It is worth thinking about how they do it, using round numbers. Consider a drug company that performs $1 billion of R&D per year. It has an expectation of turning out two successful new drugs per year and must synthesize 20,000 molecules to do it. Assume 10 percent of its research budget, or $100 million, is spent on synthesizing and testing new molecules. That works out to $5,000 per molecule.

Assume further that 50 percent of the R&D is spent during the fourth stage of research, phase II and III clinicals, and in other parallel R&D required to launch a drug. Also assume that one in two drugs reaching this stage is approved and commercialized. That works out as $125 million per molecule. So the final stage represents a situation where costs per molecule have escalated by a factor of 25,000, but the risks have also been lowered by a factor of 5,000. The process is an incredible achievement in risk management.

An enormous amount of intellectual and human capital is needed to effect this transformation. Organic chemists are likely to be using advanced techniques, such as molecular modeling of protein active sites, to tell them what kinds of molecules may be most promising. Or they may use combinatorial chemistry to synthesize vast numbers of similar compounds at a very low cost. The protocols used to screen for commercially interesting biological activity are crucial to making the right choices of which drug candidates to advance to preclinical testing. And a network of alliances with clinicians in hospitals across the country is a vital asset for launching human studies. In short, it is strategic capital—having the right skills, connections, and information at hand—that powers the research plan. Again high-risk investing links to great prosperity.

Note that the cast of characters changes rapidly, from one category of specialist to another. The research chemist who invented the drug cannot contribute much to the pharmacology studies in the animal labs. And the transition from the animal studies to human clinicals involves turning the major project elements over to the medical profession. A team of chemical engineers will be assembled to carry out the parallel task of producing adequate quantities of the drug, initially enough to support trials, and then enough to support a product launch. Regulatory specialists will oversee the entire process, with its massive paperwork requirements.

■ COOPER'S RULES FOR MANAGING DEVELOPMENT

Cooper has written strategically about the general process of staging R&D and has encapsulated it into some pithy wisdom, with which few experienced practitioners would argue. However, Cooper never links these rules with options theory, even though they keenly illustrate the value of the option to abandon. Shortly, we will show quantitatively, with options theory, why following these rules contributes enormously to value creation. And it is no coincidence that Merck, the leading pharmaceutical company, has pioneered the use of options theory[11] to manage its R&D portfolio.

Cooper's rules, somewhat paraphrased, are:

1. When the uncertainties are high, keep the investment at risk low.
2. When uncertainties decrease, the stakes can be increased.
3. Incrementalize decision making—break the process into a series of stages and decision points.
4. Be prepared to pay for information that can reduce risk.
5. Provide ample bailout points.

In essence, his advice means spending as much money for make-or-break information about unique, irreversible risks as can be obtained before major dollars are committed to more expensive activities, such as long-term animal tests and pilot plants.

So, a corollary to rule 4 is that intellectual activity should generally precede physical activity. It is usually cheaper and more effective. Obvious perhaps, but not all that obvious. I can recall an incident where the highly regarded president of one of W. R. Grace's operating divisions was encountering a serious technical crisis with a customer and asked the R&D chief to put a top scientist on the problem. The project was launched. About two weeks later, a loud complaint was heard that the scientist was still in the library and not a single experiment had been run! The boss's frustration was understandable, but the communication gap between the scientists and the operators about the value of information was difficult to bridge. For in this case, the cost and the time involved in running the wrong experiments would far outweigh the trivial expense of two weeks of literature analysis.

There is another important point about stages and gates. Any company that has consistently categorized its research into stages has created a database for estimating success rates from stage to stage. The database is itself an asset. It provides a statistical sample relevant to the enterprise, just as Edmund Halley developed mortality data relevant to scientific management of life insurance. We had just such a database[12] at Grace, and we shall see how it proved useful in projecting financial impacts of R&D investments.

We have several times noted that an enterprise controls its destiny when it comes to managing unique risk. For us, our unique knowledge of the mortality statistics of R&D projects was an important asset in managing the go/no-go decisions of the labs to maximize value creation.

■ SQUEEZING VALUE FROM THE OPTION TO ABANDON R&D PROJECTS

How much value can option theory add to an R&D portfolio? Or, put another way, how much opportunity is lost when options and the management flexibility they represent are not considered in decision making? The answer in both cases is "a great deal."

A fictional case, but one based on typical business and statistical data, was developed in *The Valuation of Technology*. It was labeled the "Polyarothene" case,[13] and the reader who is interested in how the numbers in the following paragraphs were derived is encouraged to look there. Yet the value added by exploiting real options is almost as spectacular as a Mark I microcomputer running at Internet speed.

In this case study, we used four research stages, although the odds of success were not nearly as steep as in the pharmaceutical example mentioned earlier. In fact, the odds of success were round-number approximations from a sample of about a hundred projects that the author and his colleagues had developed at W. R. Grace. Not a large sample in statistical terms, but a lot better than nothing, and directly applicable to Grace's circumstances.

We first assumed four two-year research stages with success rates of 1 in 3 (33 percent) between the first and second stages, 1 in 2 (50 percent) between the second and third stages, 3 in 4 (75 percent) between the third and fourth stages, and 5 in 6 (83 percent) between the fourth and fifth (final) stage—R&D and successful commercialization. The overall probability from concept stage to successful commercialization is 10.4 percent. The second key assumption based on an analysis of the R&D budget was that costs doubled in each successive stage. In a word, this research was undoubtedly high risk!

Let's first consider an unsophisticated approach to this project. It involves a commitment to invest $11.3 million over eight years for a 10.4 percent chance of gaining a revenue stream estimated to have a net present value (NPV) of $31.0 million. Sounds like a loser, doesn't it? In fact, it's not quite that bad because some of the large development expenditures are discounted by the same cost of money as the commercial reward, but it's still a loser by discounted cash flow (DCF) analysis to the tune of –$2.60 million.

This approach has been called the "rifle shot," because it assumes we go full-bore through the whole development process and only find out at the end whether we succeeded or failed. It is almost as insane as if Merck took the first molecule it synthesized and pushed it through phase III clinical tests. It is irrational because management needlessly gives away its flexibility as defined in the option to abandon. Unfortunately, kamikaze commitments by corporations are not unknown. All researchers have heard this piece of misguided advice: "Do the last experiment first!" I have seen more than one project in which commitment and executive hubris outweighed information, and death occurred at the point of market entry.

Next consider what happens if we exploit the opportunity to terminate, using the historical success rates cited earlier. The decision tree was presented in detail in *Valuation of Technology*.[14] The result was that the introduction of four abandonment options increased NPV from a negative –$2.60 million to a positive $1.67 million. Call this case the "decision tree." It implies a value of about $4.27 million for four options to abandon; that is, it is $4.27 million more valuable than the "rifle shot" case. This result is powerful. First of all, just as in the Mark I and oil well cases, we learned that what seems like a good decision based on economic value is a poor decision strategically. The NPV tool, shorn of options, gave us the wrong answer again. And equally important, we have found a quantitative tool for decision making in circumstances of high risk.

In fact, we can calculate that if we could increase the selectivity in stage 1 without affecting the overall odds of success, the increase in value would be even higher. This result argues for a bias *against* advancing projects.[15] In the end, an informed judgment must be made by the R&D chief and his or her advisers as to when too much selectivity is strangling potentially valuable ideas.

To be fair, this approach is based on an arguable premise, because it implicitly assumes the odds that a project will in the end succeed (here, 10.4 percent) are inherent and not affected by the resources committed to it. This assumption is certainly reasonable for some projects but less valid for others. Also, there may be hidden options to change strategy in light of future developments. This consideration implies a slight bias *for* advancing marginal projects.

The motion picture industry employs a process for creating new products that is strikingly similar to that used in industrial R&D. It seems however, that few movie moguls are consciously aware they are using abandonment options.[16] Script development takes an average of two years at a cost of $2 million per script. Ninety percent of the scripts are abandoned or sent back for rework. The 10 percent that reach the production stage consume an average investment of $51 million over 1.5 years, and 20 percent of these are abandoned. The remaining 80 percent proceed to box office release. But the game is not yet over.

A decision tree of high-, medium-, and low-value cases exists in the movie business with the division of the products into A, B, and C films. Movie studios monitor initial box office reaction, sort out the winners, and then decide whether to invest heavily in advertising and promoting the best of the crop. In this way, optionality is used explicitly to maximize profits. Returns from a few blockbuster hits are the fuel that enables the prosperity of this high-risk business.

What is this form of flexibility worth? Its value was in fact calculated for the Polyarothene case,[17] and it is substantial. We evaluated an "A-B-C" model with a 50 percent chance of achieving base-case assumptions on price and volume; a 25 percent chance for a more aggressive case, where volume would be twice as great and the gross margins 5 percent higher; and another 25 percent chance for a downside case, where the volume would be halved and the margins 5 percent lower. The real-world rationale was that an upside case might be enabled by strong patents and weaker-than-expected competition; and the opposite would be true for the downside case. This form of optionality creates an upside skew and yields an NPV of $2.59 million, or an additional 55 percent above the base case.

■ BUILDING IN MARKET RISK

We have yet to take into consideration market risk. Using a Black-Scholes model, a volatility of 50 percent (characteristic of DuPont and Dow stock today), and an overall chance of success of 10.4 percent, the value of the Polyarothene project is $3.57 million versus $1.67 million based on the decision tree alone. This result does not consider the option to abandon at each of four stages; it is based on a straight 10.4 percent unique risk. So it is the rifle shot, but it takes into account the volatility of the marketplace.[18]

This result is also interesting—because of market volatility alone, it might still pay to do this rifle shot project, just as it would pay to drill the exploratory well in Chapter 5. NPV gave the wrong answer for another reason!

Of course, we should take into account both kinds of risk. This requires us to work backward from the end result, using the probabilities of success cited in the previous section. First, value an option of entering stage 4 with an 83 percent chance of successful commercialization, using Black-Scholes. With this value in hand, go back a stage: Value the option of entering stage 3 with a 75 percent success rate and the reward (underlying security) being the value of the stage 4 option, discounted for the probability of success.

Do it twice more until you are back to the beginning of the process, stage 1. We have created a series of linked, nested, compound options. Although the detailed calculations are beyond the scope of this book, the result is interesting: $4.75 million.

In effect, we have now moderated the negative impacts associated with unique risk using multiple options to abandon and have taken full advantage of the positive values associated with market risk.

To summarize, without the option to abandon, the project has an NPV of –$2.60 million. With four options to abandon, which relate only to unique risk, it is worth $1.67 million. Adding market risk to the equation improves the value to $4.75 million. In relative terms, each step in risk management represents an enormous increment in value. Note also that these results depend critically on the systematic reduction of risk at each stage and the acceleration of costs from stage to stage. But that is how R&D should be managed.

■ A REAL OPTIONS APPROACH TO PROJECT CONTROL

Managements considering the adoption of real options methodology will inevitably look beyond using their use for project selection and will ask whether they are sufficiently robust for project control.

I now believe real options provide a wholly new and potentially improved approach to issues of project control. In project management, two primary control tools have been milestones and net present value. Let's review them briefly and show why an options approach provides a workable, and more flexible, alternative.

Milestones help control unique risk and are a characteristic control tool in R&D. Project managers set forth a schedule of times and costs (the milestones) by which certain achievements will be met. A typical technical milestone may be "R&D will demonstrate an 80 percent yield in a 30-gallon reactor for the proposed process by September 30."

Unfavorable variations from the milestones indicate that risks may be growing beyond planned levels and signal that a re-evaluation might be called for. If September rolls around and the yield has not exceeded 70 percent, management may suspect that the unique risks in the project are higher than estimated, the timeline is longer, the operating margins are lower, and the capital requirements are higher.

A missed milestone signals either a failure in execution or, more typically, an error in planning. It may be sufficient reason for management to abandon the project.

DCF/NPV, as calculated from a pro forma business plan, is the second traditional control tool. Using the milestones example, NPV can be used to recalculate the value of the project, assuming that 70 percent yield is the best that can be done. If NPV is negative, the project would be terminated. If NPV is reduced but still positive, the bad news from the laboratory may still not drive a no-go decision.

In addition to the technical issues in the milestone, DCF/NPV will incorporate commercial factors. For example, if during the course of the project, the industry sees price erosion, this unfavorable news can be factored into the economics, resulting in a decision to terminate or defer the project.

The *real options* equivalent would start with some of the same tools. The first step, as always, would be to update the business plan, for example, with the latest yield projections and pricing information, to estimate a target NPV, assuming a technically successful project. The target NPV would then be reduced by the probability of technical failure to give an expected NPV. This figure would be the value of the underlying security in a new Black-Scholes estimate of the option value.

If the calculated option value has now fallen below the premium—essentially the price of continuing the program—the time has come to bail out. This criterion replaces positive/negative NPV for the go/no-go decision.

What is different? For one thing, the options approach allows specifically for the possibility that prices will again improve as supply and demand balances in the industry adjust. Second, each of several alternative scenarios to handle the unique risks of this particular business situation could be evaluated. In the case mentioned earlier, one option might be to build the plant designing for a 70 percent yield; a second option might be to defer the plant six months while R&D tests a new approach to the 80 percent target; and a third option would be to kill the project.

■ RISK-WEIGHTED HURDLE RATES:
A DANGEROUS FALLACY

The reader who has persisted in slogging through the details of how options theory adds value to his or her investments should be rewarded by finding that those values are in fact rewardingly large. But the reader can also be rewarded by looking over his or her shoulder at the horrors of the alternative: the risk-weighted hurdle rate (RWHR).

Financial analysts, as we have seen, are comfortable with the idea of translating increasing risk into higher costs of money. That is what the weighted average cost of capital (WACC) is all about. Therefore, it is common for people to say that different discount rates should be assigned to different categories of investment. For example, one financial textbook cites these different discount rates:[19]

30 percent for speculative ventures,

20 percent for new products,

15 percent for expansion of existing business, and

10 percent for cost improvement of known technology.

These numbers appear to be based on managerial experience. There is an element of practical wisdom in this approach—demand high returns from your riskier projects—but two serious analytical errors lurk therein. First, even if industry experience has validated that 20 percent is an appropriate hurdle rate for screening a new product proposal, it is not reasonable to discount the entire project's costs or its rewards at 20 percent to establish *value*. As described earlier in this chapter, well-managed R&D is in part a process of risk reduction. If risks are not being reduced with each progressive R&D expenditure, the project is likely to be unsuccessful and probably should be terminated. During the project's life, monies will be spent in stages of progressively lower risk, starting with conceptual research (with risk of failure at 90 percent or higher) and ending in product launch (where the risks may be 15 percent or lower). And because development is much more expensive than laboratory research, most of the expenditure should occur at the less risky end!

Put these comments in the context of a new drug. In its early stages, this project is extremely risky. But when the NDA is approved, the risks have been reduced to a business-as-usual level for a drug company. Yet major investments in manufacturing, advertising, and promotion are still part of the project, and the analyst must choose a rate at which these are to be discounted.

Clearly, the correct discount rate for continuing investment in a successful product becomes the cost of capital. And the economic value added is determined by the return on invested capital (ROIC) minus the weighted average cost of capital (ROIC – WACC), not the difference above the risk-weighted hurdle rate (ROIC – RWHR)!

It is conceptually incorrect to apply a uniform risk-weighted discount rate to a situation where risk is changing, but that is just what the RWHR approach entails.

A second criticism can be leveled against this method. The

approach to risk is all wrong. The basic concept behind the capital asset pricing model (CAPM), that a higher cost of capital should be applied to more volatile securities, is an argument about market risk. We know that investors can diversify unique risk but cannot diversify market risk. We know market risk actually increases the value of an option. In effect, the RWHR method takes an idea from the arena of market risk and applies it to unique risk, *which has entirely different characteristics*.

The idea of evaluating project proposals using RWHRs is primitive and should be replaced by the methodologies of real options, which handle unique and market risks independently.

Worse, RWHRs are dangerous because they cause management to turn down any long-term project for which the calculated return is less than 25 percent or so. It usually requires extremely aggressive pricing and growth assumptions to get a 25 percent return on a long-term project. Yet, a retrospective look at business history most often shows that the largest and most profitable innovations had long gestation periods. It was fortunate they were somehow protected from naïve analysts wielding this crude form of DCF analysis.

■ DIVERSIFICATION IN THE R&D WORLD

Markowitz and his followers have demonstrated that investors can use diversification to eliminate unique risk. We have further learned that systematic risk cannot be diversified away and that this risk is directly proportional to the correlation of individual investments to the risk in the market as a whole. These conclusions are well understood by investment portfolio managers but far less well understood by those who manage R&D projects and portfolios.

In this section, we discuss the implications of diversification for an R&D portfolio. We will then look at why a broad portfolio of quality ideas, each of them individually risky, may have more value than a narrow portfolio of low-risk concepts. This line of thought leads directly to why R&D creativity should be more highly valued and encouraged than the reduction of R&D risk at *early* project stages.

Many experienced business managers will take exception to this position—*focus* is a shibboleth for business excellence—but I believe their position is derived from a misunderstanding of which options are and are not included in their strategic capital. Options that are inconsistent with the strategic intent of the corporation, or its core competencies, or that cannot be exercised because of its corporate culture are virtually worthless. The options may exist somewhere in the realm of dreams, but they are not "owned" by the business. As we showed in Chapter 5, one doesn't own an option until one has paid the necessary price. Becoming a dot-com is not an option for a steel company until it both invests with conviction in the necessary expertise and creates a culture capable of translating such intellectual capital into tangible capital. Until then an e-business project is just expensive window dressing.

It is a fair assumption that all financial investors wish to maximize return while minimizing risk, although they may have different profiles regarding how much risk they are willing to tolerate. This notion has led to a financial theory of *efficient portfolios*—portfolios that provide the highest expected return for a given amount of risk.[20] The theory of efficient portfolios is beyond the scope of this book, but the important conclusion is that such portfolios have standard deviations (or variability of return, a proxy for risk) that are substantially less than that of the average security in the portfolio, and sometimes less than *any* individual security in the portfolio. Standard deviation, representing unique risk, is minimized by (1) including many stocks in the portfolio and (2) selecting stocks whose correlations with each other are low.

Correlation factors can be determined statistically from historical stock price data, but they also correspond to informed intuition. The price history of General Motors and Ford will be highly correlated, whereas that of Duke Energy, Campbell Soup, and Microsoft would be less correlated. An efficient portfolio of 20 stocks would not likely include *both* General Motors and Ford.

The most obvious distinction between financial and technology portfolios is *liquidity*. Most financial assets can be bought and sold quickly and with very little transactional friction because they are traded in highly efficient markets. Given this liquidity, the investor can construct a portfolio virtually overnight, incorporating within it securities with whatever characteristics she seeks. Diversification can be achieved over different classes of assets, within industry groups, between industry groups, over geographic regions, or over other categories.

Diversified portfolios of technology assets are much more challenging to assemble and to liquidate than portfolios of either securities or businesses. Technologies exist for the most part in an organizational context. To obtain the full value, you must have *all* the relevant assets of the business in which they are embedded. This notion implies that the assets may often be most valuable in the company in which they are created. If that company were to be liquidated or the assets sold, the assets might be subject to a large liquidity discount.

Though it may be difficult to obtain through buying and selling, diversification in the R&D portfolio nevertheless helps us maximize value for a given level of risk. In fact, we'll get more value per increment of risk than if we remain undiversified. I have earlier noted that in the world of stocks and bonds, this diversification effect is known as "the investor's free lunch." A technology firm faces the same two types of risk that a stock investor faces: unique risk and market, or systematic, risk. Together, these represent the company's total risk. We have seen that unique risk is associated with the activities of an individual business and is reducible through diversification. For example, a computer company with one or two new product projects in its

R&D portfolio has a high level of unique risk. If either or both projects bomb, the company will be in a very bad position. It can reduce this risk by adding more projects to the portfolio, as long as those projects are not highly dependent on each other (thus correlated).

Market risk is the risk associated with the industry or technology category in which the company is immersed. This risk cannot be reduced through diversification as long as the company stays in the same "system." For example, no amount of diversification in its computer product portfolio will save our computer company if personal computer (PC) markets go into free fall or are displaced by a new and heretofore unknown technology, such as web-based computing. For a pharmaceutical company, its entire drug discovery portfolio may be subject to systematic risks relating to changes in health care reimbursement, regulatory trends at the FDA, changing demographics, global competition, and a host of factors large and small. These risks are largely undiversifiable within the context of being in the business.

Let's look at how one can diversify unique risk in a situation in which unique risk is very high. Assume drug companies all have similar productivity in drug discovery; that is, their hit rates in the discovery of new drugs are 9 ± 3 hits per 100,000 molecules synthesized, where "hit" means a drug sufficiently promising to enter clinical trials. Statistically, the standard deviations are known to vary as the inverse square root of the number of trials.

For a drug company synthesizing 100,000 molecules per year, the year-to-year variation in hits is 33.3 percent, a high level of risk. On the one hand, a small drug company, say one that synthesizes only 20,000 molecules per year, can expect only 1.8 hits per year; and it will have a standard deviation of ± 1.34, or 74.5 percent. At this rate, it is bound to experience quite a few "hitless" years, which may be an intolerable level of risk for its owners. Certainly, investors should think twice before investing in a tiny company capable of synthesizing only 1,000 compounds a year (at this level of productivity). On the other hand a large drug company synthesizing 400,000 molecules per year will experience a standard deviation of only 16.7 percent, in line with the standard deviation of a typical Standard & Poor's (S&P) 500 stock. In other words, its research output will be reasonably predictable.

In an industry where value is largely driven by drug discovery, diversification in part explains the forces driving drug company mergers. If two companies, each synthesizing 100,000 molecules per year, merge their R&D portfolios, their standard deviations of 33.3 percent would drop to 23.6 percent—an enormous risk reduction. This "mass effect" also supports the growing investments in combinatorial chemistry and high throughput experimentation (HTE), where robots synthesize enormous numbers of new molecules (each in tiny quantities) and other robots screen them for desirable biological properties.

Diversification is clearly an important value, but it is at odds with another R&D value: productivity. And R&D directors must find a happy balance between the two. Research directors have strong reasons for *linking* R&D programs, both because of synergies between them and because of the perceived value of focusing on core competencies. By linking, they leverage their intellectual capital. For example, a company that is good at synthesizing gene therapy drugs carried by viral vectors may focus on that specialty. It can produce more drug candidates at lower cost, and it will have better methods of evaluating and improving them. Its research productivity will be higher.

However, in so doing, it will be creating a portfolio of highly correlated projects. If the FDA raised general objections to viral vectors, the company would be in serious trouble. The focus strategy creates efficiency but increases exposure to unique risk. It is a matter of judgment whether focus or diversification is the better value-creating strategy. The financial tools we have developed in this book can help a manager make that judgment.

■ VENTURE CAPITAL AND DIVERSIFICATION

The behavior of venture capitalists (VCs) is interesting in regard to technology risk management and diversification, for many of the companies in which they invest are pure technology plays. Not only do the VCs seek diversified portfolios overall, but also they strongly prefer a diverse R&D portfolio *within a single company*—a one-product company is often shunned. However, VCs still are constrained to building relatively inefficient portfolios because start-up capital is concentrated in relatively few fields, such as biotechnology and software, and the performance of stocks within these groups is highly correlated.

We discussed the role of venture capital in creating value from business plans in Chapter 6. However, we are now focusing on how VCs augment their returns because their high-risk portfolios are diversified. We noted that the hypothetical VC's experience may indicate there is a one-in-ten chance of meeting or beating the plans of the founders, doing an initial public offering (IPO) and hitting a "home run." There are three chances in ten of a total failure, three chances in ten of a partial failure where the company is acquired and salvaged by a competitor, and three chances in ten that the company survives but produces average business results—a "single." The VC may create a portfolio of several dozen, or even several hundred, investments on this basis, depending on her financial resources.

To create further diversification, she may work with other VC firms whose business judgment she respects on a tacit understanding that "if you invest in some of my companies, I'll invest in yours." In effect, further diversification can be created by syndication. As long as overall quality is uniform, the larger the portfolio, the more predictable the results. If the expectation for home runs is 4, the standard deviation is the square root of 4, or 2, or 50 percent. If the expectation for home runs is 16, because the portfolio is four times as large, the standard deviation is 4, or 25 percent. By eliminating risk through greater diversification, the VC reduces her cost of capital.

However, she has other considerations that exactly parallel the concerns of an R&D director. Unlike the mutual fund investor, but like the R&D director, the VC is in a position to diversify both unique and market risk. This situation arises because companies whose stocks are not publicly traded are available to a limited universe of investors. Also, like the R&D director, her intellectual capability of determining quality is limited by her training and experience and by that of her associates. If she is based on Sand Hill Road in Palo Alto, she likely will have contacts with Internet start-ups and local biotechnology firms. But she may know little about natural resources, entertainment, or financial services. If she concentrates on Internet start-ups, she diversifies her unique risk, but her market risk is high. The values of these securities move up and down by and large as a pack. If she diversifies into natural resources, entertainment, and financial services, she surely reduces her market risk but may be misled by cleverer folks from Texas, Beverly Hills, or Manhattan.

So, she must make the judgment either to leverage her expertise and knowledge and expose herself to market risk, or to diversify across relatively uncorrelated markets and take bigger chances on the unique-risk side.

■ A VALUE PROPOSITION FOR EARLY-STAGE R&D

Having established the power of diversification in reducing portfolio risk, we now look at its power to create opportunity. For the sake of making the point, let's make these assumptions:

1. We have perfect knowledge of economic outcomes (we don't).

2. The returns on capital of a portfolio's early-stage projects will be distributed around a mean value.

The second assumption means that if all the projects were to be completed, there would be an average return. Most projects will cluster about that average return, but some will be total losers and some will be big winners. That average return may be at the cost of capital and very conceivably below it. This hypothesis would appear to be consistent with the experience of VCs cited earlier. Presumably, the partial successes and home runs earn the VC's cost of capital and more, but the others do not.

Let us further assume that we intend to terminate all projects that do not meet our hurdle rate and that we intend to invest in those projects that offer exceptional returns. (Here we are vulnerable to the presumption of perfect knowledge.) If so, simply having more projects overall means having more projects at the upper end of the curve and therefore a better portfolio of investment opportunities.

It follows that having enough conceptual projects in the portfolio to generate high return opportunities is a key to value creation. Keeping the projects relatively uncorrelated minimizes risk. Terminating them as early as possible frees up money to investigate the next generation of new ideas. Options analysis leads to the same conclusion—that a diversified portfolio of high-risk projects should outperform a focused portfolio of low-risk projects.

Of course, in the real world, we don't have perfect knowledge of outcomes—few experienced research managers are confident that they can pick the ultimate winners in a portfolio of early-stage projects. That is why it is wise to pay for critical information and to act on it. Winners emerge as projects progress. Furthermore, there is no assurance that an R&D organization will come up with *any* winners. That will depend on its quality and creativity and on the arena in which it attempts to innovate.

■ SUMMARY

The message for high-risk investors is that every piece of new information changes value. The underlying security is a business plan whose value drivers are revenue, cost, and capital. Because the plan is also an option, the elements of risk, time, and volatility affect its value. (Time, however, is defined not as time to project completion, but as time by which the option to enter the market will have disappeared.)

A successful experiment reduces unique risk and may reduce cost and the time line to marketplace entry. A disappointing experiment will do the opposite. It will likely affect the strike price (the initial investment) by increasing capital. Changes in the commercial marketplace affect selling prices and volumes and change the value of the underlying security. If major surprises are commonplace in the business, they may also affect the implied volatility of the marketplace and thus increase the value of the option.

Competitor developments may increase, or decrease, estimates of unique risk. They may also affect projections of market share and gross margin, which are built into the underlying security. A favorable patent development may even lock rivals out.

Lastly, changes in the financial marketplace affect discount rates and thus net present value. If the business has an international component, exchange rates will be built into the model.

In baseball, the score and situation can change every inning. So it is with high-risk ventures.

Chapter

11

The Enigma of Intellectual Capital

For high-risk investors the realization of wealth creation takes place in the domain of strategic capital. It is there that an executive departure or a patent setback can rock a stock. What would Celera Genomics be without Craig Venter, Microsoft without its copyrighted Windows operating systems, or Amgen without its erythropoietin patents? Even in old-economy industries, such as automobiles and clothing, the intangible element of design is what separates winners from losers. In all these cases, intellectual capital forms the timber from which real options are framed.

But intellectual capital is also an enigma, and its valuation has been problematic. Despite the obvious importance of intellectual capital in enterprise valuation, investors and managers have had few tools with which to appraise it. A recent Brookings task force report summarized the confusion in this area: "Companies have no coherent, consistent, or regular approaches to representing, managing, and valuing their intangibles. . . . Investment decisions in the area of intangibles seem more a matter of faith than fact."[1] This conclusion by a group of distinguished experts suggests that there is very fertile ground in thinking through the value proposition for intellectual capital in our society.

The enigma is largely resolvable when it is recognized that the value of intellectual property is *situational*. The value is dependent on the businesses or the business plans in which it is embedded. When a plan is involved, the value is strategic, and the real options solution provides the key to its valuation.

All intellectual and human capital originates, virtually by definition, with individuals. In some cases it is owned by them; in others it is sold or rented to others. And although parts of this chapter will deal with transactions that are very familiar, they appear in quite a new light when viewed through the lens of a Total Value Model.

■ THE INTELLECTUAL CAPITAL LANDSCAPE

Intellectual capital can be grouped into three general categories, each with its own characteristics:

1. *Education and experience.* Together with talent, these are the key components of human capital. They are typically summarized in an individual's resume, a document designed in part to establish an individual's value in the employment marketplace. But the value of individuals is not absolute: It is situational. That is why one is well advised to customize one's resume for the particular requirements of each prospective position.

2. *Traditional intellectual property.* Patents, copyrights, and trademarks comprise this domain and are protected by law. In many cases, their value can be appraised, for example, the copyright on an enduring piece of music or a famous movie generates a royalty stream of reasonably predictable value. The same is true of a patent on a commercial drug. Such well-

defined, income-producing properties are, in fact, equivalent to tangible capital; whether they show up on the books is a matter of accounting convention and/or a business decision. In what may be a new trend, large firms, including Dow Chemical,[2] are employing internal or external consultants to appraise and to manage their patent portfolios.[3]

3. *Unstructured intellectual capital.* These assets are much more amorphous than those in 1 or 2. Trade secrets, unpublished research and development (R&D), business processes and other forms of know-how, customer relationships, strategic alliances, and informational networks fall into this broad category. They may be governed by law, by custom, or by contract. Their value is more difficult to appraise, and the task of managing them is one of today's most perplexing and promising business issues.

In terms of the model in Figure 4.1, some of these assets will contribute to economic capital, while others contribute to strategic capital. Melding the latter to create new investment opportunities requires that they be embedded in plans.

■ EDUCATION

Let us begin with education. As with any asset, there is a difference between cost and value. The cost of education is reasonably well defined. Its value can vary tremendously.

Clearly, individuals in modern societies make an enormous investment in education. In the more-demanding medical specialties, the total training period is comparable to the expected working lifetime. In less-developed societies, the investment is to a lower level, but an investment is always made. In Western societies, the investment begins with the basic skills characteristic of primary education—reading, writing, and arithmetic. It moves to a higher level in secondary education, developing introductory knowledge of science and advanced mathematics, history, literature, and foreign language. At this point academic education may be curtailed in favor of practical training in a trade. A college education may confer a measure of specialization (which may bestow an economic advantage but starts to preclude other career options). Full professionalism is conferred in graduate schools and may be augmented by fellowship and residency programs.

There are two major costs involved: (1) out-of-pocket costs and (2) hidden costs. The out-of-pocket costs are paid from many pockets. Payment takes at least five forms: (1) a subsidy from the state (as in "free" public education and subsidized state universities), (2) charitable gifts (college scholarships, endowments, donated facilities), (3) a gift from parents (private school and college tuition), (4) direct cash payment from the individual ("working her way through college"), and (5) debt (student loans).

The hidden cost is the opportunity cost of foregone earnings. If the individual entered the labor force at age 16, after high school graduation, or after college, he would have more earning years than if he earned a master's degree in business administration before getting a job or if he became a doctor. Periodically, detailed studies of the labor market are made regarding whether the increased earnings that higher education confers over a working lifetime are sufficient to amortize its costs. This calculation will be situational, depending on the specific educational costs, the salaries for each occupation and profession, and the return on capital that one is seeking. But when this condition is met, the value of an education seems to be greater than its cost. Of course, this standard is based solely on personal income. There may be substantially more value to society than that. Hence, it is not unreasonable that education tends to be funded from both personal and societal sources and in quite different proportions depending on the profession. Using this criterion, society may pay the full freight for professional military officers and research scientists, but lawyers are on their own!

Personal decisions about education involve classic decision-and-risk considerations. The commitment to pursue, or not to pursue, a professional education is made many years before the student enters the profession. Aspects of the decision are irreversible. A student who chooses at age 16 not to pursue further mathematics or science cannot expect to become an engineer. A student who has not passed organic chemistry by his third year in college will not be admitted to medical school. In either of these career paths, full professional employment is 5 to 10 years ahead of the initial decision to invest. There is a serious risk that the employment prospects for engineers or the compensation paid to physicians will significantly deteriorate during the intervening period. There is also a "risk" that shortages will develop and conditions will improve. So market risk, in the form of volatility, is real. Unique risks, such as academic failure or physical injury, are also important. These cannot be diversified by the employee—only by the employer. The new graduate's investment in education is thus subject to nearly the same considerations as a capital investment in a shop or a factory!

The student also has some classic options. One is to terminate the educational process and perhaps recover some of her investment in a more promising profession. Thus, we hear of physics Ph.D.'s who are unable to get jobs on accelerators or as teaching faculty finding jobs that utilize their sophisticated mathematical skills to price derivatives for Wall Street firms. The option to abandon is alive and well.

Four other points regarding hidden costs are:

1. Subsidization of education by government may be economically viable, when one considers the additional lifetime tax revenues.[4]

2. From the viewpoint of an employer, each employee should add value above the cost of employing her. Therefore, in the long term, a professional employee must justify the salary premium she receives, which in turn reflects the investment in her professional education.

3. It is perfectly possible for an expensive education to create negative value for a society, particularly in a socialistic society. A bright and talented graduate may take a government job that confers dignity and status but makes no contribution to economic value formation.

4. The opportunity cost of education is by no means restricted to developed economies. In developing nations, young boys may work in the fields while young girls weave carpets or textiles, even when public schooling may be had. Their parents have decided the opportunity cost of education is too high.

From the standpoint of our Total Value Model, societal and personal investment in education flows into an economic organization via the hiring process. Education is not free, and the costs are recovered via both salaries by individuals and taxes by government. (The process is depicted in the connection to the "outside world" box of Figure 4.1.) The quality and the cost of that education will have a great deal of influence on the value-creating capabilities of the organization. In particular, the availability of high-level skills will create strategic capital.

■ EXPERIENCE

The value of experience can be found in the humblest situations. Until recent times, the Khoi-san of the Kalahari Desert in southwestern Africa were nomads who lived a hunting-and-gathering existence in a submarginal agricultural area. Their stock of physical capital was pitiably small. Formal education was unavailable, and life was challenging. If young men and women did not learn and absorb the details of terrain, weather, vegetation, and animal characteristics from their elders, their survival would be in jeopardy. But for generation after generation they did learn these things—at the first level of experience—and their way of life continued.

A second level of experience, beyond that of illiterate nomads or peasants, is developed through an apprenticeship system. Apprenticeship has been the traditional vehicle by which the crafts (carpentry, blacksmithing, glassblowing, etc.) are transmitted. The apprenticeship system reached its pinnacle in medieval guilds, which established and administered a progression of skill from apprentice to journeyman to master craftsman. Today the system is supplemented by formal education, but it is far from dead and takes different forms in different countries. Indeed, apprenticeship takes place at some of the highest levels of education: For example, a graduate student in science typically serves as an apprentice to a tenure-track professor who trains her in the basic skills of research in a chosen field. Further apprenticeship opportunities are available for postdoctoral fellows ("postdocs"). Physicians in internship and residency programs are basically apprentices. So are aspiring lawyers who begin their careers as clerks to judges. Such apprentices normally accept low wages for performing very sophisticated jobs in order to be able to claim the requisite experience to command higher salaries (and greater prestige) later.

The third level of experience is through lifetime development. The essential questions in many fields are "What can you do?" and "Who do you know?" Generally several years in a related lower-level job are a prerequisite for a higher-level job. And job levels in mature fields follow well-established hierarchies and pay scales. One usually has to be a car salesman to become a sales manager for a major dealership. One is required to fly thousands of hours in a small jet to qualify as a pilot for a large one. The premise is that the jobholder is developing intellectual capital as he learns—from peers, from supervisors, and from direct contact with the external environment—how to perform his occupation with increasing expertise. And he naturally expects to be paid commensurately with the experience he is adding to his resume. This process occurs within both the operations and the plans loops of Figure 4.1 and is an important source of value creation for the company (as long as the value of the skills learned exceeds the salary increases!).

In the New Economy, lifetime development may be foreshortened to the amount of time it requires to become proficient in a new skill—say HTML (hypertext markup language) programming. The individual will be paid the market rate for a good HTML programmer, regardless of the cost and the length of her previous education and experience. In effect, the cost of that part of her education that is no longer relevant to the job at hand is being written off.

At the fourth and highest level, experience becomes virtually unique. There are only a few individuals qualified to be a professor of inorganic chemistry at Harvard, a secretary of state, or for that matter a Hollywood leading lady or a quarterback for the Buffalo Bills. Most of the basically qualified people are well known to their peers, and their capabilities are classifiable into strengths and weaknesses. Unique skills are not interchangeable in the way one would expect of an airline pilot qualified on a 777 or a board-certified anesthesiologist. Any fourth-level-experience individual selected for a position will do the job differently from the way another individual would do it, and his or her performance will profoundly affect the outcome of the organization and the value of the products it brings to market. In some cases (the quarterback and the actress), this condition justifies very large differentials in rewards. There is much grumbling about the "undeserved" compensation of such individuals. However, value in these cases is very situational. For those organizations where such human capabilities drive value, the right price must be determined by competition in the marketplace.

■ REAL OPTIONS AND THE VALUE OF BUSINESS LEADERSHIP

Executive compensation is one of the controversial issues of our times. I believe an understanding of real options will enlighten the dialogue. In one sense, compensation has been driven by the marketplace: Most jobs in the U.S. economy have well-established salary pay ranges. There are consulting firms that make their living by gathering and compiling industry data on compensation practices and advising clients as to what they may need to pay to be competitive. Such ranges are published for all kinds of jobs—a legal secretary, a research scientist, a director of sales, a chief executive officer (CEO), a board member. The ranges tend to be industry-specific with scale and regional adjustments.

The trend in compensation for higher-level employees has been to align compensation with value creation. A bonus based on increased earnings is tied only to *economic value*. A stock option that appreciates with stock price is tied to *market value*. Market value reflects both economic value and perceived *strategic value*, as we have defined it in the Total Value Model. The wealth-creating potential of the strategic component was a principal motivator for the employees of the Internet start-ups and for executives in many other industries.

The ability to create strategic capital has a great deal to do with the ability to frame real options (i.e., to form business plans and strategies). These options can be as diverse as picking the right product (Michael Eisner at Disney), reorganizing for value (Lou Gerstner at IBM), focusing on market leadership (Jack Welch at GE), betting on the right research programs (Roy Vagelos at Merck), conceiving mergers and acquisitions (Bernie Ebbers at WorldCom or Steve Case at America Online), or recognizing investment potential (Warren Buffett at Berkshire Hathaway). These CEOs, for the time at least that they were on top of their game, played the strategic capital game with skill and were rewarded for it.

Those CEOs who were content only to shepherd the economic engines under their control but who destroyed or failed to build strategic capital did little for shareholders and little for themselves.[5] Others grasped some of the wrong strategic options (Roger Smith at GM acquiring Perot and EDS in 1984). From a shareholder viewpoint, it makes sense to pay the big bucks to those with the skills to make the right plans. Indeed, shareholders must ask, "What is the opportunity cost of having a placeholder or a fumbler, rather than a value creator, as the chief executive?"

Employees who are good at framing options—especially CEOs and R&D directors in technology-driven companies—have the opportunity to add large increments of market value. Thus, there is a growing trend to align compensation with gains in *market* value.

■ HUMAN AND INTELLECTUAL CAPITAL

Human and intellectual capital are only valuable when embedded in an enterprise. This point is seemingly obvious but needs to be repeated now because it has some less obvious ramifications.

If I am unemployed, my education and experience are doing me little economic good. But the day I show up on the job, I create a revenue stream for myself. If my employer chose wisely in hiring me, I will subsequently add value to the enterprise as well.

Indeed, the value of a human asset will depend enormously on the nature of the enterprise in which it is embedded. A great quarterback will be more valuable on a good team than on a mediocre one—if only because he will be given more time to throw and because his receivers are more likely to be open. Furthermore, if he is traded to a contender, he may take that team to the Super Bowl—he is more valuable on the contending team. From a value viewpoint, his present team should value not only his direct services, but also the option of trading him to a competitor, provided that is a realistic business option. In effect, he has no intrinsic value; his value to the Chargers is the difference in their value playing with and without him; his value to the Bills is likewise the difference with and without his services. If the first number is substantially larger than the second, the Chargers and the Bills have room for a deal that creates additional value for both teams. Of course, his value is zero to an organization that isn't into football, say a ballet company, which cannot use his talent at all.

Intellectual property is equally situational; a patent will be more valuable embedded in a firm with a position in the market than in a firm without such access.

When the value of an asset is sufficiently situational, there may be important opportunities to create value by framing options. Specifically, the asset, like the quarterback, may be less valuable in the enterprise in which it is currently embedded than in alternate uses.

■ DISTINGUISHING VALUE PROCESSES FROM TRANSFORMATIONAL PROCESSES

Employees in a growing firm may find themselves in one of two roles: (1) supporting the operating business and its value processes or (2) being focused on the transformational processes of value creation and value extraction on the strategic side of the enterprise. Many employees, especially at higher levels, have job definitions that encompass both roles!

At lower levels considerable tension can arise between the two groups—even to the point where each may regard the other as the enemy. R&D people may be viewed as expensive supernumeraries by operations people, who may resent having to disrupt established business processes with troublesome new inputs. Those charged with fostering innovation may view the operators as hopelessly resistant to change. Incentive systems can exacerbate the problem: Operating people are typically rewarded for reducing costs and will be resistant to incurring new costs on behalf of the innovators. They focus on economic value. The innovators can only demonstrate their value if their innovations are adopted. They focus on strategic value.

People with job titles involving R&D, central engineering, business development, commercial development, strategic planning, marketing, or market research are usually paid to facilitate the growth plans of the company, whether through internal development or acquisition, or both. They are there to conceive and to develop plans that will create additional growth or earn a superior return and then to proceed to execute those plans. In many companies, there is a sense of functional entitlement to such roles: "Our competitors have central engineering staffs, so we should, too!" A clear vision that their contribution is only made in the context of framing and implementing business plans would be salutary.

An acid test for distinguishing between these roles is whether an employee would expect to continue to be employed in the event of a leveraged buyout (LBO)—where the objective is to maximize short-term cash flow rather than opportunity creation. If the employee expects to be retained, his or her contribution is primarily economic; if not, it is likely strategic.

Of course, this built-in conflict comes to a head in the office of the CEO, who is increasingly rewarded for maximizing Total Value.

■ PRODUCTIVITY

The productivity of an individual is defined by his work output over a given period of time. If that output exceeds its full costs (including the cost of the capital employed), the activity is value creating. This relationship can be direct in the operating world.

Productivity gains in an automobile assembly plant may be reflected in a speedup of the line. These gains will not only lower unit labor costs but also reduce the fixed capital charges per vehicle produced. Each car will then be cheaper for at least those two reasons, and shareholders will benefit.

Note that such a productivity gain is not necessarily achieved by each worker working harder. It can occur through the identification of bottlenecks in the process, the addition of capital equipment, better training, elimination of wasted motion, and a host of other improvements.

Productivity is not only relevant to lower-level tasks; it is also applicable to the higher-level tasks that create strategic capital and extract value from it, for example, R&D. In *The Valuation of Technology* it was demonstrated in quantitative terms how the productivity of a research organization links directly to the company's rate of growth and, hence, its ability to create value.[6] In this model, the metric for productivity was defined as sales of new products per dollar of R&D investment (assuming new sales meet the company's profitability criterion or hurdle rate). Because R&D has a cost, there is actually a measurable point at which declining productivity begins to destroy value. This observation is just a special case of the law of diminishing returns. Calculating this point can allow an R&D manager, at least in principle, to recommend a value-maximizing research budget. It makes financial sense for a firm to pursue R&D projects in which anticipated new product sales from a dollar of R&D expenditure exceed the economic threshold and to reject all projects below that level. Because a more productive R&D organization can complete projects at a lower cost, it is able to address a greater number of value-adding opportunities.

■ CREATIVITY

Creativity, another major factor in value formation via innovation, is indispensable to building strategic capital because a creative idea is invariably the initial step in the innovation process. Most experts agree that creativity is a function of both *personal qualities* and *organizational culture*. Organizations that are dependent on creativity for success—be they in fields as different as advertising or invention—will address both factors to stimulate creativity. Their methods can range from reward systems for patents or suggestions to brainstorming sessions facilitated by well-paid consultants.

In terms of this book, *creativity* is congruent with *skill at framing options*.

Most of the useful creative ideas generated in an organization seem to come from a small minority of its members. In my personal observation, the most creative individuals are not necessarily the most articulate. Finding them is less a matter of observing their performance in the conference room than of listing the past innovations of the company and tracing good ideas to those who proposed them! To create strategic value, recruit people whose backgrounds indicate creativity, and nurture that trait during the course of their employment. High creative performance is correlated with talent at reaching out to others for information and ideas. Low creative performance is to be expected from those who seldom communicate beyond their own disciplinary group.

Environmental obstacles to creativity abound, and many organizations perform poorly in this dimension because they have not identified the cultural and sociological factors that depress creativity. Paramount among those factors is the receptivity of the organization to new thinking, which must first be actively encouraged and then embraced during its highly vulnerable gestation stage.

Some opposition to creativity is to be expected in an organization focused on operational excellence. Creativity is not essential to extracting economic value, whereas a lack of discipline and focus can interfere with efficiency. So it is hardly surprising that creative geniuses are not welcome on the plant floor.

Japanese companies and universities have had a notoriously difficult time fostering creative research (though there are exceptions). But it has been my experience that Japanese employees in a Western company are equally as creative as employees from any other group—and Japanese scientists working in U.S. universities have made discoveries, and even won Nobel prizes, for research that they probably could not have performed at home. In Japan, an industrial culture focused on operational excellence and quality may be coincidentally inhibiting creative behavior.

It is tempting to speculate that the recession in Japan, which has persisted stubbornly for a decade and has resulted in the Nikkei stock average losing about three-fourths of its value (during a period when the Dow tripled), is a result of creative failure. The postwar Japanese boom was almost singularly dependent on one idea: Copy advanced Western products, but bring to their manufacture a higher degree of operational excellence and discipline. The strategy worked brilliantly while Japan was in a catch-up position, but it provided nowhere to go when the opportunities were exhausted. Only creativity—the ability to frame new options—could do that. Growth rates based on revenue dropped far below history and expectation, and value plummeted accordingly. The conventional wisdom today is that Japan can recover when it jump-starts consumer spending. The hypothesis just described would put that prescription in doubt.

I have some issue with the notion that Japan will revive when its enormous load of bad private and public debt has been written down. The high values of Tokyo real estate, Japanese stock prices, and golf club memberships in the late 1980s and early 1990s were largely predicated on the value-creating capabilities of Japan's economic paradigm: efficient, high-quality manufacturing. Japanese executives had their brief turn as "masters of the universe," and it seemed to make eminent sense for them to congregate near each other in elegant office buildings and to relax on weekends in luxurious clubs. But as competitors whittled down Japan's advantage, growth rates slowed, margins eroded, and the economic values of Japanese enterprises were undermined. Not only were stock valuations vulnerable, but so were the derivative valuations of prime real estate, whether urban or recreational. The Maranouchi district of Tokyo was no longer the hot spot of global value creation, real estate prices inevitably dropped, and the banks that funded loans to both industrial firms and real estate magnates, based on a continuing upward economic projection, lost much of their capital when it turned out the ride was over. Writing down the loan losses is a necessary condition for recovery, but it is not sufficient for a full return to peak conditions. A new value-creating paradigm of comparable power needs to be established.

The United States has been a remarkably creative society for at least two centuries, but there are still many U.S. organizations whose performance on the creativity scale is very disappointing. U.S. management can be remarkably shortsighted, owing in part to the financial metrics it has chosen to adopt. The good news is that when ours becomes the first global economy to recognize that metrics such as net present value do not begin to capture Total Value, U.S. economic performance can be, and is likely to become, considerably better.

■ WHO OWNS HUMAN CAPITAL?

This question takes on considerable importance in our valuation approach because business plans are the vehicle by which the value of human capital is realized. To the degree that ownership is an issue, valuation will be uncertain.

The question is complex and is subject to vigorous dispute, especially when serious money is involved. It is useful to explore the fundamentals and to look at some common-sense examples. There are two complementary ways to look at the question: one from the point of view of an individual and the other from that of an organization, for example, a corporation.

In the areas of education and talent, it is clear that ownership resides within an individual. Slavery is dead. We begin by investing in our own education and in the development of our talents. That having been said, many of us soon *rent* these same talents out to employers and expect to receive a premium reflecting our qualifications. In return, those employers will almost certainly insist on an exclusive right to our services within the area in which they compete. They may also claim a first call on any other intellectual capital we happen to develop.

Consider chemist Jones, for example, who is hired by General Camera to perform research in photographic emulsions. He will be required to sign an employment agreement on joining the company. He will not be allowed to consult for a competitor in this field, even if he scrupulously respected General Camera's trade secrets. However, he might have the right to engage in other activities that could result in the creation of intellectual property. General Camera would probably not object to his selling tulip bulbs over the Internet because that is clearly outside its business field—although it might claim the right to do so under some of the more restrictive employment agreements. General Camera would probably agree to let Jones teach polymer chemistry at Central Community College because the activity would be viewed as noncommercial and a contribution to the community. Yet the rights to a valuable invention made under these circumstances could end up in dispute among the three parties (Jones, General, and Central) if the rights are not spelled out clearly in advance.

Of course, Jones can quit after giving reasonable notice and then attempt to rent his talents to a different employer. His leaving should not be a problem if the new employer is in a different field of business and if Jones respects his confidentiality agreements. It does become a problem, however, if his *experience* makes him far more valuable in his specialty (say, photographic emulsions) than in any general employment.

So who owns the chemist's experience? The answer seems to

be that it is jointly divided between the employee and the employer, with the employer keeping most of what is unique to its business. Such unique knowledge is considered a trade secret (as discussed later in this chapter), and the employer can attempt to enforce its rights to any secrets under the law. But insofar as the chemist learns valuable general skills on the job, he carries with him those skills and may advertise them on his resume. Examples of these skills might be operating certain types of scientific instruments, programming a computer, supervising technicians, and planning projects. These aspects of experience will likely be valued by future employers. In this sense Jones is increasing his personally owned human capital by working at General Camera. If he earns a major promotion, the fancier title may also increase his economic value correspondingly. But he may never have an opportunity to use his acquired experience in preparing photographic emulsions in subsequent employment.

So, in general, we have seen that employees "at will" (the large majority whom employers can fire after giving reasonable notice) own and can continue to rent their education, experience, and talent—with the significant exception of unique parts of our experience within a former employer's domain.

Although this condition is generally true, there are ways to lose these rights, especially via long-term agreements or contracts. A baseball player under contract is not an at-will employee. The team must pay, according to the contract, whether he plays or not; and he is not free to find another employer in the field of baseball. The player's human capital is owned—sometimes for the effective duration of the player's career. The only way out of his contractual commitments is to negotiate a mutually advantageous new agreement with the team.

A departing executive may sign a noncompete agreement in exchange for an enhanced severance package, which may well be envisioned as fair compensation for the lost premium she could otherwise earn by using her talents in her recent field of expertise. The employee has in effect *sold* that portion of her experience. In return the employer retains some of the value of that experience by ensuring that it is not made available to a competitor.

The other side of the issue can be seen from the organization's viewpoint. A large organization rents large amounts of human capital from its employees. The skills rented are very diverse— from such interchangeable skills as bookkeeping and truck driving (which lend themselves to union representation) to such unique and critical skills as pharmacology and deal making. The organization pays wages and benefits to its employees. To create value for the organization, these people must add value in excess of their cost. (For noncommercial organizations, value may be measured in other than financial terms, but the principle would still hold.) From this viewpoint, the common lament "I'm worth a lot more than they pay me" is entirely justified—if you were paid *more* than you were worth, your employment would be destroying value.

This equation is evident in baseball. Consider a star pitcher like Roger Clemens, a great pitcher for the Boston Red Sox whose late career took him to the Toronto Blue Jays and the New York Yankees. It is no longer unusual to trade or to release the star player of a team, likely the player with the highest salary. Clemens's performance continues to be great on any objective performance scale; but if the Red Sox could use the salary savings to put together an even more effective mix, they should.

The value proposition for employees is not always a linear one, for it is the interaction of human beings with each other and with the physical and intellectual assets of the firm that determines their ultimate value. Great teamwork is a great asset. Internal dissension destroys value.

Not all employees are simply rented. An important change is going on. Those with a major equity stake in the firm (as *in extremis* Bill Gates of Microsoft or option-laden corporate executives) are likely to view the value of their equity stake as far outweighing rental (salary) considerations. Such alignment of employee financial interest with shareholder interest has been growing rapidly in the United States, and it is being extended to progressively lower levels in the organization. It is a source of vitality in U.S. business that seems to give it an edge over more traditional compensation models used in Europe and the Far East, which are based on salary and attempt to foster loyalty through lifetime employment.

In a day when outsourcing is an increasingly important mode of business, there is also increasing recognition that not all of the rented brainpower is in employees of the firm. Accountants, lawyers, engineering firms, maintenance contractors, and a host of other service providers are part of the value equation. They too should be paid less than they are worth! In many cases employees of the service provider are virtual employees of the client, spending large portions of their careers on the problems of that single client. Like regular employees, they develop experience unique to the firm that increases their value in human capital terms beyond their general skills.

■ CLASSIC INTELLECTUAL PROPERTY

Classic intellectual property (IP) is comprised of patents, copyrights, and trademarks. These properties are sufficiently well defined that they are frequently bought, sold, or rented (licensed) in the marketplace. Their legal status is established, and their importance to value creation is enormous.

IP also includes industry trade secrets, such as the Marlboro recipe or the legendary Coca-Cola formula, which is said to be stored in a vault in Atlanta, Georgia. IP also embraces many other classes of business secrets, such as customer lists and laboratory data. The definition and the legal status of secrets is murkier, and we shall deal with this form of intellectual property in a subsequent section.

➤ Patents

In the world of high-risk investing, there can be nothing quite as exciting as the prospect of getting a patent or quite as depressing as the likelihood of losing its protection. The reason is that patents are licensed monopolies and fantastic value drivers. The best patents are valued at hundreds of millions, if not billions, of dollars. They propel prices and gross margins upward. One of the world's most successful industries—pharmaceuticals—is absolutely dependent on them.

The prospect of patenting business models as embedded in software was upheld in a recent court decision,[7] *State Street v. Signature Financial* (1996), and added significant value to some Internet stocks. As a result of *State Street*, several high-profile patents were asserted, notably those of Priceline.com and Amazon.com (versus Barnes & Noble). The area is destined to be controversial for some time as the U.S. Congress, the courts, the Patent Office, and myriad businesses struggle to deal with the implications. Very interesting, and risky, opportunities for value creation have opened up as a result of that one case.

Patent systems are, in fact, an established, effective, and proven method of risk reduction and have fostered significant investments in both intellectual and physical capital. They represent a tacit understanding made between inventors and society. Society provides inventors with a monopoly for about 20 years (in the United States) in return for donating the information to the public at the end of that period. That expiration date is highly significant: It marks the point at which an ethical drug becomes a generic drug and its price falls like a stone. It is clear that without the patent system—and the ability to keep generic competitors out of the market—the costs of drug discovery could never be recouped, and the multibillion dollar research budgets of "big pharma" could never be justified. The ability to receive and to enforce a patent is itself subject to the many risks discussed later in this section, but the very possibility of eliminating a large component of competitive risk makes innovation in pharmaceuticals an attractive business strategy.

Patents themselves are highly technical and generally dull reading. They are written by lawyers for an audience of patent examiners and patent attorneys. Claims can be voluminous and seem repetitious. There are millions of patents, and any one can take hours to read and comprehend. The vast majority are of no commercial value. And the most useful technology is often deliberately obscured because the patent holder has no desire to reveal practical details that might benefit competitors.

In a nutshell, a U.S. patent allows its owner to prohibit others from making, using, selling, offering for sale, or importing the subject invention into the United States for a period of up to 20 years from the date of filing the application. (Patents issued prior to mid-1995 expire 17 years from the date of issuance.) The invention must be novel, useful, and nonobvious. It is typical for subjects of invention to be functional items, functional methods, functional compositions, or functional designs.

The heart of a patent is its list of claims. If you are a patent holder and another company practices technology within your allowed claims, you have a negotiating position. You can demand that the competitor desist, or you can permit it to continue if it pays a satisfactory royalty for the privilege. Your claims do not, however, give you an unconditional right to *practice* your own patented technology—you must also be free of everyone else's patents.

The patent value chain has three key elements:

1. Writing the patent.
2. Obtaining and maintaining the patent.
3. Enforcing patent rights.

All are important, and all involve different processes and different people.

The initial step in the patent process is the basic invention itself. The invention must be documented, preferably in a signed, sealed, and witnessed bound laboratory notebook. The first step for an inventor seeking to patent an invention is to prepare a patent "disclosure"—a document that enables a patent attorney or agent to write a patent application.

The patent attorney must deal with both intellectual property and business issues. He knows that his patent application must meet the criteria of being (1) novel, (2) nonobvious, and (3) useful. Demonstrating novelty means finding and citing all relevant "prior art" (a term encompassing patents and publications related to the invention) and then distinguishing the invention from that prior art. (Missing some of the prior art can cause problems down the road in obtaining and enforcing the patent.) "Obviousness" can be a tricky issue—it can be argued that any combination of existing technologies is obvious to "one skilled in the art"—therefore it is important to show that something unexpected was discovered. "Useful" means that the invention may have commercial value—the solution of a mathematical problem is of no relevance to the real world; thus a brilliant proof of Fermat's last theorem is, by itself, not patentable.

The best patent attorneys specialize in relatively narrow fields. They know not only the patent literature (or "prior art") but also the thinking of the (equally specialized) patent examiners in the field. As such they can do a superior job of structuring the claims and maximizing the chances that a patent will eventually be granted.

The patent writing step is a game of disclosure and concealment for the patent attorney. Obtaining the patent usually creates value for the company; however, the disclosures required to obtain the patent may aid competitors. Thus, the patent attorney must balance business issues against technical issues in gaining the claims. He may not wish to disclose to potential competitors the most valuable known use of the invention when the patent is published. And he certainly won't provide a roadmap for making the patented material that others can follow. Let competitors learn at their own expense—he merely wants an allowed claim that happens to *include* the most valuable cases. Patents typically contain a section of examples meant to illustrate the usefulness of the invention, but the actual examples given may be decoys.

The inventor and the patent attorney have two other key tasks to perform to ensure that value is maximized. First, they must broaden the claims as much as possible, both to increase economic value and to make it as difficult as possible for ingenious competitors to invent around the patented position. Second, they will "teach" downstream applications to make it more difficult for competitors to show nonobviousness if they attempt to patent such applications.

Care must be taken that publications by the inventors themselves do not undermine the patenting process. This problem is serious because publications are the coin of the realm for scientists. They are the basis for advancement for academic scientists and an absolute requirement for graduate students seeking Ph.D. degrees. Even for industrial scientists, publications are a means of gaining and maintaining status in the field. So scientists are eager and motivated to publish. (Giving a talk at a scientific meeting is equivalent to publishing for this purpose.) Unfortunately, publication preceding a patent filing may invalidate that patent by creating its own prior art and denying the condition of novelty. The rules and the timing differ in different countries, but the principle is universal. So businesspeople usually argue against publishing any material for which a patent has yet to be filed.

Although this issue is nontrivial, it can usually be successfully negotiated. Industrial scientists don't have much choice but to play by company rules. Most research contracts between industry and universities have a section dealing with the problem. Even so, very valuable technologies, such as the basic claims on hybrid monoclonal antibodies, were "donated to the public" because the inventors published the technology (in 1975) before filing for patents. This event had significant international trade significance—the invention was British (César Milstein and Geörges Kohler), but U.S. firms primarily exploited the myriad real options created by it.

The second step in the patent value chain is to actually obtain the patent. In its straightforward form, this step involves a negotiation between the patent examiner of a national patent office and the patent attorneys who represent the owner of the patent application. Few patent filings are simply accepted. The examiner usually rejects or strives to narrow the applicant's claims. It is his or her job not to grant broader claims than the inventor deserves. When very broad claims are granted, as for example for Cetus's PCR patent mentioned near the end of Chapter 2, considerable controversy can ensue. In any case, the inventor's attorneys attempt to counter the examiner's arguments until a final decision is reached.

Patent applications may result in multiparty proceedings. In the United States, a patent examiner may declare an "interference" if he or she believes that two patent applications have overlapping claims. The judgment is made in part by the earlier date of filing, but there are other criteria. Each of the parties may present evidence to support its priority. Outside the United States, patent applications are often published before the patent is issued, and in some countries anyone may argue against the issuance of that patent in a process known as an "opposition." Large local competitors routinely oppose patent applications in their fields of interest, and defeating a German or a Japanese industrial giant on its home turf can be a formidable task.

There are, of course, costs associated with obtaining and maintaining patents. National patent offices charge fees, usually several thousand dollars per application, to cover their costs. They may also charge additional fees for maintaining the patent, and these often escalate as the patent gets older. These costs represent incentives for inventors to drop valueless patents. The second major cost is the patent attorney. Costs may range from a few thousand dollars to hundreds of thousands of dollars in the event of a major interference proceeding. These costs have increased significantly in the past decade.

Insofar as patents represent strategic capital, maintenance fees imply a hefty tax on that capital, and firms must review which parts of their patent portfolios should be sustained and which should be abandoned. For patents with proven economic value—patents that protect a new product or earn licensing income—the decision to maintain is usually a no-brainer. Others require study.

The global aspects of patent strategy are important. A number of different patent systems and patent philosophies are found around the world. All national patent offices seek in some measure to favor local businesses and inventors. For U.S. inventors, the decision to seek patent protection abroad must be made promptly. The urgency is due to the requirement of novelty. Absolute novelty is a prerequisite to obtaining a patent in Europe. Commercialization or the publication of technical information in the United States will violate this novelty requirement and most likely destroy any chance of obtaining overseas rights.

In some countries a patent provides very little protection. Courts may favor local infringers, and law enforcement agencies may be reluctant to pursue local pirates—or they may even be susceptible to influence or bribery. Some third world politicians view patents as a form of neocolonialism and think that patented drugs should be available to them at cost. The prospects of patent enforcement in these countries are poor.

Businesspeople and inventors face a clear trade-off between investing valuable funds on patent protection in dubious locales and risking future competition from an overseas bastion. A first priority is to cover one's bases in those European and English-speaking countries that respect patents and that have substantial markets in which the patent may be applicable. The second priority is to seek patents in selected smaller countries and in less-developed nations. Japan represents a special case. It is very difficult to compete there; but if one intends to compete, it is extremely important to patent one's products. One can anticipate that their patent system will be biased against foreign interests and will move slowly. Skill and dedication are needed to gain protection.

The third and final step in the patent value chain is enforcement. Neither the cost nor the value of enforcement should be underestimated.

We have already seen in our discussion of licensing that some patents have generated enormous cash streams from licensing. Searle's aspartame patent was valued at over a billion dollars when Monsanto acquired it. Patents on blockbuster drugs protect many billions of dollars of shareholder value. These stakes explain why competitors and potential competitors carefully scrutinize and challenge any important new patents. Challenges take several forms: as disputes in the patent offices of various nations; as interference actions in the United States; or as formal opposition procedures in Europe or Japan. After patents are issued, the challenges move to the legal arena. Competitors may knowingly infringe, saying in effect: "Sue me!"

A patent challenge should not cause the inventor firm to panic—it represents business as usual. This circumstance explains why any income model that includes extra gross margin based on patent protection should include some expenses for patent enforcement! In one sense, a challenge is good news, a clear indication that the invention has real and substantial value and that the inventor is in a position to negotiate and to capture that value. Unfortunately, some business and financial executives draw the opposite conclusion—they perceive only an inconvenient, unbudgeted, and uncapped legal expense. Their thinking is again economic, not strategic. Surely, the costs of a patent challenge in court can be nontrivial—a million dollars or more. Yet this cost is all part of the process of validating a patent and extracting its full value. Risk aversion in this case can be a form of myopia and is rarely in the shareholder's long-term interest.

One way to reduce the cost of patent enforcement is to negotiate a licensing arrangement with the challengers. Often, if a respected industry player accepts a license, the rest of the industry will fall into line, and the validity of the patent will be established for practical purposes. However, to get that first licensee, the patent holder must be prepared to defend the patent vigorously, even if it means settling the case on the courthouse steps.

In summary, patents create powerful and valuable real options available to their owners. They can be abandoned, sold, traded, licensed, or enforced against infringers. Each of these options can be evaluated using the general methodology in this book: (1) develop a pro forma cash flow statement,[8] (2) correct for unique risk, (3) apply the Black-Scholes method, and (4) calculate Total Value.

➤ Trademarks and Trade Names

Trademarks and trade names are a second class of identifiable intellectual property. Trademark law is intended to prevent consumer confusion as to the source of products or services. The great names of the old economy are largely trademarked: Coca-Cola, McDonald's, Xerox, Sears, Gillette, DuPont, and Kodak all inspire trust on a global basis. They create shareholder value above the intrinsic value of the goods and services in the marketplace.

The proliferation of web sites has made trade names even more important in the New Economy. Witness the flood of dotcom advertising during the Christmas season of 1999 aimed at creating brand awareness. The very names America Online and AOL, Amazon, Yahoo!, and eBay are now important commercial franchises. The traffic that comes with consumer awareness generates real options to supply *new* services on these sites and thus leverages value beyond that earned from the *existing* services.

The owners of trademarks and trade names thus go to considerable lengths to protect them from infringement, dilution, or conversion to a generic term (as in the common misuse of the term Styrofoam, a Dow Chemical trademark, to represent any type of polystyrene foam, or of Xerox to connote generic photocopying).

In legal terms, a trademark is anything that indicates source, sponsorship, affiliation, or other relation of a product or a service to a business. A word used as a trademark is properly an adjective—not a noun or verb—as in Styrofoam™ polystyrene foam. Trademark protection lasts as long as it is being used, with some exceptions. Registrations often require renewal.

Trademarks can be used commercially almost as aggressively as patents. Monsanto spent millions to establish the Nutrasweet trademark and required soft drink suppliers such as Coca-Cola and PepsiCo to put the Nutrasweet swirl logo on every can and bottle. They succeeded, despite considerable resentment from their customers, because of their patent position on the composition of matter. The objective was to use the trademark to differentiate Nutrasweet from generic aspartame and to protect its market position after the patent expired. The strategy appeared to work for a while, but the swirl now has been harder to find on the cans of the major soft drink brands.

➤ Copyrights

Copyrights are a big, big deal in the New Economy. Two of the newest industrial giants in the United States, Microsoft and Oracle, owe their positions to copyrighted software. Disney, with its large portfolio of copyrights, had intangibles valued by the marketplace at $85 billion in August 2000, about 8 times their recognized book value.[9] These copyrights provide the firm platform from which their executives could frame a host of real options to expand their lines of business.

As much as copyrights create huge opportunities and incentives in the digital age, their erosion is equally a threat. The exchange of copyrighted material over the Internet is putting severe strain on parts of the old economy. So the rock band Metallica sued Napster on the grounds that its server was facilitating the exchange of pirated MP3 copies of their music. Then along came Gnutella "freeware," which gave teenagers the same capabilities without a central server—and hence left the musicians with no one to sue! The free exchange of music is a severe and current threat to the music industry's copyright-based revenue model. The motion picture industry may be equally threatened as broadband becomes more widespread. Book publishers too are very much at risk. Many newspapers see no alternative but to go on line: I now regularly read the *New York Times* on line (for free) and the *Wall Street Journal* (for a fee which is less than the subscription price of the hard copy).

Copyright is a tool that can be used by computer programmers, actors, musicians, authors, photographers, artists, or any other creators of original work. Any original expression now receives copyright protection when it is fixed in a tangible form. Some examples include literary, dramatic, and musical works; pantomimes and choreography; pictorial, graphic, and sculptural works; audiovisual works; sound recordings; and architectural works. The former requirement that the work be *labeled* as copyrighted no longer exists. This chapter, for example, will be copyrighted when I save it to my hard disk. However, the copyright will not be officially registered unless and until I apply for a copyright from the U.S. Copyright Office. The registration process is fairly straightforward, and the fees are not exorbitant. Why register if it is already protected? Because it strengthens my protection by improving my legal position.

If someone chooses to make an unlawful copy of this book,

say by posting the chapters on his web site, I could force him to cease and desist without having first obtained a registered copyright. (I would, however, first have to register, and only then would I have standing to sue.) But I could only sue him for actual damages, based on my showing how many copies were not sold as a result of his activity. However, if I had had a registration, I could sue for additional statutory damages, which could be significantly punitive and a serious disincentive for him to engage in this activity.

We have seen that the protection from copyrights is broad and the ability to obtain a copyright is far easier than is the case for a patent. The area typically in dispute with regard to copyrights is "fair use." "Fair use" has generally been taken to mean that an individual can make a copy for noncommercial purposes, especially if that use promotes knowledge and progress. Thus, as a Yale professor, I can make a single copy from an article in the *Harvard Business Review* to prepare a transparency for my class. I can hope that this activity promotes knowledge and progress. But this right is not very broad. Because this reprint is available over the Internet for a few dollars, I would hesitate to make 40 copies of the same article for my class because doing so would presumptively harm the copyright owner's right to collect rents for use of the work.

Even the right of original photocopying has been severely restricted. *American Geophysical Union v. Texaco* (1992) ruled that a consortium of 83 publishers of scientific articles were entitled to compensatory damages for individual copies made by scientists from journals that had been *purchased* by Texaco and placed in their library. The publishers then went to every important industrial research library in the country and demanded payment (successfully) based on the *presumed* photocopying done by their employees. At the time, I had the responsibility for one such library and was outraged—in particular because some of the publishers were scientific organizations that we supported financially. It can be presumed that the distinction was that Texaco was a commercial organization and that Yale University is not.

This vexing problem was of course created by technology—in particular the development of efficient, low-cost copying machines. The digitization of images and sounds, combined with the Internet, will make earlier versions of the problem seem trivial by comparison. But it is wholly predictable that fortunes will be made and lost in the copyright wars of the coming decade.

➤ **Secrets**

We turn now to some of the other forms of intellectual capital, moving from the relatively well defined to the amorphous. Of course, what is amorphous is often the most interesting.

Trade secrets such as the formula for making Coca-Cola are often worth billions to their owners. But trade secrets include other utilitarian information: such things as test procedures, engineering drawings, software, and even administrative procedures. These types of intellectual property are a form of economic capital when incorporated in an existing business.

Other secrets are in the domain of strategic capital. Such secrets may include R&D, seismic and geological surveys, and business plans. For legal purposes, the latter are viewed similarly to trade secrets employed in operations. However, from a financial viewpoint, valuing these properties, along with idle patents, trademarks, and copyrights, is more problematic. The logic in this book suggests strongly that they are properly evaluated as real options.

A vast bulk of corporate intellectual capital is in the domain of trade secrets. The investor, assuming that she is not an "insider," will not know what they are, although she may be told or infer they exist (like the Coke formula). If she did know, they would no longer be secrets and would be in the public domain. Once a secret is known to the public, its owner has no way to get it back—although he may sue the leaker for damages. If a competitor unlawfully obtains the secret, the original owner has a right to insist it not be used. This situation occurs regularly when an employee resigns and is hired by a competitor—a routine letter from the original employer may follow him, putting his new employer on notice that the employee knows trade secrets in certain areas.

Laws regarding trade secrets, as well as those governing the rights and obligations of former employees who have signed employment agreements, vary from state to state. However, most states have adopted the Uniform Trade Secret Act or have enacted laws similar to it. Under the Uniform Trade Secret Act, a trade secret is information not generally known and not readily ascertainable, and it must have independent economic value due to secrecy and be the subject of reasonable efforts to protect secrecy. This broad definition of a trade secret thus encompasses almost any confidential business information. Information is protected as long as the information fits the definition of a trade secret. The time can be a matter of minutes or decades. Handling confidential information can lead to some unusual situations: On several occasions I asked a business client questions to which I already knew the answer, not to waste her time but to establish that these facts were known to her and that I had learned them from her and not another source whose confidential information I was committed to protect.

From the viewpoint of this book, that of high-risk investors, three types of trade secrets are of the greatest interest. They relate to strategic capital: (1) business plans, because these generate options and create value; (2) business processes, because when new opportunities can be combined with advantaged business processes, further value can be created, as the Peggy Sue scenario in Chapter 4 illustrates; and (3) research and development, to which we turn next.

➤ Research and Development

A portion of a firm's R&D budget is undertaken to create opportunities for profitable investment. The opportunities may be in the form of ideas for new products, for improved processes, for software, and so forth. But the category does not include information that is developed to help customers, which is often categorized as "technical service" and is typically aimed at retaining and growing existing accounts.

R&D is an investment; technical service is clearly an expense. R&D creates options for the future; technical service is part of operations and supports economic value. Many companies' financial statements do not make a clear distinction between the two categories. Accounting does not require it, and often R&D and technical service is performed within a single organization, by people with similar backgrounds, and sometimes by the very same people on different days of the week. An incentive may exist for pooling R&D and tech service in income statements because the result creates an impression of more strategic investment than is actually taking place.

From a valuation perspective, however, and from the viewpoint of corporate competitiveness, it makes a huge difference if a company that reports an R&D budget of 4 percent of sales is spending 3 percent on the future and 1 percent on technical service, or vice versa.

To illustrate these ambiguities, consider this scenario: A chemist assigned to an R&D project to develop next-generation catalyst technology for automobiles (R&D investment) is asked by sales to assist with a problem with a catalyst bought by Ford (technical service). This diversion of resources may save an important piece of existing business, but it may slow down the arrival of the next generation of catalysts. Trade-offs like this one are a lively source of debate in real companies.

Also, R&D has a limited shelf life. Its financial value depreciates. R&D investments must sooner or later be translated into commercial plans, or a decision has been made by default to write off the investment.

As with education, there can be a huge difference between the *value* of unpublished R&D and its *cost*. That is why putting R&D on the books (as per EVA [economic value added] accounting, described later in the section "Valuation and R&D Accounting") is far less useful for valuation purposes than evaluating it as an option generator. Much R&D is valueless because it fails in meeting its objectives. In *The Valuation of Technology*, I describe a model R&D portfolio, where about 47 percent of the effort, on a historical cost or book value basis, is "wasted."[10] However, the economic value created by the other 53 percent is greater than 400 percent of the total cost! So book or historic value is not in any sense economic value, and economic value typically underestimates market value.

R&D achieves its greatest value when it becomes the basis for aggressive and innovative business plans. The cost of the key discovery that enabled a great business plan could itself be very small, just one of many experiments that otherwise led nowhere and proved valueless. The serendipitous discovery that a methyl ester of the two amino acids aspartic acid and phenylalanine had incredible sweetening powers—and could be made from materials common in nature—provides an example. This discovery was part of a broader research program aimed at different business targets. The cost of this particular experiment may have been only a few thousand dollars, but when finally translated into the commercial products Equal and Nutrasweet, it created value for shareholders of G. D. Searle and Monsanto in the billions.

Between the time that aspartame's sweetening power was identified and an initial patent application filed, the R&D investment grew and grew, as did the expected value of that research—much of it unpublished and proprietary. Data needed to be developed to discover the most efficient processes for making the raw materials and the most efficient processes for making the sweetener itself, to establish its shelf life under a variety of conditions, to test its performance in a variety of applications (aspartame was never stable enough to be used in baking, for example), and above all to check its toxicity under both acute and chronic conditions.

Clearly, during this time, the project's value was increasing more rapidly than its associated cost, making all the development cost a value-added investment. But this investment was also at high risk; U.S. Food and Drug Administration (FDA) approval was a serious challenge. Some academicians were expressing concerns regarding its safety, and competitors had potentially excellent sweeteners under development.

In short, for G. D. Searle, aspartame became an important piece of strategic capital, representing a growing sunk cost and even greater expectations of future profit. The value of that capital undoubtedly fluctuated with each major development—favorable or adverse—until it was transformed into an operating business whose value could be established by conventional yardsticks.[11]

➤ Strategic Alliances

Service relationships—with vendors, consultants, and law and accounting firms—have been mentioned as a hidden part of a company's intellectual capital. Partnerships and alliances can be even more important. To the extent that a company can effectively muster the energies and the brainpower of a powerful strategic partner, it can speed its product development, reduce the cost of manufacturing, and rapidly penetrate its target markets—all enormous competitive advantages. Major companies such as IBM enter hundreds of such relationships. These relationships are intellectual capital of a most important type—mutual understanding of capabilities and costs and trusted working relationships.

From the viewpoint of the real options solution, strategic alliances only create value when they enable plans. It is possible they will be formed because of personal relationships and a vague sense that working together can help both parties, as when two top executives meet on the golf course. But value will not be created until an option is framed. In time, when that option is exercised, the strategic capital represented by the alliance is translated into economic capital.

Cisco, which produces networking devices (the king of routers) and software, owns only two of the 38 plants that assemble its products.[12] It connects component manufacturers, assemblers, logistics providers, systems integrators, and its own employees and customers in what is known as a b-web (business web). The arrangement leverages the strategic capital of the participants and appears to provide exceptional value. Nortel has embraced the same approach.

In 1999, the pharmaceutical giant Eli Lilly[13] screened some 1,500 external R&D proposals. From this broad field it signed some 350 cooperative development agreements, each representing one or more external research projects. Each of these agreements constituted an option to proceed with the business plan enabled by a technical success.

The financial implications of alliances should not obscure the fact that the human elements are extremely important. Alliances and partnerships are typically put together by small groups of champions in each firm. A study by Gene Slowinski[14] showed that disruptions in the human links (owing to job changes, for example) can undermine the value of alliances. There is increasing interest by financial analysts in placing a valuation on alliances and a general lack of agreement as to the methods by which this should be done. Real options are the methodology of choice. Even so, analysis from the outside cannot be straightforward or transparent because the relationships are complex and the details may be very closely held.

Alliances are thus part of the strategic capital of the firm. A company has a plan and intends to use its strategic ally to help it execute part of that plan—in a way that it hopes is faster, at lower cost, at lower risk, and more effective than what it could do by itself. The value added can in principle be measured quantitatively: It is the difference between the value of the option (as determined by the typical business factors of timing, unique risk, potential revenues, margins, and capital investment) with the strategic alliance and the value without it.

When the plan is transformed into an operation, the alliance value may well continue. What was once strategic capital is converted to economic capital. So we see alliances of airlines, such as the Star and One World alliances, which initially enabled the allies to market to more destinations and to enhance the value of their frequent flyer programs, becoming integral parts of their operating business.

➤ Networks

Networks are examples of intellectual capital that are even more amorphous than alliances, because the members of a network come and go, whereas the network lives on. There is widespread interest today in the role of networks in value creation. Some members of professional and trade organizations believe networks have become the single most important benefit they receive from membership. A popular title as this book is being written is *The Social Life of Information*.[15] Its starting point is the massive amount of information that is made available to professionals today. And we know that few professionals take steps to cut back on information flow, though we are sorely tempted.

But we know information is not enough in itself: It must be prioritized, validated, and put into context. Information overload has become the enemy of effective work habits. Information in the wrong format or hidden in a mass of garbage is expensive to extract. Yes, good databases, the Web, the spiders, and the search algorithms help; but finding what one is looking for can be frustratingly difficult, whereas a knowledgeable colleague in the network might be able to locate it in seconds.

Our personal behavior provides anecdotal evidence for the value we place on networks: Each of us spends a considerable amount of time and energy maintaining all sorts of networks. For it is to the network we turn when the right information is not in front of us. Business and professional meetings, e-mails, cocktail parties, Christmas cards, and newsletters all play a role. Our networks extend in all directions—bosses, peers, subordinates, and just people we have found very helpful in the past. We do many favors, most small, but some substantial, just to maintain the network. This time is an investment, and the evidence points to the view that it is not at all foolish. Nevertheless, the effort may run entirely outside formal business processes, and attempts to stifle it in the name of efficiency or reengineering are hardly unknown.[16]

Why do we network? Because our contacts help us to frame new options. The options become strategic capital, whether for us as individuals or for the organizations we represent, or most often for both.

Although individuals have long networked, corporations are just beginning to. The transition from mostly a collection of two-way strategic alliances centered on a hub as earlier described for Cisco, IBM, and Lilly to a true multicentric network appears to be a logical evolution of the b-webs discussed before.

Again, networks are a form of strategic capital. The cost of maintaining them is at the expense of economic capital, but their rapid growth attests to their contribution to strategic and Total Value.

■ HOW VALUE IS CREATED THROUGH
INTELLECTUAL CAPITAL

So far, we have explored the types of intellectual property assets. It is equally useful to examine the *transformation processes* by which these assets are converted to value.

Consider first a hypothetical example of how important a seemingly mundane intellectual asset such as validated test procedures can be. Professor Stern, who teaches chemistry at a small college in Delaware, has synthesized and patented a new molecule, which is of a class that has previously shown biological activity as an insecticide. However, he has no clue as to how to demonstrate its efficacy or how to test for possible safety problems. On the other hand, a firm that develops and markets pesticides, such as Acme Chemical, has been testing new chemical entities for biological activity for decades. It would be straightforward for them to test this substance on a spectrum of insect species and also to screen it for key environmental properties such as biodegradability and fish and avian toxicity. Acme scientists would be able not only to quickly quantify each property but also to place the results in the context of hundreds of other experimental and commercial materials! Their database and methods, which took decades to develop, now confer a huge advantage over any rival that might be starting from scratch. It would behoove Stern to make a deal with Acme rather than to form his own company to commercialize this material.

In effect, Acme has invested in a transformation process for converting a new chemical entity into a product—in this case a pesticide. When combined with Stern's property, that process has an opportunity to create value.

Let's look at a second example of how intellectual property is developed and the ways in which it can create value. When a researcher or an engineer is hired, it is often in part because the employer is seeking a specific expertise that the employee has gained through education or experience. Assume a recently hired engineer, McCarthy, is an expert on extruding plastic film. McCarthy has just been hired by Pinnacle Plastic Products. In effect, Pinnacle rents her specialized expertise in the form of a salary that reflects the value of her skills in the marketplace. This general expertise is sometimes referred to as *background technology*. As individuals learn and study on the job, this background expertise, this portion of the individual's and the company's intellectual capital, will grow. It is, in effect, jointly owned and belongs to the company as long as the engineer is employed. The company may also gain proprietary *foreground technology*, which will initially be a trade secret.

Let us imagine in this example that McCarthy develops a technique for running an extruder 30 percent faster than the competition can. This invention improves Pinnacle's capital productivity in extrusion. Normally, the intellectual property would be recorded in McCarthy's notebooks, translated into drawings, and embodied in physical modifications of the extruders. It will be shared with some other individuals in Pinnacle.

Pinnacle now has choices regarding how it will treat this intellectual property. It can patent its new extrusion technology or leave it as a trade secret. Patenting might prevent others from using the invention, thus enhancing Pinnacle's competitive edge. Or Pinnacle could license the technology exclusively to a leading manufacturer of extruders. A third alternative is that Pinnacle could license it nonexclusively to all comers.

The first choice, to treat the invention as a trade secret, may be feasible if few knowledgeable outsiders visit the company's manufacturing facilities. It might be possible to restrict knowledge of the invention on a "need-to-know" basis, reducing the likelihood that the secret would get out through ex-employees. The device itself may be concealed in a "black box" to keep it away from the eyes of visiting repairpeople, tech service representatives, customers, and others. These types of precautions are hardly unknown in industry and, in fact, may be legally required to prove the technology was indeed a trade secret.

Valuing this intellectual property in the marketplace would be straightforward in principle. Let's say that the company had 10 extruders prior to its productivity invention. The 30 percent improvement in output is worth at least 3 extruders, minus the cost of modifications. This calculation would define its *economic* value. If an extruder cost $250,000, McCarthy's contribution is worth $750,000.

But it may be worth far more if the company has an attractive option to expand its extrusion business based on its new competitive advantage. Such an opening would be a strategic plus.

If licensed, the invention would have an economic value equal to the discounted cash flow of the anticipated royalties over the life of the patent, an entirely different calculation. The actual decision to license or not to license will hinge, in part, on the valuation exercise, but also on judgments regarding whether the trade secret can be kept, whether competitors will invent (or worse, patent!) something similar, and whether a patent will be granted and be enforceable. In other words, the risks that are unique to this situation must be estimated and included in the analysis.

■ VALUATION AND R&D ACCOUNTING

As we discussed in Chapter 2, accounting for intellectual property and valuing it are two different matters. In most companies, the time spent by McCarthy and her associates in developing the technology and procuring the patent will be expensed. Hence, the book value will be zero; patents are not normally shown as assets on the company's books. The real value of the asset would emerge only if the extrusion business were to be sold. The enhanced productivity would surely create a purchase premium, and that premium would be booked either as goodwill or as an appraised value for the patent by the buyer.

In an important example, Monsanto acquired the pharmaceutical company G. D. Searle in 1985. One of Searle's key assets was the patent on its blockbuster new sweetener, aspartame, trademarked as Nutrasweet, which had 5 years of remaining patent life, thanks to a special patent extension granted by Congress. Rather than ascribe the aspartame technology to goodwill, Monsanto valued the key composition of matter patent at over $1 billion and wrote it off over the remaining 5 years of patent life. The cash flow implications were important: Monsanto received its tax benefits in 5 years versus 40. But the important point is that intellectual property valued at zero by Searle was converted in the marketplace to a valuation of over $1 billion.

In principle, the alternative to zero valuation is to capitalize R&D, just as the labor involved in constructing a physical facility is part of the capital investment. Management could divide all R&D activity into projects and charge direct time and materials to the various projects and add a further charge for laboratory overhead. This approach would treat each project as an investment, much as a production plant is an investment. This sum could then be depreciated over the useful life of the technology. For valuable technology protected by a patent, the time period might be the remaining life of the patent. Of course, the book value of this asset would be based purely on cost, which would not, in any case, reflect the economic value of the technology.

This approach has strong advocates and has been implemented at companies that use EVA as a management tool.[17] In that model, R&D is treated not as a cost but as an investment. Typically, the investment is amortized over an appropriate time period, say 5 years. The result is that current earnings are not charged for current R&D but for the depreciation of the R&D investment now on the EVA books.

To make it simple, assume R&D is amortized over 5 years, and the historic costs of R&D in the past 5 years have been (in millions) $60, $70, $80, $90, and $100. The R&D "depreciation" in the current year would be (in millions) $12 + $14 + $16 + $18 + $20, or $80 million. Because R&D expenses have been increasing, EVA earnings will be debited $80 million instead of $100 million, leading to a $20 million increase in EVA earnings. But the R&D investment remaining on the "EVA books" will be (in millions) $14 + $32 + $48 + $80, or $174 million. A charge for this capital investment will be levied. If the cost of capital is 12 percent, the capital charge will be 0.12 × $174 million, or $21 million. Depending on the cost of capital and on the R&D spending pattern, this set of adjustments can put a positive or a negative tone on performance. But because it is averaged over 5 years, it eliminates the incentive for managers to slash R&D to make the numbers in their short-term bonus plan.

Capitalizing R&D, as just described, has important pros and cons. As a practical matter it is usually not done and is not consistent with generally accepted accounting principles (GAAP), which stipulate immediate expensing of R&D costs (FASB 2).[18] The accounting logic is based on the view that most R&D efforts are too uncertain to warrant capitalization and that writing them off immediately is the *conservative* course.

Let's start with the "cons" first.

1. If an expensed project fails, and it has been capitalized, it must be written off. If some, but not all, of the project's goals have not been met, it might be written down, a partial write-off. This accounting requirement, when extended to a broad portfolio of R&D projects, would engage an R&D manager in countless discussions with auditors as to which projects to write off and when. It could give management another tool by which to "manage earnings" by electing to defer or to hasten R&D writedowns, a generally unwelcome situation given the large discretionary factor in R&D decisions and the SEC's (Security and Exchange Commission) sensitivity to any hint of managed earnings. Write-offs might also need to be described to investors, giving competitors access to some very interesting information.

2. If R&D were capitalized, the company could not expense the R&D costs on the income statement. Normally, legitimate business costs can be used to reduce taxable income from all sources, thereby improving cash flow. Those tax savings take some of the sting out of R&D expenditures. Most financial managers prefer the benefits of better cash flow to better reported earnings. Moreover, because some valuation methods are based on cash flow and others on earnings, this financial decision does affect valuation. For capitalized R&D, deferred income taxes become an *asset* (and an unproductive one) because the full tax deduction is yet to be realized. (We have seen that accelerated depreciation is more usefully classified as a *liability*.)

Here are the "pros" for capitalizing R&D:

1. R&D costs can be depreciated over time. This practice will not be as tax-advantageous as expensing costs immediately, but it helps to match the costs of R&D with the income it produces.
2. No single year's earnings are torpedoed by huge developmental expenses, which often bunch up in one or two years. These costs may be no small matter if they have the effect of reducing operating income below what management considers acceptable or of slowing the apparent growth rate of operating income.
3. The books will reflect that an investment is being made. Confusing investment with expense is probably the biggest mistake that corporate executives make in dealing with R&D. Capitalizing its costs is a visible signal that the organization sees R&D as a bridge to the future, not as a cost center that needs to be limited or reined in.

In principle, there remains the possibility of keeping three sets of books: writing off R&D as performed for the tax books, capitalizing R&D for reporting to investors (currently contrary to FASB 2), and basing management bonuses on the EVA methodology.

In summary, accounting methods, based as they are on historical expenditures and mostly tangible assets, have very serious problems in dealing with technology. To the degree that investments are confused with expense, accounting numbers can mislead management and investors with regard to both current and future profit levels. Accounting earnings are particularly pernicious in judging small, rapidly growing businesses, which typically must make above-normal investments in R&D, in problem solving, in market development, in the training of personnel, and in plant start-up costs. As the business gets larger and the bugs are worked out, these expenses are likely to be spread over a larger base, thus improving apparent margins.

One other consequence of not recognizing technology as a balance sheet asset is that one misses the phenomenon of technology depreciation. And technology *does* depreciate. Under accounting rules, however, you can't depreciate something that is not on your books (although some technology depreciation may be recognized in the useful life of equipment, such as computers, which has technology embedded in it).

Technology depreciation is driven by the fact that the performance parameters for most technologies improve continuously, at rates that are characteristic of the technology's position on the S-curve (see Chapter 12). "Moore's Law," that the density of circuits on a chip doubles every two years, indicates just how quickly technology can improve in some business sectors. Speeds of Fourdrinier paper machines and of oil drilling rigs also increase, as does the fuel efficiency of vehicles, but in these cases much more slowly. And when radical innovations occur, the value of existing technology may not just depreciate, it may collapse.

Technology depreciation has serious financial consequences. For business people, the first signal that their once-golden technology has depreciated may be mysteriously eroding margins. The market value of their shares will be the next to slide. To prevent this slide toward devolution, R&D programs must ensure that the bar of competitive performance is being set higher. Thus, to stay even with an advancing pack of competitors, a company must continue to invest in R&D, just as it offsets the depreciation of its equipment with new investment. This portion of R&D investment is intellectual maintenance capital, and its bottom line impact can only be measured against what would have happened if the money had not been spent. The cost of just staying even in a competitive environment is often high. For a group of specialty chemicals businesses with R&D budgets in the range of 4 percent to 5 percent of annual sales, one expert told me that he believed that about half of the amount of those budgets was required to just stay even, with the other half employed in projects that might create new value.

Revisiting the Nutrasweet example is helpful in reinforcing the difference between research cost and value. No matter what the historical cost of James Schlatter's research program on amino acids in 1965, and the subsequent developmental costs of shepherding the sweetener through the FDA and scaling up for global commercialization, the value of this blockbuster discovery exceeded it. Monsanto, a strategic buyer, estimated that value and elected to pay for it. The author indeed was part of a sophisticated rival group that considered making a competitive bid and concluded the price to be high—indicating that G. D. Searle received fair value or more based on the facts known at the time.

■ SUMMARY

The intellectual capital of an organization includes tangible, registered elements of intellectual property, such as patents, trademarks, and copyrights. It includes a host of other technical information embodied in manuals, drawings, procedures, and correspondence. It includes all of the company's unpublished R&D. And it includes the education and experience of its employees and, to some extent, of its strategic partners, its contractors, and vendors. Many of these resources are utilized in running the operations of the company.

Intellectual capital also includes the ability to relate and organize these individual elements in creative new combinations or to deploy them in new situations. Employees learn each other's capabilities and traits. They learn the potentials and the limitations inherent in the company's technologies. They form teams and networks, formally or informally. And with these resources they pool their intellectual resources to frame opportunities. Opportunities are formulated into plans, plans become options, and strategic capital is created. In time, the options may be exercised, with economic capital resulting.

Innovation: The Fountain of Prosperity

There is a truism that innovation is much more than invention. Inventions, by conventional definition, must be novel, nonobvious, and arguably useful. But these features are not enough to change the world, which is why the inventions in the great majority of patents are never adopted in the marketplace. *Innovation* refers to the process by which human ingenuity contrives to actually change the world in small ways and large. To endure, the innovation must in time create *value.* This prescription is conventional wisdom. However, from the new real options perspective, innovation is the process of framing options and implementing them.

Innovation is inherently unpredictable, virtually by definition. It is a prime source of business volatility. In our process diagram, Figure 4.1, we depicted innovation as affecting both value creation loops—the operations loop, involving economic assets, and the plans loop, involving strategic assets. In this role, innovation is a two-way street. Our innovations affect the world;

but, very importantly, the world's innovations affect us. Depending on position, the effects can be positive or negative.

Consider a contemporary example, a conventional landline telecommunications (telecom) company in the new age of cellular telephones. On the one hand, the cell phone innovation will have a largely negative effect on the company's operations because many phone calls initiated over cell are phone calls not initiated over wire.

On the other hand, the telecom has a great deal of expertise in communications technology and access to individual and business customers who have relied on it for years. It appears to have an advantage, even if only temporary, of credibility and perceived reliability. Its mailing list gives it access to a vast installed customer base when it seeks to offer new services.

This company has the option either of pioneering its own cellular system or of acquiring one based on its strong financial position. When these options are perceived in the marketplace, the company's stock is likely to rise. However, its stock may fall when quarterly reports indicate weakening revenues in its conventional business.

Just such factors, working in opposite directions, affected AT&T. In September 1994, AT&T acquired McCaw Cellular Communications, Inc., for $11.5 billion—then the fifth-largest merger in U.S. history. The acquisition of McCaw wireless gave AT&T tremendous options for future growth, but its conventional long distance business was declining relentlessly.

Of course, unwise innovation can extract a penalty. Boeing had committed itself to the first stages of an option to build a new jumbo jet, dubbed the 747-X, capable of carrying 500-plus passengers. It had communicated this option to investors and potential customers. Then, in early 1997 it announced that it was canceling the program, which was costing $3 million per day.[1] The stock rose several points on the news. Clearly, the stock market viewed this enterprise as a likely destroyer of value (the Asian market looked dubious at the time) and welcomed Boeing's exercise of its option to abandon and the boost to its free cash flow.

Boeing was on the opposite tack from AT&T: The economic side of the company was strengthened while the strategic side was diminished, but with a net gain in market value. The wisdom of this decision for the long run is still unclear because Boeing's archrival, Airbus, continues its jumbo jet development program and is actively taking orders for its A380.

■ INNOVATION'S IMPACT

Let us turn first to the question of how the world's innovations affect us. Figure 4.1 showed innovation impacting both the operations loop and the plans loop of companies. These impacts seem to be growing with time and can be very disruptive to companies and entire industries. Yet, by their very nature, innovative developments are hard to anticipate in specific terms and, therefore, are hard to include in a realistic valuation.

When innovations come from the outside, they can be severely threatening to free cash flow, just as plastic bottles took business from glass, cellular telephones from land lines, and personal computers from mainframes. They can also be threatening to a firm's strategic capital in that growth plans may have to be abandoned and the existing stock of human capital becomes obsolete. Thus, the once-proud technology centers of the large steel companies are largely a thing of the past, as minimills and efficient foreign competitors eroded the industry's margins.

On the positive side, the advent of cheaper and better performing materials and more efficient machinery create options to improve margins. Even so, capturing value from these innovations is not automatic because improvements that are available to all competitors tend to be passed down the economic value chain by competitive forces. More important, new technology combinations will create new product opportunities, adding options to the firm's strategic capital. These options, too, need to be framed in ways that are differentiated from the competition to have much hope of capturing significant value!

Of course, when innovation occurs from within the firm, the benefits need not be shared. That is why firms seek to foster innovation and why they perform internal research and development (R&D); and it is largely this activity that is addressed in the remainder of this chapter.

■ SOURCES OF INNOVATION

Innovation has two wellsprings:

1. Inspired response to new circumstances.
2. Directed "random" experimentation.

Inspired response to new circumstances is the larger source of innovation, at least in terms of the *number* of successful innovations. This category is closely allied to "market pull" thinking, and technology synergies will be a big factor. Companies regularly travel for opportunities created by changing needs in the marketplace. The birth of a new technology or market also affords opportunities for combination with existing businesses and technologies. Smart people with intellectual property assets and market positions look for these opportunities and chase them. The frequent occurrence of new combinations in rapidly developing fields, such as computing, ensures a high flow of new opportunities. In more mature fields, such as primary metals, inspired response may not be enough to drive adequate value creation or top line growth.

A potential disadvantage of the inspired-response approach is that the world is full of smart people, and competitors and potential customers are more than likely to see the same opportunities at about the same time, which diminishes the opportunity for a long-term franchise and high margins. The dot-com gold rush was just such a situation. Young entrepreneurs tested every conceivable business model with little recognition of how transparent their actions would be to direct rivals or to entrenched old-economy companies with interests to protect. The potential for value creation boils down to the degree of inspiration built into the inspired response, with obvious solutions headed for trouble.

Directed random experimentation refers to the concept of proactively investing in R&D in areas that appear especially fertile from either a technological or a marketing viewpoint. I admire the cartoon showing two vultures perched on a telephone wire. One vulture says to the other, "Patience, my ass. Let's go out and kill something!" The research equivalent of the high-risk vultures is to find and patent a new idea, combine it with the universe of applicable markets, and exploit it to the fullest. The danger of this approach is the very real possibility of developing a technology for which there is no market.

In retrospect, nearly every innovation can be traced to one of these two approaches. Each has produced fantastic successes. Because of the intellectual and the competitive dynamics, one can anticipate higher success rates but lower rewards with the first approach and higher risk but larger potential for home runs with the second. One of my favorite examples of directed random experimentation was Bell Lab's research into solid-state physics in the 1960s, which led to the transistor and the integrated circuit. This advance enabled most of modern computing and electronics technology; indeed, the transistor's potential was too great for AT&T to capture by itself. An example of inspired response to changing market conditions was Chrysler's brilliant investment in light trucks, such as the SUV (sport utility vehicle), in part a counterresponse to federal gasoline mileage regulations. It revived Chrysler, but a competitive counter-response in time eroded most of its advantage.

■ THE TECHNOLOGY S-CURVE

From these two sources, innovation appears to follow an inexorable process. It is incorporated in the notion of the S-curve. The S-curve concept, based on many case studies, is that at its beginnings a technology is not cost-effective and, for that reason, does not attract much investment. There is a lot of experimentation, and progress is made in fits and starts.

But at some point, investment in the new technology makes economic sense. Richard Foster[2] defines this condition as the point where the fully loaded cost of the new technology matches the incremental cash cost (or contribution) of the existing technology. This condition need not occur across the board—it need only happen in one niche in the general marketplace. A process of profitable substitution begins in which the attacker firm, the one with the innovation, has the advantage. As further investments are made in the technology, performance improvements come rapidly, and the attacker captures additional market segments.

Later, as performance approaches physical limits, diminishing returns set in, improvements become increasingly expensive, investment slows, and maturity follows.

This description aptly fits the two technologies discussed earlier. Conventional jetliner design is now fairly mature. The 747 airframe, introduced in 1969, is still an economically competitive design, though there have been many incremental improvements. Boeing judged that leapfrogging this design was not cost-effective. A similar degree of maturity affects the very efficient land-based U.S. telephone network. But the wireless revolution is still at an early stage—we are just now looking at the introduction of handsets with serious microprocessing and Internet capabilities.

Students of innovation often distinguish between *continuous* (or incremental) innovation and *discontinuous* (or radical/disruptive/breakthrough) innovation. Progress in technology for the 747 is clearly incremental and *continuous*—better avionics one year, longer-range capabilities in the next, less noise in the next. All of these are needed to match or to exceed the performance of Airbus and to convince customers that Boeing is adding value in terms they understand.

The telephone situation is one in which there was an opportunity to switch from an aging S-curve (copper wire) to a new S-curve (wireless), with an enormous performance advantage (mobility) that has allowed quick entry into a market niche. Figure 12.1 shows the substitution dynamics that are to be expected in the presence of discontinuous innovation.

Today, there are few meaningful opportunities for cost reduction in conventional telephone handsets, although some "smart" features have been added. But the cost of mobile handsets has dropped from thousands of dollars when initially introduced to the ballpark of one hundred dollars or so. Even so, the newer models far outperform the earlier ones. In recent years,

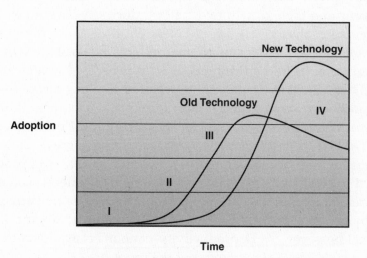

I = Incubation stage; II = Growth stage; III = Mature growth; IV = Maturity/Decline

Figure 12.1   Technology Life Cycles

mobile units have been on a much steeper part of the S-curve than conventional twisted-pair handsets.

■ CONTINUOUS INNOVATION

The case for continuous innovation is powerful. The key idea is that a company in time calibrates the slope of its technological S-curve in financial terms.[3] It gains that knowledge through an analysis of the costs of its R&D programs, counting both successes and failures. At the same time, it learns the impact of improved performance on sales growth and margins. The combination tells it how fast it can move up the S-curve for a given level of technology spending.

Faster growth and higher margins translate directly into value. A higher, sustainable growth of free cash flow significantly boosts discounted cash flow (DCF) valuations. And higher margins improve return on invested capital. The combination of high returns and high growth rates can produce sensational gains in economic value.

Of course, an R&D investment reduces free cash flow in the short term, as in the Boeing case, so it is necessary to factor in R&D productivity to determine whether the long-term growth creates more value than the short-term penalty extracts. Several metrics have been proposed for measuring R&D productivity.[4] In *The Valuation of Technology*, I proposed using a growth-related measure: the ratio of annual new product sales to the portion of the R&D budget dedicated to innovative new products. Other companies have developed algorithms for calculating return on investment (ROI) on R&D investment. In the long term, however, R&D productivity cannot be expected to remain constant. As one mines out the more attractive opportunities at the foot of the S-curve and as its slope flattens, it makes sense to reduce R&D and to eliminate programs that no longer add value.

Taken individually, incremental R&D projects incur three risks: (1) a technical gamble, (2) a gamble that customers will react as the marketing experts predict, and (3) a gamble that the marketplace will not change materially during the project. Thus, each individual project is quite risky. But a well-managed *portfolio* of incremental innovations, such as those conducted by IBM, DuPont, Procter & Gamble, and 3M research in the 1970s, was not risky at all, as long as overall R&D productivity was high. The performance of their research departments guaranteed consistent and profitable growth for many years.

■ DISCONTINUOUS INNOVATION

Discontinuous innovation means jumping to a new S-curve with better performance and cost parameters, as illustrated in Figure 12.1. It signifies a clear divide between one era of technology and another. The historic examples are numerous: sail to steam, steam to diesel, glass bottles to steel cans, steel cans to aluminum cans, vacuum tubes to transistors, individual transistors to integrated circuits, propeller aircraft to jets, copper wire to wireless and fiber optics.

There is abundant empirical evidence for the link between radical (or discontinuous) innovation and wealth creation.[5] Examples include nylon (DuPont), the techniques for making synthetic diamonds (General Electric), the transistor (Bell Laboratories), aspartame (Searle), personal computing concepts like the mouse and the user-friendly computer interface (Xerox PARC), and hundreds more. Much of the thinking that led to these breakthroughs was nonstrategic: General Electric was not in the diamond business; DuPont was not in the synthetic fiber business; Searle had no strategic intent to dominate synthetic sweeteners; AT&T/Western Electric, the owner of Bell Laboratories, saw itself as an equipment supplier for captive markets; and so on. These breakthrough discoveries created high-value opportunities for the parent investors to exploit. Although some of the opportunities were lost by their discoverers and captured by others, there is little doubt that none of this work could have occurred in a corporate environment that was restricted to incremental extensions of existing successful products.

Richard Foster has articulated the competitive advantages that are conferred by discontinuous innovation on the attacker who makes the bold leap to the new S-curve, as well as the often brutal consequences for the defenders. The attacker gains in economies of scale, in increasing margins, and in accelerating growth. These result in greater investor interest in the attacker's stock and the ability to finance further attacks.[6]

The defender is on the other side of the stick. He suffers diseconomies of scale and may have to close plants to reduce fixed costs. He must also reduce "overheads," which often turn out to be the innovative people charged with developing and executing value-creating options. Assets may have to be written off. Investors pay less for the stock, which makes raising new equity expensive. Through the eyes of the defender, the entire process is one of value destruction and devolution.

The attacker, armed with a "disruptive technology," enters a niche where the new technology's reinvestment cost is competitive with an older technology's cash cost. A recent business book by Clayton Christensen[7] contains interesting case histories that further illustrate the dynamics of substitution. In the steel industry, for example, minimill technology found its niche in the low-end rebar market using scrap steel. There, the attackers were companies like Nucor and Chaparral, and the defenders were vertically integrated steel producers like U.S. Steel, Bethlehem, and Japan's mighty Nippon Steel.

The defenders' instinctive response was to cede what was viewed as an insignificant, low-margin segment and to focus on the needs of their largest, most profitable customers, such as the purchasers of high quality sheet steel. This move brought temporary benefits to the defenders. However, as minimill technology climbed its own S-curve, it found opportunities to move upmarket. With the development of continuous thin-slab casting, the minimills were able to gain a beachhead in sheet steel, and they work diligently to expand it. From the inception of their attack in the mid-1960s, the minimills have captured nearly half of the market from the integrated producers.

The attack from below is startlingly reminiscent of the Japanese strategy of out-competing U.S. car manufacturers in the small-car segment, where they had performance advantages in fuel economy and quality. The profits on compact cars were small relative to larger models, so the U.S. Big Three manufacturers ceded position, only to watch their overseas competitors move all the way upmarket to the point where a Lexus enjoys greater prestige than a Cadillac. In this case the defenders eventually fought back (the integrated steel companies didn't) with quality programs and much better small cars (the Saturn succeeding the hapless Vega). In addition, the Japanese themselves were bumping up against the law of diminishing returns: Fuel performance with conventional engines had physical limitations, and quality was intrinsically limited to zero defects. Today, Japanese market share appears stabilized at about 30 percent, and several of their manufacturers appear to have decapitalized themselves in a futile war to expand their positions. But 30 percent of the U.S. car market still represents a huge reward for an aggressive and skillful attacker.

■ FOSTERING DISCONTINUOUS INNOVATION

Many companies, as a matter of policy, insist that their technical staffs maintain a balance between continuous and discontinuous innovation. 3M is a leading example; we have noted that each business unit there must support at least one pacing project—

one that can change the basis of competition in its markets. This definition of *pacing* does not necessarily require a project to be technically dramatic or even exceptionally high risk. Two of the examples discussed earlier, minimills and auto quality programs, succeeded through the application of a new idea in a safe niche and proceeded by continuous innovation thereafter. Nor was the personal computer (PC) created from a single technological breakthrough. But all these developments changed the basis of competition. However, the jet airliner was definitely a high risk: The pioneering British Comet suffered a fatal design flaw and was surpassed by Boeing by the time the flaw was identified and fixed.

The important point about the requirement for a pacing project is that it creates a company mind set: "We will revolutionize our markets, even at the cost of cannibalizing our existing business. If we don't, someone else will." This attitude is hardly universal. We've all heard the phrases associated with the opposite viewpoint: "The bleeding edge," "We're fast followers," "You can spot the pioneer by the arrows in his chest." It would have been relatively easy and cheap for the integrated steel producers to develop their own minimills. They did not have the mind set to do it.

In fact, a recent study indicates that management practices required to break through to the next S-curve must be substantially different from those used for continuous innovation. This study looked at some 27 projects in 20 firms and examined 11 projects in depth. It used as a definition of *breakthrough* a "potential (1) for a 5X–10X improvement in performance compared to existing products; (2) to create the basis for a 30 percent to 50 percent reduction in cost; or (3) to have new-to-the-world performance features."[8] Examples included GE's digital x-ray; TI's digital light projector; GM's hybrid vehicle; IBM's silicon-germanium devices; DuPont's biodegradable polymer; and the Otis bidirectional elevator.

The most striking characteristic of these projects was that

they had "long time horizons, starts and stops, and periods of seemingly going nowhere. Like a river, they have a general direction but they don't go there directly. . . . Sometimes they give rise to new streams." It was also observed that most fit with the strategic direction of the corporation and were targeted from the outset. About half of the projects were inspired by a company request for ideas leading to breakthrough innovations, but an almost equal number of projects represented the initiative of individuals or small groups.

These breakthrough projects often required protection from normal business forces while they were in the embryonic stage. Many were located in corporate research labs with a belief in the power of directed random experimentation, and they often sought and received government funding. Informal networks, both inside the company and outside links to other companies, universities, and government, were critical in all of the 11 in-depth cases. Corporate culture was equally critical.

The study's conclusion is of interest: "Conventional management techniques are unsuitable until uncertainty is sufficiently reduced, and therefore it appears that the primary imperative driving these projects is to reduce uncertainty to the point where tried and true conventional management practices are appropriate, or where it becomes apparent that the project should be abandoned."[9]

To realize the value of innovation, sooner or later it must be converted from strategic capital to economic capital, from plans to operations and free cash flow. Almost all established technology companies have a mechanism in place for that conversion— particularly for continuous innovations. But when it comes to discontinuous innovation, the mechanisms may be absent or may fail to engage.

Xerox invented many of the key pieces of the personal computer, including the graphic user interface, the Ethernet system, and the mouse, at its legendary Palo Alto Research Center (PARC). But corporate management had a sales mind set and was concerned principally with its core copier business. Eventually and inevitably, PARC's ideas trickled out to others, including the founders of Apple, and an exceptional opportunity to capture a dominating position in every office and home in the United States was fumbled.[10] Even the core copier business was not in the end secured, and today Xerox's franchise has been heavily eroded by Hewlett-Packard and Canon, among others.

The PARC debacle has been attributed to a cultural issue: Stick to the business we know, and don't run the risk of challenging giants like IBM and Digital head on. As it turns out, IBM and Digital were surprisingly vulnerable[11] at the low end of the computer business; and what looked like a toy for gamers rapidly produced the ability to handle spreadsheets and to become a respectable word processor. The rest is history.

■ SALVAGING VALUE FROM FAILED INNOVATION

Not all innovation succeeds, and in that event we must look to other strategies for converting strategic capital to economic capital. Indeed, because innovation is risky, innovators face this situation much of the time!

The first alternative is to license the technology. Licensing makes sense when it becomes clear that the innovator is not in a position to develop a viable business plan, while others may be better situated. In general, licensing should always be considered when it adds more value than direct investment in operations. In addition, licenses earn a return on what had hitherto been financially invisible strategic capital. This "bonus" makes the apparent return on the tangible capital in the financial statements appear very attractive. The company looks smarter.

Intellectual and human capital can also be salvaged through a merger. If there are two or three companies in a new field, each having a few experts and some valuable patents, the least successful may have trouble raising capital and will be forced to merge with one of the survivors. The surviving firm ends up owning additional intellectual property and is clear of pesky patent encumbrances. It may also gain a small group of experts. Not only are these experts valuable in a direct sense, but hiring them takes them out of play—it eliminates the threat of their leaving to form the nucleus of yet another competitor. Further salvage is possible. Unneeded staff members are released, increasing free cash flow (or reducing the burn rate). Lab equipment can be sold and lab space rationalized. The end result is that the strategic capital of the acquired firm is converted to shares of stock in the winner, at a negotiated value. In the process, the former owners of the acquiree gain economic capital in the form of stock certificates.

■ NOT ALL INNOVATION IS TECHNOLOGICAL

The world of technology and R&D is a wonderful classroom for learning about risk management and wealth creation. In today's world, as much as half of the economic growth of the developed nations (which is most of the world's growth) comes from technology.[12] But nontechnical fields, such as finance, produce remarkable innovations as well, albeit these are often facilitated by improvements in technology.

Innovation in finance has a long and colorful history. Fernand Braudel describes how bills of exchange passed through medieval fairs from merchant to merchant led, in the sixteenth through eighteenth centuries, first to international clearinghouses and then to the beginnings of a banking system.[13] Certainly these early innovators accepted enormous risks of default, theft, and government confiscation, as well as the unremitting hostility of the ecclesiastic authorities.

The credit card is another excellent example of financial innovation. Its history has been retold by John Gordon in a recent and fascinating account.[14] Gordon notes that until the twentieth century, bank credit was restricted to people who had collateral. Without it, potential borrowers had to go without, use pawnshops, or accept usurious rates from loan sharks. Banks were uninterested in small loans and extended credit only to the rich. The founding of General Motors Acceptance Corporation (GMAC) was an important first step in altering this situation. GMAC helped consumers finance the purchase of GM cars and helped propel GM to its position as the world's largest automobile company.

Around 1950, U.S. banks began to take an interest in small consumer loans, but they still required a detailed application and often some cosigners. The real breakthrough in unsecured lending to small customers, according to Gordon, came from an employee of Franklin National Bank in Nassau County, New York—William Boyle. Boyle combined two ideas: (1) the charge account that merchants had long offered to their better customers and (2) the line of credit that banks were offering to commercial customers. The alchemy of this combination was the Franklin Charge Card, which entered the marketplace in 1951. Initially designed to meet the needs of local fuel dealers, who lacked back-office support to handle many thousands of small bills, the charge card soon expanded to many other types of merchants. By 1952 almost a thousand merchants and 30,000 consumers were using the card. Franklin National won in two ways: (1) it charged merchants a small percentage of each transaction, and (2) it also charged customers a high rate of interest on unpaid balances. Fifty years later, these remain typical features of the ubiquitous credit card, which has both expanded business for merchants and assisted them with billions of individual credit transactions. And it has allowed consumers to expand their purchasing power through debt—a mechanism some use to advantage and others abuse to their disadvantage.

The charge card idea spread rapidly to other banks in the 1960s. Associations of banks followed, and in the 1970s Visa and MasterCard became ubiquitous in the United States and most other parts of the world.

The charge card is a good example of a nontechnical innovation whose full potential was enabled by a technical solution. It surfaced during a period when computers were major investments and highly technical. Banks were among the first commercial users of computers, while small businesses were a long way from replacing their trusted bookkeepers and clerks with IBM mainframes. As such, banks had huge advantages over their customers in the economies of scale in processing financial information. Franklin National understood and exploited this advantage. But the real innovation was in grasping the opportunity and creating a new business process that gained universal acceptance.

■ THE FOUNDATIONS OF INNOVATION

Today's stock market valuations show that we are literally counting on innovation for our future. But we have seen in Chapter 8 that innovation and the spirit that propels it have hardly been the rule. So it is important to consider the foundations on which our current innovative renaissance is laid. Many of these foundations are surprisingly recent, and most of them have their roots in the Enlightenment period that began in the eighteenth century.

That century and the century that followed were enormously innovative and barely needed educational establishments to fuel the mind and the spirit. Innovation was fostered by freedom and ambition as the yoke of monarchy was loosened and eventually cast away. Innovation was also propelled by the development of scientific and technical knowledge. Technical innovation created wealth, and wealth created more investment.

From the time the cotton gin was invented in 1793 to the beginnings of the U.S. Civil War, abetted by enormous developments in spinning and weaving technologies, cotton production in the United States grew from less than two million pounds per year to two billion pounds—a factor of over a thousand![15] The impact of another new technology, the railroad, was equally impressive. These investments in industrialization were based on technological opportunity, and the forces of value creation were unstoppable. These practical commercial achievements preceded the investments in education whose goal was to perpetuate the pattern of success, and not the reverse.

Despite the initial absence of formal education, great engineering advances were taking place in the country: We noted the invention of the cotton gin by Eli Whitney in 1793. His application of the principle of interchangeable parts and mass production to the manufacture of army rifles, as early as 1798,[16] was an achievement of equal magnitude. The engineering knowledge of early inventors such as Whitney was mostly self-taught, for absence of an alternative. Through this period, technology more often preceded science[17] than the other way around—quite the opposite of the twentieth-century paradigm. Scientific advances had long been led and enabled by practical advances: The science of astronomy by the technology of the telescope and the science of bacteriology by the microscope.

In contrast, the innovative culture of the *modern* United States is closely tied to its schools of engineering and its research universities. Yet in 1800 there were neither engineers nor engineering schools in the United States. In 1875 there were a handful of engineering programs but still no research universities in the country. And the two concepts were initially very different. How did this come about?

The origin of engineering schools was clearly military. In the midst of the French Revolution, the École de Polytechnique was founded by the Convention in 1794 to train engineers and scientists for the military and for civil service. The École was associated heavily with artillery engineering and was committed to meritocratic social principles. It was to become closely associated with Napoleon (who began his career as an artillery officer). The École played a major role in the development of mass production, as French engineers deployed drawings and automatic machinery to enforce production standards for artillery pieces.

In the first half of the nineteenth century, the leading U.S. engineering school was the U.S. Military Academy at West Point.[18] The army's early interest in engineering was stimulated by Sylvanus Thayer's visit to France and the École in 1815 and 1816 and developed at West Point during the period that Thayer was superintendent (1817–1833). The government often gave permission to its engineers to supervise civilian enterprises, and many of West Point's graduates became involved in the development of the emerging railroad industry.

The first dedicated U.S. engineering school was Rensselaer Polytechnic Institute founded in 1824 in Troy, New York, "for the purpose of instructing persons, who may choose to apply themselves, in the application of science to the common purposes of life." In terms of reference, the Massachusetts Institute of Technology (MIT) did not admit its first students until 1865.

Theologians heavily dominated the traditional universities of the time, a situation that lasted well into the nineteenth century. There were a few teachers of natural philosophy, as science was then called. One of the first to establish a research laboratory on campus was Benjamin Silliman at Yale, who in 1804 received an allowance of $9,000 for books and apparatus. Silliman had learned chemistry from John McLean at Princeton.[19]

Gradually more and more scientists—Joseph Priestley, James Maxwell, Josiah Gibbs, Gustav Kirchhoff, and Dmitry Mendeleyev—made teaching universities their natural home. So it was in the science departments of the great universities of England, the United States, Germany, and France, and in the new engineering schools that the modern concept of the research university was born.

However, support for research, whether basic or applied, was meager throughout most of the nineteenth century. The universities were still seen as teaching institutions, despite the growing importance of science in the curriculum. That began to change with the founding of the University of Chicago by William Rainey Harper in 1891 (with subsequent significant funding from John D. Rockefeller) and the endowment of Johns Hopkins University (founded in 1876 in Baltimore by the railroad investor and philanthropist of the same name).

Professors of science in these and other U.S. universities looked to European universities for their advanced training, and it was largely on European models that the modern doctoral degree program evolved. As Richard Atkinson tells us:

> It was not until World War II that what we think of as a modern research university began to emerge. Prior to then, the United States depended on Europe for basic research (while excelling in applied research). America attracted a cadre of European émigrés (Albert Einstein, Enrico Fermi, John von Neumann, et al.) during the 1930s, but only when the importance of radar, electronic communications, cryptology, and the atomic bomb became apparent was science recognized as critical to the national interest. The recognition of the importance of science was crystallized in Roosevelt's letter to Vannevar Bush and Bush's subsequent report to Truman entitled *Science—The Endless Frontier*.[20]

In reviewing these events, it is evident in hindsight that military competition has been one of the more important foundations of innovation—and value creation. Indeed, government funded the first experiments in mass production in the United States and France. The development of the airplane was accelerated by its military possibilities during and between the two World Wars. Nuclear power had its birth in a desperate race for the ultimate bomb. Satellite communications were accelerated by the rocketry competition between the United States and the Soviet Union. And the Internet grew out of an attempt to improve communications among military researchers.

In summary, the notion that U.S. universities should be funded by government to produce innovative developments for defense, health, and commerce is very recent. So is the concept that basic research in science promotes innovation and enables wealth creation.

■ THE OUTLOOK FOR INNOVATION

If innovation has been the source of our extraordinary prosperity, it is important to inquire about its future. The good news is that the rate of discontinuous innovation in Western society appears to be accelerating.[21] This rate is likely to hold if the two bedrock premises of innovation also hold over time: (1) the willingness of investors to accept high risk and (2) the continued existence of opportunity.

Today, investors seem very willing to accept high risks. The level of financing is virtually unprecedented, with the prospect of more than $50 billion being invested per year by venture capitalists alone, a 10-fold increase over the previous decade.[22] Whether this pace of investment will be sustained is another issue. Too much capital chasing too few good ideas is a sure way to drive down returns. But if we believe Daniel Bernoulli's ideas about utility, the fact that investors have a greater stock of capital than ever before virtually ensures that they will, over time, be more tolerant of high risks.

What about the continued existence of opportunity? At the end of the nineteenth century, the commissioner of the U.S. Patent Office famously recommended that the office be shut down because everything that could be invented already had been. His colossal misjudgment is as widely quoted by speakers at innovation conferences as is Malthus in economics textbooks—but the number of issued patents continues to grow exponentially.

The future is not without problems. The old bogeyman, the

law of diminishing returns, remains a permanent feature of science and technology. In science, the law of diminishing returns means that it costs more and more to discover a significant new piece of information. Most fields of physics and mathematics are now mature. Even chemistry has matured significantly since I wrote my thesis on boron hydrides in 1965. Biology is another story. Even with the sequencing of the human genome, we are only on the threshold of understanding how a cell really works and reproduces itself.

Many of our technologies are likewise in their golden years: the rifle, the automobile engine, refrigeration, jet-powered aircraft, to name just a few. In high technology, we know that we are within a decade of hitting the wall with silicon-based computing power. Moore's Law, which states that the number of integrated circuits per unit area on a chip (and hence its computing power) doubles every 18 months, is bound to crumble in the absence of discontinuous innovation in microelectronics. Perhaps one of many new atomic-level technologies, such as the quantum mirage effect[23] being pioneered by IBM, will provide the necessary breakthrough. It is almost certain that good ideas in this field will be funded.

Nevertheless there is plenty of reason for optimism. With worldwide R&D spending at about half a trillion dollars per year,[24] new technologies are bound to emerge and take root. And practical combinations of existing technologies, such as computers and the Internet, are still bound to surprise us. Markets are also growing at impressive rates. More important, the number of educated and motivated people in the world is much on the rise; and as interactions between these individuals inevitably increase, so too will innovation. The Internet is already bringing bright, ambitious people in China, India, and many developing countries into the mainstream of commerce and creative endeavor. These people are bound to connect with capital markets; and when that happens the cauldron of innovation will truly bubble. The networks being built by global corporations and other communities of common interest[25] are bound to produce a similar result. Their effectiveness will be enhanced by new technologies such as context-tagged information (i.e., the XML programming language).

Our vision of the future for networks, in the broadest sense, is still hazy, but surely networks are not mature and may even be embryonic. If so, the potential for innovation and value creation, and even for another period of increasing returns, remains formidable for some time.

■ A PRESCRIPTION FOR SUSTAINING INNOVATION

Sustained innovation, diversification, and corporate value are closely linked. The linkage is apparent when we observe the fates of mature companies and industries that have failed to create opportunities to invest above their costs of money. The result, inevitably, is little or no growth in corporate value. R&D productivity in these companies and industries has been slipping, often to the point at which the output of their research laboratories no longer justifies its cost. This slippage is the consequence of riding the S-curve for too long, of not knowing when to get off, and of investing beyond the point of diminishing returns. This situation is bad for scientists, who find it increasingly difficult to justify their work. It is even worse for shareholders because lower growth generally translates into falling price/earnings (P/E) ratios and the destruction of value.

The classic management response to this situation has been to seek improved R&D productivity through strategic and operating concepts such as so-called second- and third-generation R&D,[26] stage-gate methods,[27] total quality management, and tighter screening of new project ideas. These approaches have in many cases led to significant improvements; they have bought time and have helped companies pluck "low-hanging fruit" they would otherwise have missed. They have neutralized some effects of the law of diminishing returns, often by reducing uncertainty in the early stages of the R&D pipeline.

Unfortunately, to the extent that management methods attempt to control risk and raise certainty, they create another risk—the risk of diminishing opportunity. At its extreme, risk reduction reduces returns to the cost of money and eliminates future economic profit. Most of the changes that have occurred in R&D management in large companies over the past few decades, in my view, have favored risk reduction over increased opportunity. The emphasis on control may be self-defeating. R&D must incubate many concept-stage projects to one day produce a small number of important new products or businesses. The ideas behind such projects are incompletely developed and their implications poorly understood. They and their champions are extremely vulnerable to risk control mechanisms, which, in their zeal to avoid the costs and the embarrassment of going down blind alleys, screens them out. The frequent observation that the cutting edge of innovation and growth in U.S. industry has shifted to its smaller firms may have its origins in the focus on risk-reduction practices in the larger ones.

Excessive screening of new, untested ideas has yet another pernicious effect. When exploratory activity is limited, the pipeline becomes dominated by expensive later-stage projects with lower potential for economic profit. Big mediocre projects crowd out small untested ones. All too often, too few of the former are terminated because of the sunk costs and the risk to management reputations. In time, the internal research portfolio will become opportunity poor, and returns will suffer. Or, to put it in the context of our earlier discussion of diversification, to exploit the high-profit end of the normal distribution, we need enough project ideas to create a fertile distribution in the first place.

In brief, management shortsightedness may in part be caused by the tools with which R&D projects are measured. DCF systematically undervalues opportunity. It is time to examine R&D decision making in light of the emerging perspective of real options.

Chapter

13

Can Government Manage Risk and Value?

The question of whether government can manage risk and value is of paramount importance to high-risk investors. Government has the power to enable, or to disable, the real options and the strategic capital of high-risk investors. Fortunately, the short answer to the question is that at times governments have done a surprisingly good job of managing risk and value. That answer suggests that models of wise economic governance are available and that improvement will occur as economic experience is translated into improved institutional models. We have seen that the era of prosperity is only a few hundred years old, so learning is reasonably to be expected. But governments just as often have failed to understand the principles of value creation, which are often less than obvious, and inadvertently have undermined the process. It is no wonder that investors cringe when the unschooled get their hands on the levers of power.

In terms of our value model (Figure 4.1), government regulates the environment in which its twin loops—operational and strategic—function. Any discussion of value creation through history or speculation about future value creation must consider government's role. As discussed in Chapter 9, the preconditions for prosperity and for successful investing do not come naturally. Mankind's deeply rooted instinct to avoid risk seems to sabotage economic progress, and a balance of learnings over several centuries were necessary to create robust, enduring social forms in a few parts of the world to ensure its continuance. Laissez-faire philosophies won't cut it: Good governance is essential.

A great deal of the physical and the intellectual activity of a country takes place within its public sector; governmental budgets seldom account for less than 25 percent of the gross domestic product of nations and sometimes account for 75 percent or more. Their leading revenue source is usually taxation: taxation of personal income, of enterprise income, of consumption, of wealth, and of imported goods. In addition, they may derive other revenues, sometimes substantial, through the ownership of property and the sale of goods and services. The impact of taxation on an enterprise is particularly important to value creation and a later section will discuss it.

The philosophy of this chapter will be to strive to be nonpolitical while recognizing the inherent impossibility of that goal—politics is all about the role of government, the distribution of wealth, and the creation of economic prosperity. Indeed, the central political issue of our times seems to be whether it is better to have a bigger pie divided unequally or a smaller pie divided equitably; and a successful strategy for politicians is to promise a government that can provide a larger pie divided more equitably. However, reexamining this rather tired subject through the lens of value may provide a new perspective.

■ SECURITY AND RISK REDUCTION

The first and most essential function of government has long been to establish and to maintain order. Order, in turn, reduces risk. An adequate military force deters bands of aggressors motivated by plunder. A constabulary reduces crime. Fire protection and fire codes for the community reduce catastrophic loss. Health codes protect the human resource base. An effective judicial system makes the outcome of transactions and contracts predictable and enforceable to a level that promotes investment and commerce. We have mentioned that there seems to be a real correlation between history's brief periods of prosperity and strong and effective governments: Witness Egypt's New Kingdom, the reigns of Rome's Augustus and Hadrian, the Pax Britannica, and the present era.

Less obvious, but also in the area of risk reduction, governments backed by the power of taxation can create useful risk-free securities and insurance programs. Treasury notes, bills, and bonds are examples of the former and the insurance of bank deposits or brokerage accounts of the latter. Other forms of insurance can include health care programs and welfare for individuals financially unable to support themselves.

However, many current and formerly despotic nations, well provided for in terms of military capability and police presence, have proved remarkably weak when attempting to create a respected code of laws and are risky places to invest. Transaction costs can be very high if payments must be paid to several levels of officials to ensure execution. Even if the costs are acceptable, risk is also high because many officials can block a deal, but very few can truly ensure it. Fixed capital is particularly vulnerable to extortion—the owners of a mine or a factory have few intermediate choices between pay up and operate or exercise their option to abandon. Countries with abundant gold, diamonds, and petroleum wealth seem to attract more than their share of terrible governance. All such costs are highly destructive to value creation.

As they relate to real options, security and certainty will reduce the cost of capital and thus enhance the value of any enterprise or business plan. A reduction in cost of capital, of course, will create a positive present value for many businesses and business proposals that were hitherto value destroying. Its effect relates to market (or systematic) risk, applies to all ventures in the realm, and has great power to stimulate an economy. Hernando de Soto also makes a persuasive case that enormous capital resources could be generated in developing nations if title to property was ensured by reliable and durable legal institutions.[1]

Good government and a predictable code of law will in many cases also reduce the *unique risk* of a project by reducing its vulnerability to predatory or unscrupulous behavior. The latter effect will be situational, but it may be equally important as the effect of *market risk* on the cost of capital in its impact on development.

■ EDUCATION

Once security is established, the next level at which governments can influence the economy is to provide services. These services can be value creating or, when inefficient, value destroying. Education is one of these services. It is enormously important because of the dominant role of intellectual capital in value creation in Western economies. Today, Americans take the link between education and government for granted, and it is hard to remember that the concept of public education is almost brand new.

Wealthy Greeks and Romans hired tutors (or obtained slaves) to provide basic literacy for some citizens. Private academies also existed in the classical world. Literacy in Western Europe then dropped to a low level in the early Middle Ages (A.D. 400–1000), and was largely confined to the ecclesiastical sphere. Learning was preserved primarily by monks copying ancient manuscripts,[2] but much intellectual treasure was undoubtedly lost in cycles of war and plunder. The feudal aristocracy was often functionally illiterate, focused on military skills, and dependent on ecclesiastics for record keeping. Universities began to be founded around A.D. 1200, but their curricula were religious and philosophical. The overall situation could not have been conducive to the creation of value, whether in intellectual property or even physical property; the concerns of the time were otherworldly, and even the basic tools of measurement were missing.

But the fact that technological progress was made in the Middle Ages—as witnessed by the Gothic cathedral, the waterwheel, the windmill, a variety of steel tools and weapons, and advanced techniques for weaving—suggests that an important form of technoeconomic education was occurring in the world of the towns and of master craftsmen, based on apprenticeship rather than on academics. Little of this hidden wealth was codified in written text, mathematical formulas, or data tabulations.

The dynamics of this process involved a form of indentured servitude, where prospective students entered a guild for low wages and provided assistance to the master craftsmen, planning eventually to rise to that rank themselves. Undoubtedly power, birth, and influence played a role, as it does today, in who was admitted to education and who could proceed to the highest ranks. Clearly, the potential to add value and create wealth was present—a mason or a carpenter whose work was sought out and commanded a premium price could invest in tools, apprentices, and working space. Accordingly, he could accumulate both economic and strategic capital.

So the basic picture was zero government investment in education, highly specialized investments by churches, and a host of economically driven investments by families and individuals via the crafts. The medieval crafts often involved significant technology and were the incubators of modern science and engineering.

A conspicuous and successful precedent for government investment in education, science, and technology occurred in the late Middle Ages. It was the sailing academy founded in the fifteenth century at Sagres, Portugal, by Prince Henry, called the Navigator. This institution attracted cartographers, shipbuilders, astronomers, instrument makers, and seamen. As the caravel was developed and navigation improved, Portuguese seamen began to outflank the Islamic powers and to work their way down the coast of Africa and ultimately, 40 years after Henry's death, around its southern capes to the Orient. Commerce by sea was enormously stimulated. These wise national investments laid the basis for the enormously value-creating discoveries of the seaward passage to India and the transatlantic route to the Western hemisphere.

Modern developed countries are nearly unanimous in providing free primary and secondary education to all citizens, although the degree of acceptance of this concept still varies greatly around the globe. Nations now understand that most value-creating activities in a modern society require basic literacy. This requirement, of course, did not and still does not apply to agricultural economies in developing nations. It probably did not apply to the more basic crafts—blacksmithing, masonry, baking—either. In these situations, the economic value of the child in augmenting the household's economics by farming, weaving, or assisting the father in his craft was greater than spending time and money on formal schooling. Today, such practices are viewed by some as a deplorable waste of human resources.

The situation at the university level is somewhat different, for universities are more than advanced training schools; they are storehouses of strategic capital, and they make important additions to the stock of such capital. In most countries, universities are government-funded institutions. An interesting case study of government investment is taking place in India, which has a highly regarded program (the Indian Institute of Technology, or IIT) for training engineers. Competition to enter is understandably extreme, so the talent pool is formidable. Until recently, however, the Indian economy could provide few jobs for that talent, leading to emigration and expensive de facto subsidization of foreign economies. From India's viewpoint, this expensive program was adding little value. The situation is now changing, owing to a better investment climate in India and a global shortage of software engineers.

In the United States, however, where a very large fraction of the population receives some university-level education, the situation is more complex. Governments at all levels make enormous investments, of course, but so do individuals and families through tuition and service fees. Charity is also an important source of funds for U.S. private universities. And some indentured servitude goes on as well—graduate students, postdoctoral fellows, and even student athletes all work for subsistence wages in the hopes of recovering their investment through highly paid and prestigious professional employment.

Unlike India, there is little doubt that the U.S. economy has benefited enormously from the public and private investments in its university system. Stanford University and the Massachusetts Institute of Technology (MIT) alone have spun off hundreds of companies, many of them now large and profitable, that have created enormous value for investors and employers. MIT quotes a BankBoston study showing that there are 1,065 MIT-related companies headquartered in Massachusetts, which employ 125,000 people and represent 10 percent of that state's economic base.[3] Government has also benefited through the enormous "equity" it holds in such corporations through the corporate income tax, not to mention the additional revenues from capital gains and employee income taxes!

The Industrial Revolution provided an unexpected benefit to

the United States in a new form of strategic capital—educated women. With increasing technical progress, the relative value of labor in manufacturing was diminishing in relation to the value of physical capital, such as machinery. At the primary and secondary school levels, young women began to be encouraged to obtain basic education rather than employment at weaving and spinning as they did a century earlier. This development in turn enabled the establishment of women's colleges in the United States. Mount Holyoke, the first, was founded in Massachusetts in 1837. In a hundred years this movement, now spread to Europe, has resulted in women being almost fully represented in some professions and moving rapidly to full representation in others. The addition of women's intellectual skills to the stock of human capital has had an impact as profound as that created by public health and the population explosion, which we discuss later in this chapter.

Given the proven success of investment in public education, it is remarkable that the subject has recently turned contentious. This circumstance may well have to do with the very fact that education is almost universally recognized as financially valuable. The school voucher controversy is driven in considerable measure by a sense that some educational bureaucracies have lost touch with the marketplace, are driven by their own agendas, and could benefit from competition. Although there are other issues involving race and religion that complicate the picture, it is the loss of strategic capital both to individuals and to society as a whole that has galvanized the dialogue about educational quality. The value issue will not go away so long as public schools are politically insulated from market forces.

■ INFRASTRUCTURE

The government's role in providing infrastructure—in the form of roads, canals, water supplies, sewers, harbors, postal services, and libraries and possibly railroads, power utilities, and telephone service—is also well accepted today. This idea is an old one—the Romans excelled at it, with advanced road systems, aqueducts, and public baths. Indeed, part of the greatness of the ancient city of Rome was the ability of its engineers to support the needs of 1 million to 2 million people at a time when a city of 25,000 was very large! Those needs included a transportation system to bring from afar the needed quantities of food and fuel, plus raw materials for industry and trade goods for commerce. A large city also required advanced sanitation to prevent the outbreak of disease, then a huge threat in a densely populated urban area. The required capital investment was enormous for its day, as must have been the ongoing cost of maintenance.

However, the value-creating opportunities must have been equally enormous, allowing the development of complementary specialties in close proximity.

When Rome worked well, it could generate an enormous surplus, as evidenced by the large number of aqueducts, baths, temples, and city gates that were erected throughout the empire during the reigns of only two of its emperors. The system was also vulnerable; and it would seem, from the same evidence, that Rome more commonly did not work well enough to finance continual additions to its infrastructure.

Infrastructure seems to be a necessary condition for wealth creation in an industrial economy, for it can be persuasively argued that it is infrastructure that makes a large city possible and that serious value creation can take place only in large cities. Effective industrial innovation "depends on the close collaboration of workers with different kinds of expertise,"[4] often working in different enterprises. Flexibility is a key element of success, and such conditions are most typically found in large cities with good infrastructure.

Certainly, the absence of the type of infrastructure characteristic of North America and Western Europe will long hold back the commercial competitiveness of less developed areas, such as

Russia, China, India, and Africa. The capital requirements are simply too great to be supplied in a few decades.

How does infrastructure support value creation? It reduces transportation cost and time. Trucks laden with cargo between customer and supplier represent capital—the goods in transit and the truck itself. Ditto for rail, ship, and aircraft. More recently, just-in-time supply concepts were credited with winning an important competitive advantage for Japanese manufacturers. The labor market will be more efficient when employees can commute to work from a larger geographic area. Telephone and postal services facilitate commerce—experienced business travelers know that reliable services cannot be taken for granted. Port cities have thrived since ancient times. Today, an accessible world-class airport is necessary for a city to be considered a serious commercial center. It is interesting to reflect how once-lonely Dulles Airport, still no paragon of efficiency, is spawning a significant new center of commerce in northern Virginia.

But, as with education, infrastructure can be value destroying. Excessive public works, often justified for their job-creating potential, can stifle a thriving commercial economy. Such overinvestment appears to have occurred in Japan, which has been building hugely expensive bridges and tunnels to obscure rural regions, financed by overtaxed urban salarymen. Attempts to revive dying urban centers in Connecticut through new infrastructure led to an income tax and thus lost opportunities to attract corporations eager to leave higher-tax New York. And worst of all, huge infrastructure projects (notably hydroelectric dams) in underdeveloped countries have done much less to stimulate economic growth than the planners had hoped. Value must be determined on a case-by-case basis; and whether by government or by private industry, value can be destroyed by a bad economic decision.

Private ownership of infrastructure has often been a better solution from a value standpoint. But it usually provides less benefit in cases of monopoly than in the presence of competition and, indeed, lends itself to the same risks of excessive costs and bloated bureaucracy as any organization that has a market to itself. This proposition seems to be increasingly recognized, as in the breakup of AT&T and the deregulation of airlines.

Conversely, efficiencies are created when publicly owned infrastructure is subject to competition and forced to create value or devolve. The U.S. Postal Service is in this situation and must determine its role in the face of swift and cheap e-mail on the one hand and nimble private mail services, such as FedEx and UPS, on the other. Nationalized railroads, once the norm in Western Europe and Japan, will gradually disappear; and state-owned factories and mines, although still an important part of China's economy, are universally recognized as Marxian dinosaurs.

■ PUBLIC HEALTH

The value-added aspects of government-supported health care were once unquestioned; but it is interesting that they have now also become very controversial. This outcome is actually not unexpected under the law of diminishing returns and lends itself to value analysis.

Without a doubt the greatest loss to a city, a nation, or an enterprise is the loss of its most productive talent to an epidemic. The plagues of Egypt and Athens had devastating economic effects. The bubonic plague reduced the population of fourteenth-century Europe by 30 percent. In his book *Guns, Germs, and Steel*, Jared Diamond argues convincingly that disease brought by Europeans' superior weapons played as large a role as weapons in enabling the easy conquest of the powerful Aztec and Inca empires and later eased the western expansion of America's thirteen colonies.[5] And certainly, it is a substantial conquest of disease that has brought about a generally prosperous global economy of 6 billion people.

The first economic benefit of disease control is population

growth—long the basis of economic and military power. As soon as death rates drop below birth rates, populations begin to grow. If this drop is precipitous, as with the control of infectious disease in the twentieth century, populations can explode.

However, there is a second economic benefit. When average life spans were in the low 30s, it would have been a risky investment to train specialists until the age of 30 or even 25. But with average life spans in the 70s, the most specialized members of our society—whether physicians or research scientists—can spend 30 or more years developing their skills and still have 30 more years to employ them professionally. The ratio of investment (training period) to reward (employment period) is improved enormously by good health.

There have been three stages in the creation of value through human health: (1) sanitation, (2) modern medicine, and (3) discovery of nucleic acids as the source of genes. Good sanitation—good water and the removal of human wastes from residential areas—can be achieved through various combinations of municipal administration (strict rules about water supplies and waste disposal) and engineering (aqueducts, wells, sewers). However, under devolving conditions, when the necessary funds are not available, the rules often break down and facilities deteriorate. So the good sanitary practices that made Rome possible were not recreated in Europe until the sixteenth century.

As a case in point, the evolution of a safe and abundant water supply, beginning in the early days of the nineteenth century, had much to do with making New York City the leading world metropolis that it became in the twentieth century. Its origin was the creation of the Manhattan Company by Aaron Burr and his partners in 1799, when the city had a population of perhaps 60,000. The water was originally pumped by two steam engines to the Collect Pond on lower Broadway. Incremental facilities were added during the next three decades to keep up with the city's growth.[6]

By the 1830s the city had a population of over 200,000, and

the need for an aqueduct to import water from more distant points was apparent. In 1834, the New York State legislature authorized the Croton Aqueduct project, based on a 50-foot-high dam, a 45-mile right-of-way, an underground pipe of about 7 feet in diameter, and a distribution reservoir in what is today Bryant Park in midtown Manhattan. This project was completed in 1842, by which time the city population had reached 360,000. The city soon outgrew the original Croton facility and a new facility, the new Croton aqueduct, was completed in 1892. The new system had four times the capacity of the old and exploited technical innovations in drilling and excavation—the Harlem River barrier was crossed with a tunnel that was 400 feet below grade. The 30-mile-long tunnel was for some time the longest in the world. A new Croton dam was completed in 1905. This structure was nearly 300 feet high and created a reservoir 19 miles long. For a time it was the tallest dam in the world.

The next step took the system to the Catskills and required a crossing of the Hudson River. The work began in 1907 and continued to 1937, involving as many as 17,000 workmen at peak periods of activity. The Olive Bridge Dam, 252 feet high, was located near Kingston. The aqueduct was 98 miles long and the Hudson crossing near West Point was 3,000 feet in length and reached a depth of 1,100 feet. The water pressure there is more than 600 pounds per square inch. The cross-section of the tunnel was 50 percent larger than that of the new Croton aqueduct and 400 percent larger than the old Croton.

Even so, this facility could still not produce enough water for the growing metropolis. The final stage was the Delaware Aqueduct, which ran in a straight line underground from the Round-out Reservoir near Liberty, New York, to the upper reaches of the Croton watershed. Its diameter varies from 13.5 to 19.5 feet, and the deepest shaft is over 1,500 feet below grade. The combined length of the tunnels in the Delaware Aqueduct system is over 105 miles, the longest continuous tunnel built for any purpose anywhere.

The purpose of this tale is not to detail a somewhat forgotten series of technical triumphs; it is to demonstrate what an enormous economic and technical investment was required to make the huge metropolis of modern New York a healthy community. In terms of the Total Value Model, the water system was undoubtedly of itself a viable economic enterprise, but the *strategic options* it enabled dwarfed the value of the water itself. New York is the financial capital of the world, and it is also a world-class center for other important industries that are independent of the financial sector. These primary industries require a vast number of commercial and municipal services and draw on enormous infrastructure. New York may be what it is today because the investment in its water supply system (and hence sanitation) overcame one of the fundamental limits to urban growth that still slowed its rivals. It recapitulated a lesson in economics first taught by classic Rome, which itself built no less than 11 aqueducts.

The second stage in the creation of value through health was the beginning of modern medicine, based on observation and careful experimentation, in the eighteenth century. In 1747, the Scottish naval surgeon James Lind treated scurvy-ridden sailors with lemons and oranges and obtained impressive cures. By 1795 the British navy began to control scurvy by distributing lime juice during long sea voyages (giving rise to the name "limeys" for British sailors). Nearly two hundred years went by before scientists understood the role of vitamin C in protecting the structural protein collagen. Edward Jenner's prescient notion (1796) of vaccinating for smallpox saved untold lives. This innovation was truly remarkable because it would be well over a hundred years before the mysterious cause of smallpox, a virus, would be identified and understood—another fine example of technology preceding science.

It was not until the middle of the nineteenth century that the importance of sterility in maternity wards and field hospitals began to be recognized and addressed. Ignac Semmelweiss, a

Hungarian physician, made sanitary improvements in the maternity wards of Vienna prior to 1850, at least 25 years before the germ theory was established. Florence Nightingale made pioneering contributions to nursing in the Crimean War of 1854 to 1856. In the American Civil War, the United States Sanitary Commission's insistence, over considerable Army resistance, that military surgeons employ sterile instruments reduced death rates from wounds in the Union army to a fraction of those amongst Confederates, who had yet to absorb this lesson. The Sanitary Commission was one of the first and most effective women's activist organizations.

The germ theory had its origins in research performed by Louis Pasteur in the 1860s. The first stage of this research was actually under industrial sponsorship, work performed for a French distiller named Bigo, in which Pasteur firmly disproved the millennia-old theory of spontaneous generation. Emperor Napoleon III (government) thereafter enlisted Pasteur's assistance with fermentation issues in the wine industry, which led to the development of pasteurization in 1864. Pasteur went on to solve another problem of major commercial importance to France, disease in silkworms. The value created through the introduction of pasteurization and sterilization would be felt not only in terms of health but also in leaps in agricultural and industrial productivity.

The British surgeon Joseph Lister had read about Pasteur's work in 1865. Lister was familiar with the properties of carbolic acid, a chemical that was then being used to treat foul smelling sewers. By applying carbolic acid (phenol) to instruments and directly to wounds and dressings, Lister reduced surgical mortality to 15 percent by 1869. Lister's discoveries in antiseptics met initial resistance, but by the 1880s they had become widely accepted. This development came just a few years too late to help the wounded of the American Civil and Crimean wars.

The next step was to connect the germ theory to the human condition. Robert Koch, a German physician who worked at the German Health Office in Berlin, made this link. In the 1870s, he showed that anthrax, a disease of warm-blooded animals, and highly lethal to humans, grew from spores of the bacillus anthracis. He demonstrated how to acquire these bacteria from infected animals, how to propagate them artificially, and how to destroy them. Using the new techniques he was developing, Koch went on to conduct other studies of the bacterial agents responsible for tuberculosis, cholera, bubonic plague, and sleeping sickness. Pasteur, too, continued to make enormous contributions and went on to discover three bacteria responsible for human illnesses: staphylococcus, streptococcus, and pneumococcus.

The discovery of systemic antibiotics followed soon thereafter—initially sulfanilamide and other analogs that block the synthesis of folic acid in bacteria but are relatively innocuous to mammals. Penicillin was discovered by Alexander Fleming in 1928 and gave rise to an even more powerful generation of antibiotics based on natural products and semisynthetic analogs of natural products.

The impact of these discoveries can be felt on a personal level today: Many of us have living relatives with memories of the tragic loss of young siblings who died suddenly of infectious diseases that were to be routinely controlled with a few pills a decade later. With the identification of the pathogens causing major bacterial diseases and the antibiotics to control them came the second breakthrough in population and health. And with it came the explosion of world population from less than 2 billion to over 6 billion. Although the main value was the creation of enormous human capital, among the other results were the development of a global pharmaceutical industry and important new opportunities for the chemical industry, which was then also in its infancy. From here, the process of value creation would shift naturally from its origins in the public sector to the wealth-creating possibilities of the private sector.

The third and current stage in the saga of human health

began with the discovery of nucleic acids as the source of genes. Genes had been identified conceptually by Gregor Mendel in a paper published in 1866. However, it is astonishing that genes were not linked physically to DNA until the work of Oswald Avery, Colin MacLeod, and Maclyn McCarty at the Rockefeller Institute in 1944.[7] The unlocking of the molecular secrets of DNA's mode of action followed the discovery of the double helix by James Watson and Francis Crick in 1953.[8] This discovery opened up a host of scientific options. New research programs to read and to interpret the genetic code became possible. The growth in knowledge was explosive and finally enabled a basic understanding of the nature of viruses and, even more important, an understanding of how the various chemical constituents of a living cell are synthesized and how they function. In this way, basic knowledge created the conditions under which new technologies could emerge, and they did. Scientific hypotheses and models could be used to envision new therapies, whether through the synthesis of small chemical compounds designed to activate or deactivate specific proteins, through the manufacture of proteins themselves (such as insulin and growth hormone), or even by programming the genome itself to turn the synthesis of specific proteins on or off.

What is significant from a historic viewpoint is that advances in medicine originally driven in the first phase (Lyle, Jenner, and Semmelweiss) by observation and insight evolved in the second phase (Pasteur and Koch) to a mixture of science and empiricism, and then proceeded to a third phase that is now *driven* by programmed scientific discovery—the mapping of the human genome and the determination of the function of the protein corresponding to each gene. Early health care was technology driven, and many of the advances were of an engineering or an administrative nature. Technology preceded science. Today, it is the reverse. And with the relative certainty of scientific advance, investment in discovery research has been a creator of enormous value for shareholders of major drug firms.

Much of the value creation in medicine has moved today to private hands, but the role of government remains important. Government agencies led by the National Institutes of Health (NIH) are making an enormous investment in basic medical research, often of a nature that cannot be justified to shareholders of a drug company but that has had an impressive history of translating into future medical advances. Some of this research has been successfully commercialized by for-profit ventures, thus recouping government's costs through license fees and taxes.

An equally important role for government is in disease control. The populations of developed countries look to their governments to identify and contain potential epidemics (whether human, as in influenza, anthrax, or HIV, or animal, as in mad cow disease [BSE]). Leadership in this area has not passed over to the private sector, nor is it likely to.

Although there seems little doubt that modern medicine was absolutely essential to the wealth creation that occurred in the twentieth century and was thus overwhelmingly a creator of value, we may be reaching a point of diminishing returns *in economic terms*. The tensions are evident from the debates over the affordability of free universal health care, about Medicare abuses, about denial of service by insurers, and by the observation that the majority of health care costs are incurred in the last few months of human life, that is, mostly for the terminally ill. In short, there is a conflict between the desire to make quality health care a universal right and the recognition that its costs are already very high (approximately 15 percent of the gross national product in the United States) and could be higher if not constrained.

Put another way, unrestricted universal health care has a potential to destroy a great deal of economic value in a society that (rightly) does not recognize economics as the sole criterion for allocating resources. All hope the problem can be alleviated by more efficient administration and better technology; but as new therapies become ever more expensive to develop and administer, diminishing economic returns are a very serious threat to dreams of a universal age of healthy longevity.

■ INTELLECTUAL CAPITAL

The final area where government can create wealth is in fostering the development of intellectual capital, for example, by stimulating investments in R&D.

An accurate shipboard clock, virtually indispensable to calculating longitude, was at the peak of military priorities in the seventeenth and eighteenth centuries. Indeed, several disasters at sea had prompted the British government to form a Board of Longitude, which offered in 1714 a huge prize of 20,000 pounds for a marine chronometer capable of measuring longitude to an accuracy of half a degree on a sea voyage to the West Indies. This specification required an error of less than three seconds per day. The prize for this early innovation was claimed by John Harrison in 1763.

This example was one of the first instances of governments paying for the development of science or technology, in this case technology. (Today, government-sponsored R&D is a $60 billion-plus enterprise in the United States alone.)

The chronometer prize was a particularly shrewd affair. For one, the government bore no financial risk and was encouraging competition. For another, the payoff (value) was potentially enormous because the clock was needed to measure longitude from the position of the sun and the stars. There was no such problem with latitude, but an error in longitude of only one minute in time could represent an error of 17 miles at the equator. (The earth's circumference is 25,000 miles and there are 1,440 minutes in a day, representing a complete rotation of the earth). A six-minute cumulative error would represent 100 miles! Obviously, ships out of sight of land with a good understanding of their position had a significant tactical advantage over those lacking this knowledge, Britain badly wanted this advantage and achieved it in this way. Advanced clock making even became a military secret.

Although we have cited a few early examples of government sponsorship of R&D, from Henry the Navigator to John Harrison, until the 1850s most of the great scientists (Isaac Newton, Antoine-Laurent Lavoisier, and Charles Darwin) used private funds to support their studies. We saw in the previous chapter that the research university had its origins in the latter part of the nineteenth century, as the importance of science became manifest to the educational establishment. But government's role was still very modest. It was World War II and its aftermath, the Cold War, that created today's vast, federally sponsored R&D enterprise. Not only were universities enlisted massively in defense efforts, but also whole new institutions were created to convert scientific knowledge to military technology. Thus, the possibility of nuclear fission was known to physicists, including Albert Einstein, after the discoveries of Otto Hahn in 1938. Einstein, actually prodded by other physicists, interceded with President Franklin Roosevelt to create a U.S. fission program. A university setting was initially needed. In 1942, the Italian-born American physicist Enrico Fermi and his coworkers at the University of Chicago produced the first controlled, self-sustaining, nuclear fission reaction.

After a successful demonstration of the concept, the effort was thereafter transferred to a secret new complex at Los Alamos, New Mexico, and several other large facilities, such as Oak Ridge, Tennessee, were created to handle different aspects of the weapons programs. Almost all of these federal facilities continue as research institutions today.

Indeed, the evident success of the model led to it being emulated for other missions, such as the space program and the "war" against cancer. The latter is incorporated today in the National Institutes of Health, which performs research directly and, even more importantly, funds thousands of projects at research universities, teaching hospitals, and private laboratories.

The transfer of basic research from universities and national laboratories to commercially viable businesses is controversial and contentious.[9] In addition to the typical risks involved in converting raw ideas into financial assets, government and university sponsorship adds a number of administrative obstacles and transaction risks. Yet these barriers are regularly overcome, and the pool of knowledge and talent in the nonindustrial research community is a prime source of industrial innovation. A recent study by CHI Research, Inc., has indicated that 73 percent of U.S. industrial patents cite a publication that was federally sponsored.[10]

In general, there have been two mechanisms by which technology is transferred from the academic and the governmental sectors to industry. The first involves people who found companies based on innovative technology concepts. In many cases, such start-ups involve direct entrepreneurial activity by scientists, who will seek seed financing from private investors and venture capitalists, with plans to create a profitable business enterprise.

The second is the licensing of technology owned by universities or government to private firms—sometimes large companies and sometimes start-ups. The Cohen-Boyer gene-splicing patent is expected to bring more than $100 million in royalties to the University of California and Stanford. MIT boasts that some 40 companies have been started based on MIT-licensed technology.

Today, there are about three hundred federal laboratories carrying out mission-oriented and basic research for various government agencies—it is called the National Laboratory System and has a budget of about $15 billion.

Defense-sponsored research has continued to be an important source of funding for universities, but its former leadership has been supplanted by the National Science Foundation (NSF), which is principally dedicated to the continuation of basic research in the sciences and transfers nearly all of its budget as grants to university-based researchers.

The NIH and the NSF deserve much of the credit for creating the roots of the biotechnology industry. Not only did government-sponsored research create many of the seminal ideas, but also, as important, it trained the core of researchers that staffs the R&D centers of the industry. Strategic capital was thus built in *two* ways.

The defense effort had an unexpected but vast payoff—the Internet. This originated as a small network linking researchers in the defense community. It was originally called DARPA-net after the Defense Advanced Research Projects Agency. Internet protocols spread to other university researchers and eventually were released (in a moment of congressional wisdom) for commercial exploitation. The result is an enterprise that is expected in all its ramifications to soon encompass 20 percent of the U.S. economy.

Government laboratories are often deeply involved in productive[11] collaboration with the industrial and academic sectors. Their activity may be in the form of joint research agreements, grants, or contracts. These relationships become contentious because publicly funded research is being converted to private profit. Some cooperative research agreements have been dubbed "as corporate welfare." But as long as access to funding is administered equitably, this criticism is deeply misguided.[12] In effect, the government is a hidden partner in every commercial venture in the nation—holding a pseudo-equity stake equal to 30 percent or more via the corporate income tax. It may negotiate yet additional stakes from royalties paid to use the technology—and typically these royalties are more valuable when exclusive rights are granted. (Nonexclusive licenses are less valuable because they tend to level the playing field.) Finally, whether a venture is economically profitable or not, government obtains additional revenue from taxes paid by employees and suppliers. It is not such a bad deal for the public!

■ TRANSFER PAYMENTS

Broadly speaking, *transfer payments* are taxes paid by one sector of a population that are transferred as income to another sector. Today, the term is synonymous with welfare—income taxes paid by the working population are transferred to the poor, the aged, and the disabled, usually to ensure a decent standard of living to all citizens. Unlike taxes paid to provide security, infrastructure, or services, no overall economic value is created by transfers. Some of the money transferred will enter the economy as the recipients consume goods and services; but this will be offset, or more than offset, by monies not spent by taxpayers and by the transaction costs of the transfer.

A few centuries ago the most common form of transfer payment took the form of taxes transferred to royalty and aristocracy for their personal benefit and prestige! It resulted in magnificent palaces, jewel collections, and objects of art. Some of it was returned to the economy in the form of payments to craftsmen—masons, jewelers, sculptors, and painters—and thus provided employment; but most of it was amassed in unproductive assets that were static or that even incurred high maintenance costs. Efficient rulers could argue that their administrative and military skills amply justified these rewards, but in fact conspicuous waste was highly visible—and highly resented. In the West, these practices were largely swept away in a series of revolutions and replaced by governmental models that encouraged value-creating investments in industry and infrastructure.

But this unfortunate pattern persists today in the developing world where despots squeeze transfer payments by force from impoverished populations and often literally transfer the funds from these economies to foreign bank accounts. Whether the dictator is a Peron, a Pahlevi, or a Mobutu, the country Nigeria, Pakistan, or Indonesia, the pattern of aggrandizement sadly persists. Clearly, enormous value is destroyed that may take decades of efficient administration to restore.

The other form of transfer payment, from rich to poor, has more benefits, including the reduction of crime and disease. However, it appears to face its own law of diminishing returns from two sources. First, the greater the benefits to the poor, the less incentive they have to seek work. Economic rationality suggests they will view their "real" earnings as their nominal earnings minus the amount that would otherwise be transferred to them. It is much like a late-career manager earning $100,000 a year who is qualified to receive a $50,000 pension. He wakes up one morning and concludes that he is really working for only $50,000 a year—which may motivate him to retire to the golf course and to cease adding value.

Second, taxpayer behavior is affected negatively. Talented individuals (athletes, entertainers, and entrepreneurs) notoriously transfer their residences from welfare states to international tax havens to avoid what they view as confiscatory transfer payments—they may have an emotional stake in their home country, but to them residence is a serious value-destroying proposition. It is value destroying for the home country as well when the law of diminishing returns creates a downward sloping curve where the y axis is "taxes paid" and the x axis is "tax rate."

In summary, although there are real benefits to some forms of transfer payments, it will be hard to determine whether these payments create more value when spent by the recipients than they would if spent or invested by the taxpayers. There is ample evidence that they easily reach levels of diminishing returns— whether spent by royals for jewelry or the poor for alcohol—and they can breed disincentives and even dangerous resentments between sectors of society.

■ TAXES

It would seem that an effective tax policy is part of the foundation on which prosperity must rest. A wise state invests in security, infrastructure, education, public health, and even basic research when they are value-adding propositions. Taxes are needed to finance these investments. But it is not only the amount of taxes extracted from the economy but *how* they are extracted that counts, for the tax code will play an enormous role in investment decisions, and not all tax codes favor value creation.

The state also has the potential to destroy economic value through unwise expenditures. Indeed, because economics is only one criterion in developing public policy, a state will always do some of both. Let us consider some of the issues.

Broadly speaking, governments derive taxes from consumption, income, and wealth. These taxes can be leveled on individuals or on organizations. Generally, all of these sources are taxed in some way.

One of the most fundamental tax issues is whether to rely first on consumption taxes or on income and wealth taxes. The choice is of great importance to investors, who would be motivated to invest more if taxes were lighter at the income or wealth level and primarily levied at the point of consumption. Increased funds available for investment would also reduce the cost of capital and thus the ability of projects to create value.

Typical consumption taxes include sales taxes and the value-added tax (VAT) prevalent in Europe. Consumption taxes are, however, inherently regressive, falling relatively heavily on the poor. Hence, U.S. society in effect creates incentives to consume and relative disincentives to invest by favoring personal income taxes as its primary source of tax collection.

Capital gains taxes, of prime importance to high-risk investors, fall within the domain of the income tax. For investment gains made in less than a year, the top rate is currently about 40 percent; for more than one year it is 20 percent. It creates a strong incentive for holding investments at least one year. There is also a strong incentive to hold investments for longer than a year because capital gains taxes are not due until they are realized. This tax shield has considerable value: Financiers know that the effective rate is really 20 percent discounted by the cost of capital for each year the investment is held. For example, if the cost of capital is 12 percent and one holds an investment for 10 years, the effective capital gains rate is only 6 percent.

There is, however, a potential value-destroying inefficiency in these incentives. Let us say my stock for which I paid $100 has doubled to $200 in the past six months. After paying a 40 percent capital gains tax, I would net $160. Assume my expectation is for a 10 percent return on that stock at its new value ($200), or $20 per year. Assume I have identified another investment of equal risk that would pay 12 percent. If I invested $160 in it, I would earn only $19.20 per year. I would not pay the tax and make this investment. So this decision means that I will deny capital to a better company while continuing to invest in one that is creating less value. Taken more generally, the capital gains tax is a major impediment to a truly efficient capital market.

A third issue in taxation is to define as taxable income any *nominal* gain, rather than *real* gains, those gains that are above the costs of capital. Let us consider a case where you invest $100 in cash at 10 percent. In a 40 percent tax bracket, your after-tax return would be only 6 percent because the tax applies to $10.

If your cost of capital were 7 percent, you would be paying a 4 percent tax while incurring a 1 percent loss! You could get out of this situation if you used borrowed money because interest payments are deductible. If you borrowed at 7 percent, your profit would be $3 before tax and a positive $1.80 after tax.

The situation is exacerbated by inflation. Assume inflation is 3 percent. Now you would incur a 4 percent real loss (1 percent + 3 percent) while paying taxes of 4 percent. And even if you borrowed money, your real pretax profit would be 0 percent (3 percent minus 3 percent), and you would incur a real after-tax loss of $1.20.

In other words, income taxes can convert value-creating investments into value destroyers. The investor has no practical choice but to select investments that offer an after-tax return higher than the cost of money. He or she also has an incentive to use the tax shield of deductible interest by borrowing as much as prudence permits.

The double taxation of dividends is another tax anomaly that appears to be distorting the economy. If a corporation paying 40 percent in taxes pays a dividend to a shareholder in a 40 percent bracket, the effective tax rate is 64 percent. This transaction is usually a waste of capital, so shareholders no longer encourage corporate management to declare large dividends. (It is interesting that in an earlier day of capitalism, as late as the 1930s, dividends on common stocks typically *exceeded* bond yields on the theory that stocks were riskier investments.) Today, many of the most promising, rapidly growing companies pay no dividend at all; and even companies with modest growth rates prefer to reward shareholders by buying back stock (in hopes of creating capital gains) rather than paying cash dividends. So dividend yields of only 1 percent or 2 percent are becoming common among blue chips. In a sense, an irrational taxation policy is driving dividends toward extinction and with them the revenue this tax was intended to capture.

The final issue relates to death or estate taxes. In many countries these are high owing to a popular aversion to inherited wealth. However, taxes as high as 55 percent in the United States can force heirs to liquidate value-creating enterprises, especially family-run small businesses and family farms, thus destroying productive capital.

From a historical perspective, onerous taxes—those that destroy value—have been the stuff of revolution. Poorly advised tax policies by the English government created the climate for the Boston Tea Party in 1773 and the subsequent formation of the United States. And it was largely taxation that led to the alienation of the French middle class from the throne and the events of 1789.

■ U.S. TAX POLICY FAVORS HIGH-RISK INVESTING

It is clear that during many of the past 50 years, risk-free investments such as Treasury bonds offered real after-tax returns that were either negative or in the low single digits for high-bracket investors. (For example, a 5 percent nominal return in a 40 percent tax bracket with 3 percent inflation is a zero percent real return.) Under these conditions, a safety-minded investor cannot create much value, and during long periods she may slowly see value erode.

But a high-risk investor can actually do a fairly good job of approximating total tax avoidance. If she invests in a basket of fairly high risk, poorly correlated securities, in an average year she will have some gains and some losses, but more probably a net gain. (Common stocks have averaged about 11 percent annual appreciation over the past 70 years.) She can sell all of her losers to establish tax losses and sell winners that generate an equal amount of gains. The tax-free proceeds of these sales can pay her living expenses, and any balance can be reinvested in new stocks. Until she runs out of losses, she will pay no tax. In effect, she can use risk—here viewed as a dispersion of returns— to create a tax shield, whereas we have shown why an investor who opts for a risk-free return has no such shield.

With a tax structure that favors value-creating high-risk investing and rather heavily penalizes more conservative investment patterns, it is no surprise that the United States leads the world in business innovation. The good news is that we seem, for the moment, to be better than the other guy. However, viewed through the lens of total value, the U.S. tax system is a large encumbrance when compared to an ideal system designed to maximize value creation. This is the bad news. But it is also good news, in a sense: There is room for improvement. As we get smarter, we'll get better.

■ SUMMARY

Government's role in value creation, or value destruction, is pervasive. The government manages the general level of risk in a society, with a direct effect on the attractiveness of investments. It also makes investments. Investments in education and public health contribute to both the economic capital and the strategic capital of a country. Investments in infrastructure are primarily economic, but they enable important options for innovation and wealth creation. And direct investments by government in intellectual capital have a demonstrable history of providing society an attractive return.

Tax policy in most countries involves difficult political and economic trade-offs. It can have a huge effect on investment and innovation, and it is unlikely that any country has yet designed the most effective tax system to foster value creation.

Epilogue

Although most of the human experience has been one of grinding poverty, we have seen that there have also been fabulous accumulations of wealth. The evidence is in the gold and fine craftsmanship in Tutankhamen's tomb, the stone remnants of Imperial Rome, accounts of life at the Ming Court, and the buildings and accoutrements still visible today in Venice and Versailles. These splendors, however, were sporadic and temporary and involved very small numbers of people.

Today's world has something different: an enormous number of people who possess both wealth and education. Mendelsohn Media Research, Inc., estimated that there were 21 million "affluent" households in the United States in 1999, with affluent defined as incomes of $200,000 or more.[1] These affluent households held $4.8 trillion in stocks, bonds, mutual funds, and other securities. Few of these people will consume their entire wealth in food, clothing, basic housing, or basic transportation. Instead, they will use the surplus for investment, for charity, or for luxuries and entertainment.

Apropos to the purposes of this book, it is important to recognize that the members of the world's elite possess most of the world's wealth. And that wealth is fabulous in any real sense—thousands of individual American executives, bankers, and physicians have the wherewithal to outfit a fleet of three yachts and retrace the voyage of Columbus, and in far greater comfort and safety! They also enjoy luxuries of which Queen Isabella could never have conceived—European sedans, personal computers, instant communications, scientific health care, and air-conditioning.

But for our purposes what is truly important about this elite is their ability to finance high-risk investments without seriously jeopardizing their basic standard of living. And that seems to be what they are doing with their money, as evidenced by rising personal investments in the stock market, including seemingly risky enterprises. Indeed, the wealthiest are typically "angels" for very high risk, seed money investments. If risk equates to return, this strategy is a sound one. For the wealthy, investing makes intuitive sense: There is only so much one can eat, drink, or otherwise consume. Absent confiscatory policies by government, it appears likely that an increasing portion of the world's worth can be made available for high-risk investment.

What about the poor? Those who are today connected to the global economy—whether they are gardeners in Florida, chambermaids in Switzerland, or assembly-line workers in Malaysia—are already in the process of raising their education levels, skills, and aspirations above those of the agricultural communities from which most migrated. The penetration of cell phones and the Internet into even more remote communities will only facilitate connection to the global economy and personal mobility. This process will affect many, but it will not soon affect all. Local elites, whether in North Korea, the Middle East, Myanmar, or Central Africa, will resist the threat globalization poses to their franchise. And at the subsistence level, neither economic nor strategic capital can be accumulated.

However, a model for rapid evolution from agricultural to industrial and postindustrial societies has been demonstrated in East Asia. Although it is true that the cultural preconditions in Asia may have been exceptionally favorable, the existence of the blueprint ensures that the model will spread in time beyond that region.

■ WILL THERE BE INVESTMENT OPPORTUNITIES?

The strongest argument for the continuation of unprecedented prosperity is that strategic capital is certain to grow as knowledge expands and as increasing numbers of people are educated. This fact is apparent from crude numbers. More than half of the scientists ever trained are alive today. An enormous fraction of the technical literature and of the digital content in the world's databases has been created in the past two or three decades. If these categories of strategic capital can double in the space of a few decades, then it is very plausible that physical and financial capital will keep pace.

The prevalence of networks is also certain to build wealth—the number of nodes in the global network grows with the number of connected people, institutions, Internet domains, and telephone numbers. An algorithm beloved by communications theorists is called "Metcalfe's Law." It asserts that the value of a network increases as the square of the number of nodes.[2] If so, each time the number of nodes doubles, the value of the global network will quadruple. In passing, I wonder whether I am one node or several: I have several somewhat separated professional affiliations, web sites, phone numbers, domiciles, and personal computers and at any time can be accessed through many of these. I even send e-mail to myself for a variety of practical reasons. This phenomenon suggests that the number of nodes in the network has the potential to exceed the population itself. In short, the combinatorial possibilities are practically infinite, and at any one time there will be a significant number that afford value-creating opportunities.

Networks enable the framing of new options. A larger

economy (or a global economy) with more components adds value, as long as the components can connect to each other. In this sense a macroeconomy is more than the sum of the economic performance of the firms and the individuals within it; it also includes the strategic value of the potential new interactions among these members. (This observation is distinct from the more common observation that large markets, such as the United States, are advantaged by economies of scale.) Farmers in obscure valleys in the Balkans were poorly positioned to frame options, and their thinking seldom went beyond the next valley. Stagnation was the result. With the Internet and basic literacy, they have new avenues for value creation.

The third positive factor supporting continuing prosperity is the increasing sophistication of markets in managing and distributing risk. Risk and value, although incompletely understood, are nonetheless understood today with a far higher degree of conceptual sophistication and are supported by more extensive and accessible databases, than was the case even two decades ago. Both factors make value creation more predictable and reliable and less intuitive than ever before.

Venture capitalists are an important case; this form of risk financing has grown over 10-fold in the past 15 years, and there is no reason to believe the trend has maxed out. Venture capitalists disintermediate innovation. To quote Michael Mandel regarding the boom in venture capital financing, "Over the long run this is an extremely positive development. The availability of risk capital greatly accelerates the rate at which new firms bring innovations to the market, and the rate at which they are adopted by existing business."[3]

■ SOME CONCERNS

This book in many ways has described the enduring battle of human innovation and ingenuity versus the law of diminishing returns. That law has not been repealed, and there are two basic reasons for not being complacent about a renewed threat to prosperity: (1) the limits of the planet and (2) the limits of human adaptability.

➤ Overcoming the Limitations of the Planet

The Malthusian argument that increased population competing for limited food supplies will lead to famine has been extended to natural resources such as fossil fuels and mineral deposits[4] and more recently to the increased environmental burden created by the world's growing population. That problem is compounded by the near certainty that rising living standards will inexorably increase per capita consumption of resources.

There are two good reasons why this fear may not prove to be a real limitation at the end of the game. The lesser reason is that exponential world population growth is unlikely to be sustained. It was inevitable that the population would grow when life spans increased from about 30 years to about 70 years in many parts of the world. Indeed, as long as birth rates exceed death rates, growth will occur. And many parts of the world whose cultures are still rooted in agricultural tradition have benefited from lower death rates, but they have yet to reduce fertility rates to the level of about 2.1 children per childbearing female characteristic of a stable level of population.

However, in many parts of the developed world—including Northern and Eastern Europe and Japan—fertility rates have fallen considerably below the levels required to sustain the population at current levels. This trend, driven by later marriages and smaller families, appears to be spreading to North America and to the educated elites in developing countries.

In the first half of the twenty-first century, the global momentum effect of many young women reaching childbearing age will ensure more population growth. But the nearly universal trend to lower per capita fertility suggests that world population may peak later in the century at between 12 billion and 20 billion people—twice to three times the present number. From there it may well undergo a decline.

The needs of this number of people for agricultural commodities—food, timber, natural fiber, and so on—can surely be met from present terrestrial resources given capital investment and annual increases in productivity. Although starvation may occur as a result of income distribution, it will surely not happen because of a global food shortage. The world's agricultural problem seems more likely to be chronic overcapacity.

Energy, however, is indispensable to rising standards of living, and vast increases in production will be required if some 12 billion to 20 billion people are to be brought to average Western standards. There are two serious threats to this vision.

The first is also Malthusian—the risk that fossil fuel reserves will be depleted. Indeed, proven reserves of natural gas and oil each represent only about 50 years of current consumption. Coal reserves are sufficient for 200 years on the same basis.[5] However, the situation is not quite as dire as it sounds. There is no economic incentive to invest in exploration for fossil fuel that will not be needed for a decade or more. Such investment does not support the cost of money. When more reserves are needed, more will be found, at least up to a point.

They will be found, however, at an average cost considerably higher than historic costs, for most of the new finds will be less accessible, smaller, and of lower quality—the good fields are exploited first. Over a span of hundreds of years, fossil fuels will become more expensive in both absolute terms and relative to other energy sources. But until that happens, vast reserves of low-quality petroleum and huge coal beds are available. Many are already capable of being economically produced, as in the tar sands of Alberta, Canada, and the heavy oils of Venezuela.

The second threat is environmental. There is an environmental cost to almost any energy technology, whether it is based on renewable or nonrenewable sources. Strip mining of vast areas will be required to exploit the world's coal reserves. Nuclear power will leave long-term radioactive legacies. Solar technologies (both direct solar technologies, such as photovoltaic cells and solar heaters, and indirect technologies based on hydropower, biomass, wind, or tide) will require the conversion of huge areas of the earth's surface to energy acquisition! These areas may be named reservoirs, deserts, plantations, wind farms, or beachfront, respectively.

In land-use terms, fossil fuel (especially petroleum) has been a relatively benign energy source. The threat it poses is a different one—global climate change. Amidst the concerns (ranging from extrapolations of global flooding and desertification to the possibility of offsetting beneficial effects), it is important to recognize two important facts. The first is that the change will be relatively slow in economic terms. A few decades, in which global temperatures might rise a degree or so,[6] are sufficient for the creation of a great deal of new infrastructure or for the gradual migration of large numbers of people. We know that in historic times alone, local water levels have risen or fallen significantly. The vast Roman city of Ephesus, once a seaport, is now many kilometers inland, whereas there are classical-age Greek cities off the southwest Turkish coast that can be explored only by snorkelers or scuba divers. In Oslo fjord, bathhouses built at sea level at the turn of the century are now several feet above that level. The economy of the Netherlands prospers even though much of it is located well below sea level. People adjust, rebuild, turn on their air conditioners, and life goes on.

The second feature of global warming is that it is probably self-limiting. If *all* the fossil fuel reserves on earth were burned and all carbon dioxide (CO_2) remained in the atmosphere, the CO_2 levels would no more than triple from 350 parts per million to perhaps 1,200 parts. When the fossil fuel sources were exhausted, the known sinks would exceed the natural sources, and levels would begin to decline. The warming effect, based on current estimates of forcing constants would peak at about 4 degrees Celsius. This change will not result in a radically changed world. In the vast majority of cases, the new environments will be similar to those already existing several hundred miles north or south. This extent of change is severe, but it is still less than historically high levels for CO_2 and global temperature in the Mesozoic era—the period in which the dinosaurs ruled and our own mammalian ancestors evolved. However, because plants grow much faster in a CO_2-rich atmosphere, it is possible that natural sequestration processes will increase as well, that the planet will become greener, and that the worst case predictions will not come true. (Natural sequestration could be greatly enhanced by returning marginal farming lands in the tropics to rain forest and wilderness, through the development of ecotourism in these areas, and by promoting biomass-producing plantations to reduce the use of fossil carbon.) Similarly, mass action effects could accelerate the removal of carbon dioxide from the atmosphere by the oceans.

It is hoped that the extreme projections will never be tested (although, given the explosive political consequences of putting the world on a serious fossil fuel diet, they may well be). Some of the effects will be ameliorated by incremental improvements in energy productivity, more efficient renewable energy technologies, and capital investment in alternate energy sources. The first trend is already underway: Despite increases in their standards of living, the European and North American economies are already reducing their per capita consumption of energy. This trend is certain to continue as fossil energy costs rise, as they will when technology advance cannot keep up with the law of diminishing returns as applied to depletion.

I am focusing here on the threat of global warming to human progress, which I believe is manageable. The peril to ecosystems and to biodiversity is a different issue and needs to be taken very seriously, in particular because the notion of controlling emissions by treaty may prove naïve. The impact of growth on ecosystems has already been enormous as human populations exploded in the past few centuries and, to date, has been driven more by the expansion of agriculture, and concomitant deforestation, than by temperature change. Those pressures are continuing, and they can only be aggravated by climate change.

The concept of sustainable equilibrium is important to environmentalists and social theorists because it is evident that growth has limits in some places and times. Unfortunately, the evidence we have discussed in this chapter suggests that maintaining equilibrium may be extremely challenging.

For an organization or a society, the choices are value creation, equilibrium, or devolution. Equilibrium is reached when value is neither created nor destroyed. The organization neither evolves nor devolves. It must earn its cost of capital, but it can earn no more. The choice seems to be grow (add value) or die.

There is virtually no example of a truly stable community or business organization that comes to mind. Scientists and engineers would tend to suspect a reason. They are familiar with systems that seem stable but become unstable when they encounter a perturbation because there is no reliable restoring force. A tender ship[7] is one that may turn turtle and be unable to restore itself to an upright position. Airplanes have been designed that should have been effective flying machines but they proved to have hidden aerodynamic instabilities. (The Wright brothers' innovations had more to do with control than lift, and the name "stabilizer" persists for an important airplane part.) Finally, the failure of technologists to make nuclear fusion into a practical source of energy is largely related to the fact that magnetic bottles are unstable to perturbations.[8] Because we know that businesses and communities are regularly subject to perturbations, a state of stable equilibrium requires not only reaching equilibrium itself, but also a plausible restoring force for any upset that pushes the system toward growth or devolution. To maintain equilibrium, neither an upward nor a downward economic spiral is permissible.

Proponents of sustainable development seek to use, conserve, protect, and restore natural resources—land, air, water, and biodiversity—in ways that help ensure long-term social, economic, and environmental benefits for future generations. They have generally been wise enough to recognize that economic growth must be part of that future, for only with value-adding activity is there insurance against devolution. We have noted that devolving organizations are susceptible to plunder. A devolving society would certainly lack the discipline to protect the environment and might well hunt vulnerable species to extinction as efficiently as did the Clovis big-game hunters in North America 12,000 years ago.

➤ The Limits of Human Adaptability

The other potential train wreck for human prosperity is testing the limits of human adaptability. Alvin Toffler warned of this possibility in 1970 and linked a rapidly increasing pace of technological change with an apparent growth in bizarre human phenomena.[9] He argued that rapid change, bombardment of the senses, information overload, decision-making overload, and other features of modern life may be pushing the human central nervous system beyond its adaptive limits. Looked at in hindsight, the stress levels of the year 2000 don't look particularly worse than those of some 30 years earlier—1968 was a very difficult year for the United States, and in many ways things have improved—but the complexity of ordinary life has undoubtedly increased.

But Toffler is persuasive in arguing that there are indeed limits to human mental performance, and there is evidence to suggest that there are limits to organizational performance as well. In other words, we are likely on S-curves in both cases, and the real question may be just where on those S-curves we are. There is no doubt that our velocity up these curves is impressive, and upward progression stresses both individuals and institutions.

In my part-time role as a teacher I am familiar with one example: the chemical engineer. Traditionally, being a chemical engineer provided a well-defined and well-paying career path, with considerable upside opportunity. One received a basic college education, with midlevel training in chemistry, mathematics, and physics. This base provided versatility. To it was added another two years of training in the specialized tools of the chemical engineering trade: thermodynamics, kinetics, unit operations, fluid mechanics, transport phenomena, and material and energy balances. With that background, the engineer of the 1960s and 1970s was instantly employable in the process industries and sufficiently flexible that he could make his career in manufacturing, research, sales, or project management. If he learned a little accounting and finance at the office, he could be chief executive officer (CEO).

But the universities that produced this wonderful human product have had to contend with increasing expectations from society and the marketplace. A new model of engineer began to evolve. To the curriculum were added more electives aimed at broadening her culturally: some experience with independent research, such as a senior thesis; and perhaps a foreign language to prepare for the global economy. Then came the realization that perhaps she was not a complete engineer without knowledge of molecular biology (a field that had its origins no earlier than the mid-1950s) and that she would need advanced computer skills to communicate with her profession. To do all these tasks reasonably well would take five or probably even six years. But there is no market for five-year programs—students still prefer the four-year bachelor's degree with the option to add a master's or a Ph.D.

So the practical answer was a compromise between overloading the student and diluting the course of study. Some engineering schools have removed unit operations—the practical understanding of how reactors, heat exchangers, dryers, and distillation columns are built and operate—from the curriculum.

The pressures facing chemical engineers are hardly unique. In medicine, law, computer science, and finance, there is a proliferation of literature, new rules, new products, new institutions, and general complexity.

The underlying problem is that a professional, in whatever field, must keep up with an exponential growth of knowledge, both in his specialty and in other areas that may affect it. The innovations in a profession often come from the outside and cannot be contained. But innate human capacities are not growing at the pace at which knowledge grows.

As a society, our first defense against this problem tends to be an organizational solution: increasing specialization. To ensure innovation and economic advantage, the frontier of knowledge must be manned—science and technology are truly the "endless frontier." But as the frontier grows, we will need more and more outposts. However, this "solution" begs the question of how the outposts will communicate with each other and who will coordinate their activities. Specialized subcultures do not usually provide a platform for developing leaders with both broad vision and organizational skills. In U.S. society, at least, we rely on individual initiative to bring leaders to the fore; but all too often those who rise to the top have enormous gaps in their education and experience. Their limitations in turn impose limits on overall organizational performance, particularly for large, complex organizations with a single chief at the seat of power.

There is reason to believe that, so far, human adaptability seems to be working around this problem. The evidence is indirect but powerful: The processes of technological innovation and wealth creation remain undiminished. Yet, many fine civilizations have collapsed, and Toffler's warning about this one needs to be heeded.

Endnotes

■ PREFACE

1. The term *real* is being used to distinguish those options that arise in ordinary business and involve real/tangible assets from financial options relating to securities or commodities.
2. F. Peter Boer, *The Valuation of Technology: Financial Issues in R&D* (New York: Wiley, 1999).
3. G. R. Mitchell and W. Hamilton, "Managing R&D as a Strategic Option," *Research•Technology Management*, May–June 1988, 15–22.
4. F. Peter Boer, "Valuation of Technology Using Real Options," *Research• Technology Management*, July–August 2000, 26–30.

■ CHAPTER 1 Introduction

1. Samuel Eliot Morison, *Admiral of the Ocean Sea* (Boston: Northeastern University Press, 1983), 103.
2. Philip Snow, *The Star Raft, China's Encounter with Africa* (New York: Weidenfeld & Nicholson, 1988), 20–22.

■ CHAPTER 2   The Crisis in Valuation

1. Lawrence J. Lau, "The Sources of Long-Term Economic Growth: Observations from the Experience of Developed and Developing Countries," in *The Mosaic of Economic Growth*, ed. R. Landau, T. Taylor, and G. Wright (Stanford, CA: Stanford University Press, 1966), 79–81.

2. Fernand Braudel, *The Wheels of Commerce, Civilization & Capitalism, 15th to 18th Century*, vol. 2 (New York: Harper & Row, 1986).

3. Peter L. Bernstein, *Against the Gods: The Remarkable Story of Risk* (New York: Wiley, 1996), 42. Double-entry bookkeeping is traced to Italy, 1305.

4 . Per R. A. Brealey and S. C. Myers, *Principles of Corporate Finance* (New York: McGraw-Hill, 1996), 776: "Intangible assets: Many firms spend large sums on research and development, advertising, staff training, and so on. These expenditures create valuable assets—know-how, brand loyalty, and a skilled workforce—that may generate cash flows for many years. However, the investment expenditures are deducted immediately from earnings, and therefore the assets never show up on the balance sheet. Book rates of return, which are ratios of income to assets, end up overstated because assets are understated."

5. Sidney Davidson, Clyde P. Stickney, and Roman L. Weil, *Financial Accounting: An Introduction to Concepts, Methods, and Uses*, 5th ed. (Chicago: The Dryden Press, 1988), 386.

6. P. H. Sullivan, *Value-Driven Intellectual Capital: How to Convert Intangible Corporate Assets into Market Value* (New York: Wiley, 1998), from excerpt at www.amazon.com.

7. J. Campbell and C. Knoess, "How to Build a Future Wealth Company, Ernst & Young's Point of View on Value in the New-economy," http://www.ey.com/GLOBAL/, 2000.

8. D. Aboody and B. Lev, Presentation to the Council for Chemical Research, September 10, 2000.

9. Conference on Measuring and Valuing Intellectual Capital, New York, November 4–5, 1998.

10. David Halberstam, *The Reckoning* (New York: White Morrow, 1986).

11. www.theautochannel.com, news release dated September 1, 1998.

12. Brealey and Myers, *Principles of Corporate Finance*, 76.

13. Brealey and Myers, *Principles of Corporate Finance*, 68.

14. Last in–first out (LIFO) or first in–first out (FIFO) rules give a different cost basis to inventory carried on the balance sheet, as well as to the cost of goods sold on the income statement. This can make a substantial difference in times of inflation, when the last goods produced have a higher cost basis than the first.

15. Guy Norris, "Boeing Calls Halt to 747-X Programme," *Flight International*, January 29, 1997, 4.

16. For an excellent and detailed description of valuation methodology for purchased in-process R&D, see DuPont Company's *2000 Annual Report*, pp. 29–32, in particular with regard to its acquisitions of Pioneer Hi-Bred International and of Merck's share of the DuPont Merck Pharmaceutical Company. The method is consistent with the use of pro forma cash flows and probabilities of success as described in Boer, *The Valuation of Technology* (New York: Wiley, 1999), 213–233.

17. Robert L. Frome and Alan M. Getzhoff, "Structuring the Buyout," in *Handbook of Mergers, Acquisitions and Buyouts*, ed. Steven J. Lee and Robert D. Colman (Englewood Cliffs, NJ: Prentice-Hall, 1981), 517–529.

18. Laurence A. Tisch, quoted in *Business Week*, May 28, 1998.

19. G. M. Loeb, *The Battle for Investment Survival* (New York: Simon & Schuster, 1965), 60.

20. Brealey and Myers, *Principles of Corporate Finance*, 323–324.

21. F. P. Boer, "Linking R&D to Growth and Shareholder Value," *Research•Technology Management*, May–June 1994, 16–22; F. P. Boer, *The Valuation of Technology*, 128–130.

22. J. Campbell and C. Knoess, "How to Build." The authors estimate that only 25 percent of current market capitalization is based on cash flow anticipated in the next five years.

■ CHAPTER 3   Economic Value: The DCF "Gold Standard" and Its Limitations

1. F. Peter Boer, *The Valuation of Technology* (New York: Wiley, 1999), 121. Exhibit 5.6 shows how closely the DCF-FCF method can correlate with broadly accepted comparative valuation measures, such as ratios of price to earnings (P/E ratios), earnings before interest and taxes (EBIT), and earnings before interest, taxes, depreciation, and amortization (EBITDA).

2. Shawn Tully, "The Real Key to Creating Economic Wealth," *Fortune*, September 20, 1993, 38–49.

3. However, they can calculate free cash flow with the assumption of no further growth (Capex = depreciation, no net increase in working capital). This figure is equivalent to EBIT (earnings before interest and tax), which is widely used in valuation work. If EBIT is positive, a multiple of EBIT will give a minimum valuation for the business (F. Peter Boer, "Traps, Pitfalls, and Snares in the Valuation of Technology," *Research•Technology Management*, September–October 1998, 50).

4. T. Copeland, T. Koller, and J. Murrin, *Valuation: Measuring and Managing the Value of Companies*, 2nd ed. (New York: Wiley, 1995), 96.

5. Because debt is tax deductible, the appropriate equation for the weighted average cost of capital (WACC) is: WACC = [(percent debt) × (after-tax cost of debt)] + [(percent equity) × (cost of equity)].

6. Bartley J. Madden, *CFROI Valuation* (Oxford: Butterworth-Heinemann, 1999), 161–167.

7. The term *operating* traditionally refers to the manufacturing and marketing operations of a firm and is distinguished from its financial activities. Marketable securities or equity positions in other companies are typically treated separately as investments.

8. Boer, "Traps, Pitfalls, and Snares in the Valuation of Technology," *Research•Technology Management*, September–October 1998, 45–54.

9. Copeland, Koller, and Murrin, 303.

■ CHAPTER 4   The Total Value Model

1. F. Peter Boer, "Traps, Pitfalls, and Snares in the Valuation of Technology," *Research•Technology Management*, September–October 1998, 50.

2. Jane Jacobs, *Cities and the Wealth of Nations: Principles of Economic Life* (New York: Vintage Books, 1985), 32.

3. Laura Martin (Credit Suisse First Boston), "Using Real Options on Wall Street" (presentation at Real Options 2001 conference, Scottsdale, Ariz., March 28, 2001).

4. T. Copeland, T. Koller, and J. Murrin, *Valuation: Measuring and Managing the Value of Companies*, 2nd ed. (New York: Wiley, 1995).

5. See Chapter 9, "Building a Pro Forma DCF Model," in F. Peter Boer, *The Valuation of Technology* (New York: Wiley, 1999).

6. The term *European* is technical; it refers to options that can be exercised only on the date of expiration; the term *American* refers to options that can be exercised at any time prior to expiration. The Black-Scholes formula assumes the options are European.

7. A diskette in F. Peter Boer, *The Valuation of Technology*, includes a Black-Scholes calculator in Excel format.

8. L. Trigeorgis, *Real Options, Managerial Flexibility and Strategy in Resource Allocation* (Cambridge, MA: MIT Press, 1998), 227–271.

9. Ibid., 227–271.

10. Science and Engineering Indicators, 1998 (www.nsf.gov).

■ CHAPTER 5 Enter the Options Dragon

1. M. Amram and N. Kulatilaka, *Real Options, Managing Strategic Investment in an Uncertain World* (Boston: Harvard Business School Press, 1999), 29.

2. L. Trigeorgis, *Real Options: Managerial Flexibility and Strategy in Resource Allocation* (Cambridge, MA: MIT Press, 1998); Amram and Kulatilaka, *Real Options, Managing Strategic Investment*; T. Copeland and V. Antikarov, *Real Options: A Practitioner's Guide* (New York: Texere LLC, 2001).

3. Trigeorgis, *Real Options: Managerial Flexibility*, 227–256.

4. Peter L. Bernstein, *Against the Gods: The Remarkable Story of Risk* (New York: Wiley, 1996), 15.

5. Sheldon Natenberg, *Option Volatility & Pricing* (New York: McGraw-Hill, 1994), 8.

6. CBOE web site www.cboe.com. This web site contains useful traders' tools, such as tables of historical volatilities for common stocks, and a user-friendly Java options calculator.

7. The final profit (or loss) would of course be the gain minus the premium paid to obtain the option.

8. Calculated as $21.95 with the Black-Scholes formula, assuming a volatility of 0.5 and a risk-free rate of 5.2 percent.

9. R. A. Brealey and S. C. Myers, *Principles of Corporate Finance* (New York: McGraw-Hill, 1996), 255–264.

10. Natenberg, *Option Volatility*, see Appendix B.

11. I. M. Sokolnikoff and R. M. Redheffer, *Mathematics and Physics of Modern Engineering* (New York: McGraw-Hill, 1958), 650–654.

12. Burton J. Malkiel, *A Random Walk Down Wall Street*, 7th ed. (New York: Norton, 2000).

13. Bernstein, *Against the Gods*, 145–150.

14. Ibid., 263. The reader will recognize that the published standard deviations will depend on the selection of the data: the time period sampled, the frequency of sampling, and whether outlying data are discarded. A major move in a stock may have a profound effect on the calculated 30-day volatility during the month in which the move occurs. Standard deviations are not universal constants; for example, the average volatility of the S&P 500 averaged 17.7 percent for the period 1984 to 1990, but the average volatility dropped to 10.6 percent in the four years thereafter.

15. Our at-the-money Acme 100 calls are valued at $18.75 for volatility ($\sigma$) = 0.5. For $\sigma = 0.25$ they are $10.45, and for $\sigma = 1.0$, they are $34.77—roughly double and half, respectively.

16. Nancy A. Nichols, "Scientific Management at Merck: An Interview with CFO Judy Lewent," *Harvard Business Review*, January–February, 1994, 91.

17. Again the at-the-money Acme 100 calls are valued at $18.75 and the three-year calls at $38.64.

18. For example, Merck uses a range of $\sigma = 0.3$ to 0.5 for analyzing its drug research portfolio.

19. F. Peter Boer, *The Valuation of Technology* (New York: Wiley, 1999), 302.

20. Ezra Zack, CP Risk Management, at www.derivativesstrategy.com.

21. Copeland and Antikarov, *Real Options: A Practitioner's Guide*, 262–264.

22. In physics, at least, mean reversion implies a restoring force. The period of the time cycle varies as the inverse square root of the restoring force (Hooke's Law). The stronger the force, the shorter the cycle. Conversely, very long cycles imply weak restoring forces. Betting on weak restoring forces may, of course, be perilous in the presence of other factors.

23. Benoit Mandelbrot, "Multifractal Structure of Financial Prices and Its Implications," in *Scientific Bridges for 2000 and Beyond: A Virtual Colloquium* (Paris: Tec et Doc [Librairie Lavoisier], 1999), 131–148.

24. Stewart Myers, "Finance Theory and Financial Strategy," *Interfaces* 14, (January–February 1984), 126–137.

25. Nichols, "Scientific Management."

26. John E. Stonier, "The Change Process," in Copeland and Antikarov, *Real Options: A Practitioner's Guide*, 28–57. An excellent chapter on how options are used to structure contracts.

27. http://www.thestreet.com/_yahoo/comment/riskarb/1413588.html.

28. Brealey and Myers, *Principles of Corporate Finance*, 592–599, work out a more complex analysis of abandonment options, treating them as puts and using the binomial approach.

29. Ibid., 590–591. The cash flow schedule (M = million) was as follows: Year 1, –$450M; Year 2, $60M; Year 3, $59M; Year 4, $195M; Year 5, $310M; Year 6, $125M.

30. A colleague applied the Boston Consulting Group's experience curve methodology to value the cost advantages gained under these conditions. His estimate was of the same magnitude, $700+ million. When the competitive situation is such that a significant portion of these savings drops to the bottom line, a major element of the options value could be embedded in what "old-school" hard analysis would view as cumulative cost savings (Ranch C. Kimball, private communication). The two approaches, though fundamentally independent, incorporate management flexibility and place high value on it.

31. www.fool.com/About/staff/warreng.html.

32. Contributed by Ranch C. Kimball

33. Copeland and Antikarov, *Real Options: A Practitioner's Guide*, 344.

34. This view was contributed by Ranch C. Kimball.

■ CHAPTER 6 Why Plans Are Options

1. Greg A. Stevens and James Burley, "3000 Raw Ideas = 1 Commercial Success!" *Research•Technology Management*, May–June 1997, 16–27.

2. Experiences of Ranch C. Kimball.

3. Paul Kagan, Internet Movie Database.

4. Thomas K. McGraw, *Creating Modern Capitalism* (Cambridge, MA: Harvard University Press, 1995).

■ CHAPTER 7 Diminishing Returns: The Dusty Road to Devolution

1. Angus Maddison, *Explaining the Economic Performance of Nations* (Brookfield, VT: Edward Elgar Publishing, 1995), 260.

2. Michael Adler, "Lessons from Chaco Canyon," *Science* 290 (2000), 941.

3. Jane Jacobs, *Cities and the Wealth of Nations: Principles of Economic Life* (New York: Vintage Books, 1985), 129.

4. Ibid., 124–129.

5. Jared Diamond, *Guns, Germs, and Steel* (New York: Norton, 1999), 398.

6. Peter Liberman, *Does Conquest Pay? The Exploitation of Occupied Industrial Societies* (Princeton, NJ: Princeton University Press, 1998).

7. *Encyclopaedia Britannica*.

8. Brian Burrough, *Barbarians at the Gate* (New York: HarperCollins, 1991).

9. Connie Bruck, *The Predators' Ball: The Inside Story of Drexel Burnham and the Rise of the Junk Bond Raiders* (New York: Penguin, 1989).

10. Financial technicians refer to this as EBITDA—earnings before interest, taxes, depreciation and amortization.

11. Ron Chernow, *Titan: The Life of John D. Rockefeller, Sr.* (New York: Random House, 1998).

12. James R. Bright, *Practical Technology Forecasting* (Austin, TX: Sweet Publishing, 1978), 104.

13. F. Peter Boer, *The Valuation of Technology* (New York: Wiley, 1999), 207–208.

■ CHAPTER 8   Five Millennia of Value Destruction

1. Gerald M. Loeb, *The Battle for Investment Survival* (New York: Simon & Schuster, 1965), 17.

2. Fernand Braudel, *The Structures of Everyday Life* (Berkeley: University of California Press, 1992), 123.

3. We start with a number of $20 trillion for 1995 measured in 1987 dollars (http://www.unep.org-United Nations Environmental Program), add 36.5 percent for the GDP deflator and extrapolate 5 years of growth at 2.5 percent.

4. The liquid assets of U.S. households in 1999 were estimated at $15.4 trillion by the Security Industry Association (http://www.sia.com/publication/html/key_trends_3.html); assets held by pension funds totaled at least $4 trillion, and average home equity of $50,000 for 100 million U.S. households would add another $5 trillion. Not counted would be the enormous infrastructure owned by government and the assets and endowments of charitable institutions.

5. Braudel, *The Structures*, 104–182.

6. Peter L. Bernstein, *Against the Gods: The Remarkable Story of Risk* (New York: Wiley, 1996), 228.

7. Hernando De Soto, *The Mystery of Capital: Why Capitalism Triumphs in the West and Fails Everywhere Else* (New York: Basic, 2000). De Soto argues that the absence of clear titular rights to property is a major cause of the problem.

8. Bernstein, *Against the Gods*.

9. M. P. Charlesworth, *The Roman Empire* (London: Oxford University Press, 1951), 121.

10. Alfred T. Mahan, *The Influence of Sea Power upon History, 1660–1783* (New York: Dover, 1987).

11. R. A. Brealey and S. C. Myers, *Principles of Corporate Finance* (New York: McGraw-Hill, 1996), 24.

12. A number of versions have been published over time; the classic may be *Civilization II*, Microprose Software, 1996.

■ CHAPTER 9   Does Risk Deserve Its Bad Name?

1. M. Amram and N. Kulatilaka, *Real Options: Managing Strategic Investment in an Uncertain World* (Boston, MA: Harvard Business Press, 1999).

2. R. A. Brealey and S. C. Myers, *Principles of Corporate Finance* (New York: McGraw-Hill, 1996), 156.

3. P. L. Bernstein, *Against the Gods: The Remarkable Story of Risk* (New York: Wiley, 1996)

4. Visit www.cboe.com (Chicago Board Options Exchange), which provides options quotes, tabulates historical volatilities, and has an options calculator.

5. Barry Schachter, *Risks and Rewards*, March 1998, 17–18.

6. Bernstein, *Against the Gods*, 15.

7. This practice is reflected in the Capital Asset Pricing Model (CAPM) for equities. In its simplest form, the cost of capital is defined as a risk-free rate and a risk premium. The risk-free rate reflects Treasury yields, say 5 percent. It has been observed that the risk premium for equities has averaged about 8 percent for an *average* stock. Statisticians then determine a quantity called "beta" for individual stocks that reflects whether on the whole the stock has swung more strongly or less strongly than the Standard & Poor's (S&P) 500 (beta is 1 for an average stock). The risk premium for an individual stock is then beta times the average risk premium. Thus, if a volatile biotech stock has moved up and down twice as much, in percentage terms, as the average S&P 500 stock during a stipulated time frame, it is assigned a beta of 2. The risk premium would then be 2×8 percent, or 16 percent, and the cost of equity 16 percent + 5 percent, or 21 percent.

8. Edison's Orange, N.J., research center is often considered the first industrial research laboratory (1890s).

9. Chaos theory represents a mathematical model of the breakdown of ordered systems into chaotic ones, whereas catastrophe theory is (a generally impractical) effort to model discontinuous natural events. Both are in theory relevant to the world of financial risk: Benoit Mandelbrot, "Multifractal Structure of Financial Prices and Its Implications," in *Scientific Bridges for 2000 and Beyond: A Virtual Colloquium* (Paris: Tec et Doc [Librairie Lavoisier], 1999), 131–148, has criticized the random walk model by noting that real stock market behavior often involves larger discontinuous steps than a conventional random walk based on the Poisson distribution would predict.

10. Bernstein, *Against the Gods*, 105.

■ CHAPTER 10   Taming the Risk Bogeyman

1. P. L. Bernstein, *Against the Gods: The Remarkable Story of Risk* (New York: Wiley, 1996), 11.

2. Fernand Braudel, *The Wheels of Commerce, Civilization & Capitalism, 15th to 18th Century, vol. 2* (New York: Harper & Row, 1986).

3. R. A. Brealey and S. C. Myers, *Principles of Corporate Finance* (New York: McGraw-Hill, 1996).

4. Bernstein, *Against the Gods*, 6.

5. http://www.morningstar.com.

6. Gerald M. Loeb, *The Battle for Investment Survival* (New York: Simon & Schuster, 1965).

7. Bernstein, *Against the Gods*.

8. Discovered by Pascal in 1654.

9. F. Peter Boer, *The Valuation of Technology* (New York: Wiley, 1999), 281–289.

10. Robert G. Cooper, *Winning at New Products* (Reading, MA.: Addison-Wesley, 1993), 267.

11. Nancy A. Nichols, "Scientific Management at Merck: An Interview with CFO Judy Lewent," *Harvard Business Review*, January–February, 1994, 91.

12. Boer, *The Valuation of Technology*, 281.

13. Ibid., 217.

14. Ibid., 296.

15. The author has calculated the expected value for a situation in which the chances of advancement are equal at each stage-gate. This may not be unrealistic in terms of the behavior of some R&D organizations with a bias for *advancing* projects. If we assume an overall success rate of 10.4 percent, the chances of success at each of four gates would be 56.8 percent—higher at the earlier gates, and lower at the later ones. In this calculation the cost per successful R&D program increases by 67 percent!

16. Laura Martin (Credit Suisse First Boston), "Using Real Options on Wall Street" (presentation at Real Options 2001 conference, Scottsdale, Arizona, March 28, 2001).

17. Boer, *The Value of Technology*, 296.

18. Nichols, "Scientific Management."

19. Brealey and Myers, *Principles of Corporate Finance*, 206.

20. Ibid., 177.

■ CHAPTER 11 The Enigma of Intellectual Capital

1. M. Blair and S. Wallman (Cochairs), "Unseen Wealth," Brookings Task Force Report, Washington, DC, 2000, 13.

2. Notes to financial statements, Dow Chemical Company, 1998 Annual Report.

3. Gordon Petrash, "Dow's Journey to a Knowledge Value Management Culture," *European Management Journal*, 14, no. 4 (1996), 365–373.

4. My calculations suggest the government receives about a 6% return on its investment.

5. Peter J. Clark and Stephen Neill, *The Value Mandate: Maximizing Shareholder Value across the Corporation* (New York: Amacom, 2001), 69.

6. F. Peter Boer, *The Valuation of Technology* (New York: Wiley, 1999), 135–137.

7. Jeffrey L. Brandt, "R&D under the New Patent Paradigm" (paper presented at the semiannual meeting of the Industrial Research Institute, Washington, D.C., October 18, 2000).

8. An example of a cash flow stream from licensing is provided in Boer, *The Valuation of Technology*, 268.

9. Blair and Wallman, "Unseen Wealth," 13.

10. Boer, *The Valuation of Technology*, 284–288.

11. The author has calculated the progressive increase in value, at two-year intervals, for a research project using real option theory. These results are not published elsewhere but are based on the Polyarothene case in *The Valuation of Technology*. (PV is present value.)

	Value	Strike Price	Probability of Success
PV of commercial project	$90,400	$13,500	100.0 percent
Option to launch	$63,167	$ 6,000	83.3 percent
Option to develop	$41,957	$ 3,000	62.5 percent
Option to test feasibility	$18,271	$ 1,500	31.2 percent
Initial value of concept	$ 4,746	$ 750	10.4 percent

12. Don Tapscott, *Forbes ASAP*, October 2, 2000, 73–74.

13. David E. Thompson, "How Acquisitions and Licensing Are Changing the Role of R&D in a Large Corporation" (paper presented at the semiannual meeting of the Industrial Research Institute, Washington, D.C., October 16, 2000).

14. Eugene Slowinski, "100 Managers Reflect on Alliances," *Les Nouvelles* 29, no. 3 (1994), 135–139.

15. John Seely Brown and Paul Duguid, *The Social Life of Information* (Boston: Harvard Business School Press, 2000).

16. Ibid., 99.

17. G. Hatfield, private communication; G. B. Stewart, *The Quest for Value: The EVA Management Guide* (New York: HarperCollins, 1991); S. Tulley, *Fortune*, 128, September 20, 1993, 38–41; A. Ehrbar, *EVA: The Real Key to Creating Wealth* (New York: Wiley, 1998); G. B. Stewart, *Fortune*, 131, May 1, 1995, 117–118.

18. Financial Accounting Standards Board, Statement of Financial Accounting Standards No. 2, "Accounting for Research and Development Costs," 1974.

■ CHAPTER 12   Innovation: The Fountain of Prosperity

1. Guy Norris, "Boeing Calls Halt to 747-X Programme," *Flight International*, January 29, 1997, 4.

2. Richard N. Foster, *Innovation: The Attacker's Advantage* (New York: Summit, 1986), 181–182.

3. F. Peter Boer, *The Valuation of Technology* (New York: Wiley, 1999), 135–137.

4. Lynn W. Ellis, "Managing Financial Resources," *Research•Technology Management*, July–August 1988, 33–34.

5. Foster, *Innovation*, 102.

6. Foster, *Innovation*, 165.

7. Clayton M. Christensen, *The Innovator's Dilemma: When New Technologies Cause Great Firms to Fail* (Boston: Harvard Business School Press, 1997).

8. Mark P. Rice, Gina Colarelli O'Connor, Lois Peters, and Joseph G. Morone, "Managing Discontinuous Innovation," *Research•Technology Management*, May–June, 1998, 52–58.

9. Ibid., 58.

10. Douglas K. Smith and Robert C. Alexander, *Fumbling the Future: How Xerox Invented, Then Ignored, the First Personal Computer* (New York: Morrow, William, 1988).

11. Clayton Christensen, http://www.disruptivetechnologies.com.

12. Lawrence J. Lau, "The Sources of Long-Term Economic Growth: Observations from the Experience of Developed and Developing Countries," in *The Mosaic of Economic Growth*, ed. R. Landau, T. Taylor, and G. Wright, (Stanford, CA: Stanford University Press, 1996), 63–91.

13. Fernand Braudel, *The Wheels of Commerce, Civilization & Capitalization, 15th to 18th Century*, vol. 2 (New York: Harper & Row, 1986), 138–153.

14. John S. Gordon, WSJ.com, commentary, May 25, 2000.

15. Dirk J. Struik, *Yankee Science in the Making* (New York: Dover, 1991), 183.

16. Ibid., 183–186.

17. "Technology leads to science more often than science leads to technology." D. Shapley and R. Roy, *Lost at the Frontier* (Philadelphia: Institute for Scientific Information Press, 1983).

18. Struik, *Yankee Science*, 312–313.

19. Ibid., 214.

20. Richard C. Atkinson, "The Future of the Research University," in *Reinventing the Research University: Proceedings of a Symposium Held at UCLA on June 22–23, 1994*, ed. C. Kumar Patel (Los Angeles: Regents of the University of California, 1995).

21. Foster, *Innovation*, 36.

22. Venture capital funds raised a record $93 billion in 2000.

23. http://www.theregister.co.uk/000208-000012.html.

24. Science and Engineering Indicators, 1998; available from www.nsf.gov. In 1997, U.S. R&D spending was $205.7 million; the United States in 1995 represented 44 percent of world total R&D. Of the U.S. total the federal government funded $62.7 million and industry $133.3 million; universities performed $23.8 million, about two-thirds of which came from federal sources.

25. John Seely Brown and Paul Duguid, *The Social Life of Information* (Boston: Harvard Business School Press, 2000).

26. Philip A. Roussel, Kamal N. Saad, and Tamara J. Erickson, *Third-Generation R&D* (Boston: Harvard Business School Press, 1991), 93.

27. Robert Cooper, *Winning at New Products* (Reading, MA: Addison Wesley Publishing Co., 1993), 267.

■ CHAPTER 13 Can Government Manage Risk and Value?

1. Hernando de Soto, *The Mystery of Capital: Why Capitalism Triumphs in the West and Fails Everywhere Else* (New York: Basic, 2000).

2. Thomas Cahill, *How the Irish Saved Civilization: The Untold Story of Ireland's Heroic Role from the Fall of Rome to the Rise of Medieval Europe* (New York: Doubleday, 1995).

3. http://www.mit.edu/afs/athena/org/f/facts/origins.html.

4. Charles F. Sabel, "Italy's High Technology Cottage Industry," *Transatlantic Perspectives*, December 1982.

5. Jared Diamond, *Guns, Germs, and Steel; The Fates of Human Societies* (New York: Norton, 1997).

6. R. S. Kirby, S. Withington, A. B. Darling, and F. G. Kilgour, *Engineering in History* (New York: Dover Science, 1990), 432–442.

7. Maclyn McCarty, *The Transforming Principle: Discovering That Genes Are Made of DNA* (New York: Norton, 1985).

8. James D. Watson, *The Double Helix* (Kingsport, Tenn: Kingsport Press, 1968).

9. Wendy H. Schact, CRS Issue Brief for Congress IB85031, *Technology Transfer: Use of Federally Funded Research and Development*, Washington, DC, April 27, 2000.

10. Wil Lepkowski, "Public Science Drives Innovation," *Chemical & Engineering News*, September 1, 1997.

11. There is another issue regarding *which* companies gain the benefits of collaboration because there is a potential for government to tilt the competitive playing field. However, this issue occurs in *any* government contract and is usually resolved by a combination of open bidding and qualification.

12. The Rice study (Chapter 13, Note 7) illustrates how often government funding plays a necessary role in bringing discontinuous innovation to commercial fruition.

■ EPILOGUE

1. Monroe Mendelsohn Research, 841 Broadway, New York, NY 10003-4704. http://www.mmrsurveys.com.

2. George Gilder, *Telecosm: How Infinite Bandwidth Will Revolutionize Our World*, in press. Excerpts at http://www.forbes.com/asap/gilder.

3. Michael Mandel, *The Coming Internet Depression: How to Prosper Afterwards* (New York: Basic, 2000).

4. Donella H. Meadows, Dennis L. Meadows, Jorgen Randers, and Williams W. Behrens III, *The Limits to Growth: A Report to the Club of Rome* (New York: Potomec Associates, 1972).

5. World Resources Institute, *World Reserves 1994-5* (New York: Oxford University Press, 1995) 167.

6. The International Panel on Climate Change, Data Distribution Center, http://ipcc-ddc.cru.uea.ac.uk/cru_data.

7. Arthur M. Squires, *The Tender Ship* (Boston: Birkhauser Boston, 1986).

8. Lyman Spitzer, *The Physics of Fully Ionized Gases* (New York: Wiley-Interscience, 1956).

9. Alvin Toffler, *Future Shock* (New York: Random House, 1970).

Index